Queerly Classed

EDITED BY SUSAN RAFFO

South End Press
Boston, MA

Cover Photograph: Kelly Povo
Cover Design: Beth Fortune
Printed in the USA

Library of Congress Cataloging-in-Publication Data
Queerly classed / edited by Susan Raffo.
    p. cm.
Includes index.
ISBN 0-89608-562-7 (cloth). – ISBN 0-89608-561-9 (pbk.)
    1. Gays–United States–Social conditions. 2. Homosexuality–United States. I. Raffo, Susan.
    HQ76.3.U5Q445   1996
    306.76′ 6–dc20   96-43838
                                           CIP

South End Press, 116 Saint Botolph Street, Boston, MA 02115
03 02 01 00 99 98 97   1 2 3 4 5 6 7

Contents

Acknowledgments

N o book exists as the work of only one individual. This is particularly true in the case of *Queerly Classed*. The proposal
and initial outline for this anthology were organized by a group:
Jim Berg, Joanna Kadi, Richard LaFortune, and myself. To say this
anthology would not exist without their creative energy is more
than mere flattery. This book is one result of those meetings at the
New Riverside Cafe.

At South End Press, Loie Hayes worked first on this book. It was
her letter of inquiry and support that started the whole thing. Lynn
Lu joined later in the process and was wonderful from beginning
to bookshelf. In addition, she made it possible for me to spend
time out of the United States in my lover's home country by taking
on extra responsibility. She did more than the editor's usual job,
and she did it incredibly well.

On a more personal note, this anthology has taken far more
emotional and intellectual time than I initially imagined. Many people
worked on this book by connecting me to possible contributors.
They opened their address books, their little computer gadgets
with names on microchip, and their memories every time I called
in a panic. Others talked about the project and came up with ideas
and excitement at crucial moments. Some of the people on this list
probably don't even know the extent and importance of their
support. Some have given support through the legacy of their

memory. For their thinking and their care, I want to thank: Allan Bérubé, Jan Binder, Victoria Brownworth, Andy Elfenbein, Leslie Feinberg, Jenifer Fennell, Judith Hobbs, Amber Hollibaugh, Joanna Kadi, Pat Lindsley, Rofina Madaba-Newing, Beni Matías, Nasreen Mohammed, Donna Niles, Elissa Raffa, Jeffrey Raffo, Kay Raffo, Peter and P.J. Raffo, Eleanor Savage, Elaine Shelly, Jonna Shelomith, Ivan de Araújo Simões, Iara Volaco Simões, Nigel Singer, Cora and Maya Singer Hobbs, Carmen Vazquez, and John Watkins.

For Beth Zemsky, who lived this book with me for its entire life and who gave of her thinking, her integrity, and her belief.

And for Raquel Volaco Simões, who came in toward the end and helped tie it all together.

Introduction

I n a book intending to examine class systems and class inequality, the issue of book production seems particularly poignant. How does anyone get it together to do a book? How did the book you hold in your hands come to life? Why am I editing it? The proposal for this anthology was initially put together by a group of four people: Jim Berg, Joanna Kadi, Richard LaFortune, and myself. While our group organized to come up with a book proposal, it was agreed that I would see the ideas through to publication. Together we brainstormed an outline for an imagined "definitive" critical book on issues of class and queerness.[1] What sorts of issues, we wondered, would be addressed in such a book? We sat, drinking coffee and coming up with pages and pages of topics to cover, issues to explore, and theories to challenge. Unsurprisingly, our brainstorm asked for a many-volumed set. Cutting and pasting, we tightened our thinking until we arrived at this book.

This book is intended to act as a workbook, as part of an ongoing conversation rather than an endpoint or moment of absolute definition. There are two primary themes in this book: queerness and class. Depending on where you sit as a reader, how you identify yourself, and to what communities you belong, one theme might outshine the other. From where I sit as an editor, queerness in this book is the diving board into an exploration of and conversation about class and class systems.

Both of the primary themes in this book, class systems and classism in the United States and queer identities and communities, are subjects in flux. The definitions are as contested as the sites of social change. I do not believe there is a "correct" way to name, define, or analyze class systems and class experiences in the U.S., nor do I believe there is an agreed-upon definition of the makeup of queer communities. Rather than try and narrow the conversation ever closer to a definition that might leave out as much as it asserts, I hope this book does the opposite and makes the whole thing that much more complicated. And within that complication, I hope this book aids in determining a continuing and ever clearer strategy for ending social and economic injustice.

The questions at the end of the introduction are there for a number of reasons. They are drawn from questions originally sent out to potential contributors. They are included to show how this book was originally framed, but they are also included for your, the reader's, responses. If this were an interactive CD-ROM multi-lasered doohickey with every potential reader having access to an interactive CD-ROM multi-lasered doohickey for their home computer (ah, yes, issues of class and access), then your feedback and criticisms of the questions would be a concrete addition to this book, an additional set of essays and commentary. Since this book is in the traditional paper-and-binding format, your reactions to the questions are not included in this volume. They might remain private, if you read this book alone, or be shared with another person or group. Whatever form your responses take, they become a part of a larger conversation about class and queerness. The release of a book is nothing more than one point in an ongoing dialogue. This anthology intends to be a part of an open, critical discussion. The questions ask for your input as much as your attention.

As well as receiving the questions, contributors were asked to include two forms of analysis in their essays: the personal and the political. I believe that the construction of class origins and our experience of those class origins ground our analysis of class in the same way that the construction of sexuality and our experience of sexuality ground our understanding of sexuality, or that the construction of race and our experience of race ground our understanding of racism. I do not believe that in the United States people (and I include myself as a part of "people") generally know how to talk about class, even though we all live and experience it. We focus on individual aspects of culture and name it class, or we focus on aspects of class and name it something else. I don't believe we currently have the political vocabulary to talk about class systems in a way that automatically includes issues of economic inequality, cultural difference, race and ethnicity, internationalism, imperialism, and historical change. We err in sometimes using class to mean a specific group of people or a specific identity, saying things like "working-class/poor/middle-class/rich people tend to think/vote/act/survive this way...." At other times, class is discussed only as a social system and a function of institutions, with little attention paid to its actual effect on individual lives and individual methods of survival and interpretation. By including both personal reflection and critical analysis, this anthology aims to present a discussion of class and its entanglement with queerness that is both specific and broad-ranging.

In honor of that, let me briefly say something personal. I, like many if not most others, don't fall neatly into a class category. My family was on its way from a solidly working-class background to a professional middle-class life and lifestyle. These changes happened when I was in toddlerhood and pointed toward a life lived in the metaphoric suburbs of middle-classdom. A family tragedy changed this. Back into the working-class community with a single parent and large extended family. This particular set of circumstances placed me on an imagined edge, with a feeling of betweens. The members of my immediate family were different from the community of family and friends in which we lived. Most of our family and friends either never graduated high school or never received any formal education after high school. But my father had earned a doctorate before he died. My mother wanted us to go to college. When my brother, my mother, and I talked among ourselves, we talked of our dreams and assumed that they wandered paths other than the dreams of the people around us. We believed that when we dreamed of college and university degrees, this made us substantially different from the rest of our family.

And at the same time, when we talked among ourselves, we assumed belonging. We were of our family and our neighborhood, and we believed, in less vocal ways, that blood determined more than dreams. We knew we weren't different. We were family. We were the same. We had the same traditions, the same histories, the same recipes for cooking meat, a shared relationship to unions and to work, a shared way of talking and walking.

In our neighborhood, we were the smart and classy cousins to be teased and embraced. When I left my neighborhood, when I tried to go to college, I was the ignorant city hick. No teasing, no embracing, only a sense of watching some huge and intricate dance whose steps I never learned and that everyone else around me seemed to know. And it was more than that. Our family was made up of electrical workers and laborers, of housewives and cleaners. Even with my educated father, who died when I was seven and existed in my memory as a symbol of unattainable learn- ing, the meaning of college and education seemed vastly different for me than for most of the students around me. I had no language to explain why. I knew nothing of class and cultural difference, of how entwined and confusing they could be.

Class experience is, I believe, both fundamentally set in stone and absolutely contextual. Both at the same time. Uncontradict- ingly. Poverty is poverty. Wealth is wealth. These are concrete categories defined by experiences of entitlement or the lack thereof: lack of access to adequate housing, food, education, medical care, etc., or access to luxury goods and large-scale consumption. You might live on the wrong side of somebody's tracks and win the lottery for millions of dollars. You are now economically rich, but chances are the old boys' club won't be opening any doors to you. Winning the lottery doesn't change something more en- trenched and far more elusive than your economic status. Rich people know what rich people act like, look like, and talk like. Usually, poor people also know what rich people act like, look like, and talk like. Rich people don't usually know the same about poor people. Most of the time you know if you are rich. Most of the time you know if you are poor. It is the vast middle ground that brings uncertainty. In the 1992 presidential elections, a national survey asked voters to rank their class status by checking poor, working-class, lower-middle-class, middle-class, or upper-class. Ninety-two percent of respondents marked strictly middle-class.

Only 8 percent of Americans marked other than middle class. My interpretation of this is not that the U.S. is truly the classless society that nationalistic propaganda would have us believe, but that people in the United States are confused about how to talk about class and about how to place themselves. Or, just as likely, that people in the U.S. have had Horatio Alger's rags-to-riches story drummed into their souls to a point where admitting less than middle-classness means admitting laziness and sloth. And few in the U.S. really think they are rich. There is always someone believed to be a step higher on the ladder who must be surpassed.

Class experience is also contextual and ever changing. Your class position and status at one point in your life might appear different in another. You might be the people in your rural neighborhood who own the store where everyone shops, but as soon as you move to the big city, your relative position changes. You might be raised wealthy or middle class, particularly in the Majority World (commonly referred to as the Third World), and then immigrate to the United States and, due to cultural prejudice or racism, language difference, or any number of other things, suddenly find yourself depending on public assistance. You might be raised in one kind of neighborhood, one kind of community, and then, through education or unemployment, through a change in health or ability, find yourself in a different kind of community. Class experience and class position are contextual. It is a real experience beyond the theories that explain it. Yet individual experiences change.

In addition, class experience in the United States is tied to race and racism in an unhealthy and seemingly inseparable union. For many people, poor means Black, and widespread unemployment means that people of color, in particular immigrants of color, are taking all the jobs. To be a non-white Latino[2] in most parts of the country, Native in other parts, Asian in still other parts, and African-American all over the land is to be stopped by police who assume you must have stolen the car you are driving. The language of poverty and social programming carries implied images of people of color. The alignment of race and poverty is so entrenched in the U.S. that visual aids are no longer needed. Mention welfare and the American brain will do the rest. It doesn't matter that the majority of individuals in the U.S. receiving some kind of social aid are Euro-

American. Nor that corporate welfare demands far more cash than families or individuals.

Thus, class experience is contextual, and it is absolute. Personal experiences change, and at the same time, individuals are limited in their movement within and across classes. Contradictory and complementary.

Why class and queerness in particular? Personally, because I'm a lesbian raised predominantly working-class who sees both her lesbianism and her class to be as full of question as of definition. I have an investment in exploring the conjunction of these two interlocking spheres. That was the undeveloped and initial impetus for me many years ago. What interested me as the pieces for this book began to arrive at my home was how rarely contributors focused solely on class and queerness. Issues of race, ability, ethnicity, geography, gender, age, and education are as central to these essays as class and queerness. While class and queerness are the grouping themes that pull this book together, they are not the only themes included.

Why specifically class and queerness? Because like any other civil rights movement, social change movement, and/or identity-based movement, the queer communities and gay, lesbian, bisexual, and transgendered movements have a lot of personal baggage to contend with. Issues of class frame and run rampant through queer political issues. Workplace organizing and domestic partnership. The now defunct gays-in-the-military campaign. Gay activists who support organizing with other queers on narrowly defined "queer issues" no matter what broader political disagreements might be shared. The imagined cohesion of the national queer movement in spite of the physical and psychological distance between organizational offices in D.C., New York, and the rest of the country. The issue of leadership and access to leadership positions. Health care. Immigration. General safety and survival. And, yes, what we do in bed, what we call it, how we talk about it, and how what we say is heard.

The essays in this book range from the specifically personal to the more strictly theoretical, with the majority falling somewhere in the middle. The essays are not grouped in formal sections. In the end, there was no obvious breakdown of subject matter. Instead, each essay manages to both relate to the pieces around it while also maintaining an individual voice. Most of the contributors spend some amount of time exploring coming out within the context of their class and their culture, but none of these essays is only about coming out. The contributors in this book have leveled the same critical gaze at their personal lives as they have at the systems and institutions in which they live.

I have included some poetry in the book out of a personal bias. Partly this bias arises out of a belief that there are things that can be said in a poem that cannot be said in essay form. I think we as readers allow a different kind of emotionality in a poem than we allow or can always hear in an essay. I also think that poetry adds windows to an anthology, a series of open doors in the midst of analysis. And, while considering the structure of this book, poetry allowed the occasional pause in an anthology without section breaks.

There are two dialogues in this book, one between B.Michael Hunter and John Albert Manzon-Santos and the other between Scot Nakagawa and Catherine Saalfield. Both speak across and address differences of class and race. The others essays are written individually. Elizabeth Clare and Morgan Grayce Willow write from two very different perspectives and experiences on class and rural issues. David Becker writes from the perspective of wealth and examines queer philanthropy as a necessary piece of radical social change. Ruthann Robson engages in a lesbian and class analysis of legal theory. Allan Bérubé examines the fusion of ethnicity, class, and queerness, while Justin Chin writes from an immigrant experience on issues of class, colonialism, and imperialism. Joanna Kadi tackles the myth that working-class families are, by definition, more homophobic than rich families. Also included in this book is Victoria A. Brownworth's exploration of passing both within the context of class and of sexuality; discussions of family and home; and many complicated explorations of ethnicity, race, and culture seen through the double lens of class and queerness.

The contributors to this anthology present a wide-ranging discussion of class and queerness. There are also absences in this book. There is no representation by someone working within the labor movement, there are not enough rural voices or voices from the midwest and the southeast. There is no one here who grew up on a reservation. No one currently working on the line or in a secretarial pool. Few who have not benefited from some kind of further education. No one in these pages is currently homeless. There are only three contributors not raised working-class or poor. There are no bisexual or transgendered contributors. For me as an editor, the absences point to the amount of writing that still needs to be encouraged and initiated. For me as an activist, they point to the amount of organizing I still need to do and that still needs to be done. And for the essays in this book, they act as part of the conversation that occurs after you finish reading. The strength of these essays and the integrity of the writing open the space for more to follow.

Which is probably the best place to end this introduction: by pointing to both what is present in this book and what is absent. A book is only one point in a long discussion. If its job is social change and if it has done its job effectively, a book will soon lose potency as its arguments are considered, digested, sorted, and internalized by a movement. The contributors in this anthology present a range of thoughtful and thorough essays. May the digestive juices flow!

Notes

1. I use "queer" in this book to refer to people identifying themselves as gay, lesbian, bisexual, transgendered, or queer. Each of the contributors uses different language to identify their community. The contributors in this book primarily identify as gay or lesbian. It was my intention to include bisexual and transgendered voices. They are not here. Some individuals had to withdraw their work at the last minute due to personal emergencies or events. This leaves a book with, for me, an absence of necessary voices. I apologize for this. I continue to use the word "queer" out of the belief that any discussion of marginalized sexual orientation needs to include the voices of bisexuals and transgendered people.

2. There is a difficulty in U.S. race politics in its identification of all people emigrating from or with ancestry from Latin America as people of color. Colombians with German heritage, blond hair, and blue eyes are given the same identification as Afro-Brazilians, an identification that is then racialized. Issues of colonialism, colorism, and class are collapsed into a racial identification. This is true for most (all?) aspects of racial grouping within the U.S. as vastly disparate Asian cultures are deemed the same and as individuals with mixed parentage are expected to identify as either/or. I look forward to a political language that is thorough enough to include colonialism, colorism, class, and cultural difference in a discussion of race.

Queerly Classed Questions

Are you queer? Are you gay, lesbian, bisexual, or transgendered? Are you straight, heterosexual, undefined, or differently defined? Does your family accept your sexuality? What words do they use to embrace or reject your sexuality?

What does your sexuality mean to you? Is your sexuality a facet of your identity? Is it important to you that people know your sexuality? Why or why not?

Did you know people who were gay, lesbian, bisexual, or transgendered (glbt) as you grew up? If you did, how did you know they were glbt? How did you perceive them? How did they fit or not fit into your community?

What is the community you came out into? Was that community similar to the one you grew up in? Was it similar to the one in which you now move? Has your sense of sexuality changed over time? Do you use the language of "coming out" in analyzing your sexuality? Why or why not?

How do you define queer space? The first time you entered queer space (no matter what your sexuality or identity), how did you feel? Who did you see around you? Were you surprised at what you saw? Did you feel a sense of connection? Isolation? Comfort? Adventure? Erotics?

～

Do you talk about class and class systems as a part of your life? If so, how do you talk about class? If not, why not? When do you talk about class?

How do you think of your class position? Does it describe where you come from or how you live now? Are these the same thing? Why or why not?

What determines class location? Money? Family history? Trade and employment? Status? Health? Geography? Race and ethnicity? Ability?

Do you live in an area, neighborhood, part of the country, or country that is different from the one in which you grew up? If it is different, what is different about it? If it is the same or similar, is that by choice?

As a child, what expectations did you have about work? What were you told you could be when you grew up? What sort of role models did you have around you? What did you dream about?

What sights, smells, tastes, foods, music, etc. do you relate to your home? Are these comfortable images? What parts of them do you still carry with you?

How is where you come from depicted in the mainstream media, if at all?

What is your race, culture, ethnicity? How does your race, culture, or ethnicity affect your class experience? Do you find yourself talking about race without talking about class? Do you find yourself talking about class without talking about race? Why or why not?

～

How do you recognize class differences? Do you use terms like poor, working poor, working class, middle class, owning class, upper class, underclass? Do you say blue-collar, pink-collar, and white-collar? What do these categorizations mean for you? Where do you draw the line between them? How do you recognize the differences? Do race and gender change the categorizations for you?

How do you see conversations about class and sexuality taking place? How do you see class and sexuality intertwined?

How does sexuality play into the economic side of class issues? The cultural side? Do you see a distinction between these things?

What do the terms gay community, gay and lesbian community, glbt community, or queer community mean to you? Where do you or don't you see these communities? What goes into the making of a community?

How do we talk about work? Labor? How do we talk about labor organizing? Do sexuality and class play a role in organizing workplaces? How do we talk about the differences among organizing laborers in corporate work, nonprofit organizations, the service industry, factory work, agricultural work?

What language is used to discuss the radical right and its anti-queer platforms? By the media? By queers? Do you hear such terms as redneck, hillbilly preachers, fundamentalist hicks, and Bible Belt mentality? What class and cultural assumptions are being made?

How do we talk about the sex part of sexuality? About attraction and desire? About "rough trade," butch and femme, about queer style and fashion? About how we do it, where we do it, when we do it, and how we describe what we are doing? What are the rules for these conversations? The assumptions of appropriate versus inappropriate behavior? How do we add class to this discussion of sex and desire?

Are these issues queer issues: Immigration? Health care? Social services? Education? Environmental degradation and environmental racism? Affordable housing? What makes an issue queer?

Jerry Lee Lewis Kills His Child Bride

WILLIAM REICHARD

On the backroads of Blue Earth County, I rode
in the open back of a pick-up with my sisters,
with three drunk brothers-in-law in the cab
taking turns pretending to steer. We called this
joy-riding, though my throat was filling up with dirt,
though my sister Linda sat propped against the cab,
wheezing through incomplete lungs,
and the brothers-in-law kept opening up
the little window between inside and out
and offering us beers. Jerry Lee Lewis screamed
out from the eight-track, caught in the loop
of track two, over and over again singing
"Goodness gracious, great balls of fire!"
My sisters discussed what they had just heard
on the news: that this star who played piano
with his foot had been accused of killing
his wife, the one he married when she was thirteen.

My sisters dreamed of this
                        and I dreamed too
white trash grand passion on the top of big black piano,
of a man like Jerry Lee coming to lure us away
from the next kegger; the death, we let slip by;
it was only an accusation. But I wondered about pianos,
and saw Mrs. Jerry Lee spread out in a pink chiffon dress,
her petticoats covering the whole surface
of a piano-shaped swimming pool; on this dry day
it had to be a pool where she died, drowned
with a martini in her hand.
                        The pick-up plunged down a hill.
We all screamed, and Linda wheezed, looking like
a skinny fish; death before celebrity would be a shame.
And it's really only a matter of degrees that separates
the famous white trash from the unfamous; any one
of my sisters
could achieve a beehive, pink chiffon formal,
crinoline bigger than her whole body. Our dreaming father
bought a piano one day, on credit, and promised us lessons.
                        In the summer.
But summer never came that year, and I snuck lessons
from a friend who said he wanted to be Vladimir Horowitz.
I said I hadn't heard his songs, and could he play the piano
with his foot? I managed "Für Elise" before the creditors
closed in for non-payment, and only managed to snatch
my romance novels from the bench before they hauled
the piano out the door. Our father said nothing.
My sisters didn't notice. And I didn't care; the only time
I really wanted to learn to play the piano was when I watched
the creditors carry the spinet down the steps,
and load it into the back of their van.

Losing Home

ELIZABETH CLARE

I must find the words to speak of losing home. Then I never want to utter them again. They throb like an abscessed tooth; *homesick* is a platitude. I need to grab at seemingly unrelated words. *Queer. Exile. Class.* I reach for my red and gold *American Heritage Dictionary* but restrain myself. I know the definitions. I need to enter the maze created by lesbian identity, class location, and rural roots.

Let me start with *queer*, the easiest point of entry. In its largest sense, queer has always been where I belong. A girl child not convinced of her girlness. A backwoods hick in the city. A dyke in a straight world. A gimp in an ableist world. The eldest child of a poor father and a working-class mother, both teachers who pulled themselves up by their own bootstraps, using luck and white-skin privilege.

In its narrower sense, queer has been home since I became conscious of being a dyke. At age seventeen I left the backwoods of Oregon with a high school diploma and a scholarship to college, grateful that I didn't have a baby or a husband. A year later, after months of soul-searching, I finally realized that I was a lesbian and had been for years. Since then, I have lived among lesbians and created chosen families and homes, not rooted in geography but in identity. Our collective dyke household in Oakland, with its vegetable garden in the front yard and chicken coop in the back. The women's circle on the Great Peace March from Los Angeles to Washington, D.C. The Women's Encampment for a Future of Peace and Justice outside the Seneca Army Depot. Lesbian potlucks in Ann Arbor, where I now live. Whether I've been walking across the country for peace or just hanging out listening to lesbian gossip, learning to cook tofu or use red-handled bolt cutters to cut fence at the Army Depot, being a dyke in dyke communities is as close as I've ever felt to belonging. And still I feel queer.

Exile. If *queer* is the easiest, then *exile* is the hardest. I lie when I write that home is being a dyke in dyke communities. Rather, home is particular wild and ragged beaches, specific kinds of trees and berry brambles, the exact meander of the river I grew up near, the familiar sounds and sights of a dying logging and fishing town. *Exile* is the hardest because I have irrevocably lost that place as actual home. Let me return to *queer.*

Queer people—using the narrow definition—don't live in Port Orford, Oregon, or at least I have never found them. And if we did, we would have to tolerate lack of community, unspoken disdain, a wicked rumor mill, and the very real possibility of homophobic violence. Now, if I moved back and lived quietly, never saying the word *lesbian,* but living a life centered upon women, no one would shoot at my house, throw stones through my windshield, or run me out of town. Muscles Smith at the cannery, Bonnie Wagner at the one-room library, and Dick Tucker at the lumber mill would just shake their heads and talk about Bob Johnson's oldest, back from the city. As long as I maintained the balance—my unspoken lesbianism weighed against their tacit acceptance—I would be fine.

Urban, middle-class queer activists may mock this balance as simply another "don't ask, don't tell" situation contributing to queer invisibility. While I agree that it isn't the ideal relationship between queer people and straight people, it is far better than the polite and disdainful invisibility bestowed on us by many middle-class, liberal heterosexuals. If you don't believe me, let me take you to my maternal grandfather's funeral. At the service I sat with family, my sister to the right, my Great-Aunt Esther to the left, my Aunt Shirley in front of us, her longtime lover to her right. Marge is an African-American dyke, unmistakable whether or not she's in heels and a skirt. I am quite sure my aunt has never introduced Marge to Uncle John or Aunt Esther, Uncle Henry or Aunt Lillian, as her partner/lover/girlfriend or explicitly come out to them. Yet Marge is unquestionably family, sitting with my grandfather's immediate relatives near the coffin, openly comforting my aunt. My grandfather was a mechanic in Detroit; his surviving brothers and sisters are Lutheran corn farmers from southern Illinois. Most of them never graduated from high school, still speak German at home, and have voted Republican all their lives. They are about as "redneck" as middle- and upper-class urban folks could ever imagine.[1] Here in this extended working-class family, unspoken lesbianism balanced against tacit acceptance means that Marge is family, that she and Aunt Shirley are treated as a couple, and that the overt racism Marge would otherwise experience from these people is muffled. Not ideal, but better than frigid denial, better than polite manners and backhanded snubs, better than middle-class "don't ask, don't tell," which would carefully place Marge into the category marked "friend" and have her sit many pews away from immediate family at her lover's father's funeral.

At the same time, it is a balance easily broken. In Port Orford I would never walk down Main Street holding hands with a woman lover. That simple act would be too much. It is also a balance most readily achieved among family or folks who have known each other for decades. If I moved back and lived down the road from a dyke—closeted or not—who hadn't grown up in Port Orford, whose biological family didn't live in town, who was an "outsider," I would worry about her safety.

It isn't that outside the bounds of this fragile balance these rural white people are any more homophobic than the average urban person. Rather, the difference lies in urban anonymity. In Ann Arbor if a group of frat boys yells "hey lezzie" at me or the man sitting next to me on the bus whispers "queer" and tries to feel me up, I'll defend myself in whatever ways necessary, knowing chances are good that I'll never see these men again, or if I do, they won't remember me. On the other hand, in Port Orford if someone harassed me—the balance somehow broken, some invisible line overstepped, or drunken bravado overcoming tacit acceptance—I would know him, maybe work with his wife at the cannery, see his kids playing up the river at Butler Bar, encounter him often enough in the grocery store and post office. He would likewise know where I lived, with whom I lived, what car I drove, where I worked, and so on. This lack of anonymity is a simple fact of rural life, one that I often miss in the city, but in the face of bigotry and violence, anonymity provides a certain level of protection.

If I moved back to Port Orford, the daily realities of isolation would compete with my concerns about safety. Living across the street from the chainsaw shop, I would have to drive an hour to spend an evening at a lesbian potluck, three hours to hang out at a women's bookstore or see the latest queer movie, seven hours to go to a lesbian and gay pride march. I don't believe I could live easily and happily that isolated from queer community, nor could I live comfortably while always monitoring the balance, measuring the invisible lines that define safety. My loss of home is about being a dyke.

It is also about class. If *queer* is the easiest, and *exile* the hardest, then *class* is the most confusing. The economics in Port Orford are simple: jobs are scarce. The life of a Pacific Northwest fishing and logging town depends on the existence of salmon and trees. When the summer salmon runs dwindle and all the old-growth trees are cut, jobs vanish into thin air. Fishermen now pay mortgages on their boats by running drugs. Loggers pay their bills by brush cutting (gathering various kinds of ferns to sell by the pound to florists) and collecting welfare. What remains is the meager four-month-a-year tourist season and a handful of minimum-wage jobs—pumping gas, cashiering, flipping burgers. The lucky few work for the public school district or own land on which they run milk cows and sheep. In short, if I moved back, I probably wouldn't find work. Not only are jobs scarce, but my cerebral palsy also makes jobs that require a lot of manual dexterity—such as cashiering or flipping burgers—difficult or impossible. And if, miraculously, I did find work, the paycheck probably wouldn't stretch around food, gas, and rent.

To leap from economic realities to class issues in Port Orford holds no challenge. The people who live in dying rural towns and work minimum- or sub-minimum-wage jobs, not temporarily but day after day for their whole working lives, are working-class and poor people. There are some middle-class people who live in Port Orford: the back-to-the-land artists who grow marijuana for money, the young teachers whose first jobs out of college bring them to Pacific High School, the retirees who have settled near Port Orford, lured to Oregon by cheap land. But these people don't stay long. The artists burn out; young teachers find better jobs in other, more prosperous towns. The retirees grow older and find they need more services than are available in Curry County. The people who stay are poor and working-class. I left because I didn't want to marry and couldn't cashier at Sentry's Market. I left because I hoped to have money above and beyond the dollars spent on rent and food to buy books and music. I left because I didn't want to be poor and feared I would be if I stayed. I will never move back for the same reasons. My loss of home is about class.

Leaving is a complicated thing. I left with a high school diploma and a scholarship to college, grateful to be leaving, but this is only half the truth. The other half is that everyone around me—my parents, teachers, classmates, and friends, the women who cashiered at Sentry's Market, the men who drove logging trucks—assumed I would leave, go to college, and become "successful." No one expected me to marry a week after graduation and move up the road from my parents, to die in a drunk-driving car accident or a high-speed game of chase down Highway 101, to have a baby and drop out of school at fifteen. A high school diploma and a college scholarship were givens in my life.

This is all about class location. In Port Orford, my family was well off: We always had enough to eat; my father was securely employed as a high school teacher; my mother bragged that she had the only Ph.D. in town. We eventually owned a big wooden house. Books and records filled my childhood, not only those we borrowed from the library, but also those we bought and lined our house with. We always had health care. I grew up among people for whom none of these things were givens. On the other hand, we wore hand-me-downs and homemade clothes, rented tiny two-bedroom houses, owned one beat-up car, and balanced dental bills against new school shoes. I didn't know that in a middle-class town or neighborhood these things would have marked my family and me as something other than well off.

Who left and who stayed measured in part the class differences at Pacific High School. My best friend from sixth to twelfth grade was poor. Judy's father lost his arm in a mill accident, and they lived on his disability checks. She and I spent high school together in college-prep classes, poring over pre-calculus problems and biology experiments. We both wanted to go to college, to leave rural Oregon, and yet in our senior year as I filled out college applications, Judy made plans to marry her boyfriend of four years. I know now that her decision arose out of financial desperation—her father had just died, and her family was falling deeper into poverty—but at the time, I thought Judy was copping out. I walked away, glad to be leaving Port Orford behind me. Or so I thought.

Only later did I understand what I lost by leaving. Loss of a daily sustaining connection to a landscape that I still carry with me as home. Loss of a rural, white working-class culture that values neighbors rather than anonymity, that is both tremendously bigoted—particularly racist—and accepting of local eccentricity, that believes in self-sufficiency and depends on family—big extended families not necessarily created in the mold of the Christian right. Loss of a certain pace of life, a certain easy trust. I didn't know when I left at seventeen that I would miss the old cars rusting in every third yard. Miss the friendly chatting in the grocery store, the bank, the post office. Miss being able to hitchhike home, safe because I knew everyone driving by.

In leaving, I followed in my parents' footsteps. My father, raised poor on a dirt farm in North Dakota, and my mother, raised working-class in Detroit, both left their families to go to college. Their departures were part of an upward scramble toward the middle class, a scramble that my siblings and I inherited. Our grandparents were farmers, gravediggers, and mechanics; our parents, teachers; and we were to be professors, lawyers, or doctors. As I try to sort this tangle out, knowing I can't dodge the question of my own class location much longer, I have to ask, does this upward scramble, this endless leaving, work? Instead of professor, lawyer, and doctor, my brother is a high school teacher; my sister, a low-level administrator; and I, a bookkeeper. Did my parents become middle-class in their scramble? Did my siblings and I? And what about the loss? For decades my mother missed living in a big, industrial, working-class city; my father would drive every day to the ocean just to see a long, flat horizon like the one he left behind in North Dakota. My brother has returned to rural Oregon, my sister dreams of leaving Seattle for some small town in the North Cascades, and I entertain fantasies of a rural dyke community. Is the upward scramble worth the loss? Answering these questions brings me back to being queer, brings me to the next question: Is queer identity worth the loss?

Queer identity, at least as I know it, is largely urban. The happening places, events, dialogues, the strong communities, the journals, magazines, bookstores, queer organizing, and queer activism are all city-based. Of course rural lesbian and gay communities exist, but the people and institutions defining queer identity and culture are urban.

For me, coming into my lesbian identity and untangling my class location have both been rooted in urban life. In moving to an urban, private liberal arts college, I found what I needed to come out as a lesbian: the anonymity of a city, the support of out lesbian-feminist activists, and access to dyke books and music. In that same move, I also found myself living among middle-class people for the first time. Because in Port Orford my family had always defined itself as middle-class—and in truth we were well-educated people who fell somewhere between the working-class loggers and the middle-class retirees—I believed the class differences I felt in my bones amounted to my being a country bumpkin. I assumed my lack of familiarity with trust funds, new cars, designer clothes, trips to Paris, and credit cards was the same as my lack of familiarity with city buses, skyscrapers, one-way streets, stoplights, and house keys.

Even now, the two—the lack of familiarity with city buses, which I've lost in a decade of urban living, and my lack of familiarity with trust funds, which I have not—are hard to separate. I am remembering the first time I went to OutWrite, a national queer writer's conference. From the moment I walked into the posh Boston hotel where the conference was being held, I gawked, staring unbelievingly at the chandeliers, at the shiny gold railings, at the ornate doors, in the same way I used to gawk at twenty-story buildings. Saturday night before the big dance party, which I couldn't afford to go to, I had dinner with an acquaintance and a group of her friends, all white lesbian writers from New York City. We ate at the hotel restaurant, where I spent too much money on not enough food, served by brown-skinned men who were courteous in spite of our ever changing party and ever changing food orders. Jo and her friends were all going to the party after dinner and were dressed accordingly, in black plastic miniskirts and diamond earrings, three-piece suits and gold cufflinks, hair carefully molded and shaved in all the right places. In my blue jeans and faded chamois shirt, I felt conspicuous and embarrassed.

At some point the conversation turned to gossip about queer writers not at the conference. Cathy, an editor for a well-known lesbian press, started in on one of "her" writers, a novelist from rural Oregon. Having heard me talk earlier about growing up in rural Oregon, Cathy turned to me and asked, "When Laura asks me to send stuff to her P.O. box because during the winter rains, the mail carrier might not be able to navigate the dirt road to her mailbox, is she serious?" I wanted to laugh. I wanted some clever retort to slide off my tongue. Instead, I politely explained about dirt roads and months of rain. What this New York femme didn't know about rural living didn't offend me; rather, it was the complete urban bias of the evening that did. Was I uncomfortable, feeling conspicuous and embarrassed, because of class or because of urban/rural differences? I can't separate the two.

Experiences like this one have brought me to needing words for my class location. Sometimes I say I'm mixed-class, living somewhere between working-class and middle-class in a borderland rarely, if ever, acknowledged or defined. Other times I feel like a bridge, one foot working-class, the other middle-class, spanning the distance, able to sit in a posh Boston hotel with well-dressed New York butch and femme dykes and not feel *shame*, only *embarrassment*. Or is it as simple as still feeling like a country hick—with all of its class implications—in the city? In any case, it leaves me feeling queer in the queer community.

The twenty-fifth anniversary of the Stonewall Riots (Stonewall 25, in media shorthand), if one were to believe the mainstream media and much of the queer media, was a defining event of queer identity in the '90s. I didn't go. I can't tolerate New York City, its noise, crowds, grime, heat, concrete, and traffic. I inherited my father's rural fear of a city as big and tall as New York. I've gone to Lesbian and Gay Pride marches for the last decade, but Stonewall 25 was a commercial extravaganza of huge proportions. From the reports I heard, the tickets for many of the events cost outrageous amounts of money. Who could afford the benefit dance at $150, the concert at $50, the T-shirt at $25? I know that at the 1993 March on Washington trinkets and souvenirs flourished. Not only could one buy fourteen different kinds of T-shirts, but also coffee mugs, plastic flags, freedom rings, posters, etc. I can only assume this proliferation was even more astonishing at Stonewall 25. And sliding scales? They're evidently a thing of the past. Stonewall 25 strikes me not so much as a celebration of a powerful and life-changing uprising of drag queens and bull dykes fed up with the cops, but as a middle- and upper-class urban party that opened its doors only to those who could afford it.

Why does the money that creates Stonewall 25 and events like it rarely find its way to working-class and poor queers? Why does the money stay urban? What about AIDS prevention programs, gay/lesbian/bi/transgendered youth services, hate-crime monitoring, and queer theater in the mountains of rural Oregon, the cornfields of rural Nebraska, the lowlands of rural South Carolina? Have we collectively turned our backs on the small towns in Oregon that one by one are passing local anti-gay ordinances? Are we, in effect, abandoning them to the Oregon Citizens Alliance, the Christian-right coalition that spearheaded the outrageously homophobic Proposition 9 in 1992 and that, after losing that vote, has directed its attention toward local initiatives? Will we remember and support Brenda and Wanda Hansen of Camp Sister Spirit, white, rural, working-class lesbians who are building and maintaining lesbian and feminist space in rural Mississippi, when the homophobic violence they face—dead dogs in their mailbox, gunfire at night—no longer makes the headlines?

In her essay "Rural Organizing: Building Community Across Difference," Suzanne Pharr writes:

> If we cannot do rural organizing around lesbian and gay issues, then rural lesbians and gay men are left with limited options: leaving our roots to live in cities; living fearful, invisible lives in our rural communities; or with visibility, becoming marginalized, isolated, and endangered. Not one of these options holds the promise of wholeness or freedom.[2]

If we do choose to engage in rural organizing, to effectively build queer communities and foster queer identity in the backwoods, I want us to follow the lead of rural poor and working-class queers. I want urban activists to take a backseat, to lend their support—financial and otherwise—as rural lesbians and gays build and strengthen community among themselves. This will be the easy part for urban, middle-class queers to support. The harder part will be understanding the alliances queers—urban and rural—need to create with straight rural people, the same folks urban people call "rednecks," "hicks," "clods," and "bigots."

Building and supporting these alliances will entail many different kinds of organizing. At the heart of this work needs to be a struggle against economic injustice, since most people—queer and straight—living in rural communities (with the exception of resort towns and retirement enclaves) are poor and working-class. This means confronting unemployment, inadequate food and housing, unaffordable and inaccessible health care and education—issues that queer activists have largely ignored. It is neither easy nor glamorous work, sometimes as simple as lending support to a strike or a family out of work, other times as complex as fighting for health care reform that serves the needs of both rural and queer communities. It will be slow work, creating queer visibility and acceptance by building community among rural lesbians and gay men most accustomed to isolation, and finding common cause with the very people cast as the country's most backward homophobes. But it is exactly this kind of work that will erode rural homophobic violence.

Consider, for example, the eight months I lived at the Women's Encampment for a Future of Peace and Justice in rural

New York. As a community of women, mostly lesbians, protesting the existence of the largest U.S. Army nuclear weapons storage site in the world, the violence we faced from the local community had several sources. The Army Depot was the primary source of jobs for the people in Romulus, and we were a clear and absolute threat to those jobs. We mouthed the rhetoric of economic conversion but never seriously worked on the problems of economic injustice, never asked the hard question, "What happens to the people who work at the Depot after it closes?" Because we—mostly middle-class, urban activists working within the context of the women's peace movement—never asked the question, much less worked toward an answer, we lived in a community that never stopped being angry at us. That anger most typically came out as homophobic violence. By the very nature of activism, activists encounter anger and resistance all the time, but in Romulus, by not addressing the economic issues, the chances of diffusing the anger and working toward true justice were decreased. In addition, the chances of lesbian activists living in comfortable coexistence with the people of Romulus were zero.

Alongside the issue of economic injustice was the ever-present fact of our lesbianism—both perceived and actual. In its first two or three years, thousands of women visited and lived at the Camp, and the homophobic violence they encountered was virulent and, for a while, unrelenting. By the time I lived there, seven years after the Camp's founding, our numbers were smaller, and we had settled into a less volatile but still uneasy coexistence with Romulus. To arrive at this relationship, Peace Camp women had worked hard to build alliances with local people—farmers, business owners, the waitresses at the one restaurant in town. One of these alliances was with Bob, the county sheriff. He and his co-workers had done everything from arresting Peace Camp women to issuing us parade permits to helping diffuse violence directed toward us. During my time at the Camp, I became Bob's contact, a role that, because of my cynicism toward the criminal justice system, made me uncomfortable. I also knew that an alliance with Bob, not as our protector, but as a local whom other locals respected, was important to the Camp. While other Peace Camp women were scornful, rude, or hostile toward Bob, I developed a cordial working relationship with him. I understand the scorn directed toward a burly, uniformed white man toting a gun. But in a rural community, developing an alliance with a sheriff who is willing to go knock on doors to find the people responsible for homophobic violence, as Bob had done on more than one occasion, is part of nurturing a rural dyke community. The women with whom I lived understood my discomfort and ambivalence about our relationship with the county sheriff, but not my willingness to maintain it, to stand out on the porch and talk about the weather, the corn crop, and the Peace Camp with Bob.

I want all of us to listen to Suzanne Pharr's words, because wholeness and freedom need to be at the center of queer identity and activism. If queer activists and communities don't create the "options that hold the promise of wholeness [and] freedom" for all queer people, rural as well as urban, working-class and poor as well as middle- and upper-class, we have failed. And if we fail, those of us who are rural or rural-raised, poor and working-class, even mixed-class, will have to continue to make difficult choices, to measure what our losses are worth.

There are no real answers for me in the measure. My leaving gave me a lesbian community but didn't change my class location. I moved from being a rural, mixed-class dyke-child in a straight, rural, working-class town to being an urban-transplanted, mixed-class dyke activist in an urban, mostly middle-class dyke community. Occasionally, I simply feel as if I've traded one disjunction for another and lost home to boot. Most of the time, however, I know that living openly in relative safety as a lesbian among lesbians, living in a place where I can find work, living with easy access to books and music, movies and concerts, when I can afford them, is lifeblood for me. But I hate the cost, the loss, the measure.

The disjunction of never belonging has become an ordinary condition in my life, only noticed when I meet new people or travel to new places. Some years ago, my friend Marjorie and I took a trip to lesbian land in Oregon, visiting WomanShare, Oregon Women's Land (OWL), and the Healing Ground, hanging out with dykes, hiking in the mountains, splitting firewood, and planting trees. As we left WomanShare heading north to Eugene, a woman named Janice told us about a dyke-owned natural food store in Myrtle Creek and asked us to say hello to Judith if we stopped. Two hours later we pulled off Interstate 5 into a rickety little logging town. Marjorie, a Jewish dyke who grew up in suburban Cleveland and suburban Detroit, noticed the John Birch sign tacked under the "Welcome to Myrtle Creek" sign, while I noticed the familiar ramshackle of Main Street, the hills checkered with overgrown clearcuts, the one-ton pick-up trucks with guns resting in their rear windows. We parked and started to make a shopping list: fruit, bread, cheese, munchies for the road. I could feel Marjorie grow uncomfortable and wary, the transition from lesbian land to town, particularly one that advertised its John Birch Society, never easy. On the other hand, I felt alert but comfortable in this town that looked and smelled like home. In white, rural, Christian Oregon, Marjorie's history as an urban, middle-class Jew and mine as a rural, mixed-class gentile measured a chasm between us.

As we walked into the grocery store, the woman at the cash register smiled and said, "Welcome, sisters," and all I could do was smile back. Judith wanted news from WomanShare, asked about Janice and Billie, answered our questions about Eugene, already knew about the woman from Fishpond who had committed suicide a week earlier. News of her death moved quickly through this rural dyke community; as we traveled north, we heard women from southern Oregon to Seattle talking about and grieving for this woman. As I stood in Judith's store, I began to understand that OWL and WomanShare and Rainbow's End and Fly Away Home and Fishpond and the Healing Ground weren't simply individual, isolated pieces of lesbian land, created and sustained by transient urban lesbians; they were also links in a thriving rural lesbian network. When Judith asked where I was from, I tried to explain what it meant to discover this network a mere hundred miles east of my inarticulated dyke childhood. But all I could really do was smile some more as Judith told stories about being a dyke in Myrtle Creek, stories interrupted as she greeted customers by name and exchanged local gossip and news. Marjorie and I left forty-five minutes later with a bag of groceries and a pile of stories. As we drove north, I reached out to my ever-present sense of disjunction and found it gone for the moment.

I certainly don't believe that I can cure my sense of disjunction with a simple move to the Oregon mountains, where I could live at OWL or WomanShare and shop in Myrtle Creek. The problems highlighted by the intersection of queer identity, working-class and poor identity, and rural identity demand long-lasting, systemic changes. The exclusivity of queer community shaped by urban, middle-class assumptions. Economic injustice in the backwoods. The abandonment of rural, working-class culture. The pairing of rural people with conservative, oppressive values. The forced choice between rural roots and urban gay and lesbian life. These problems are the connective tissue that brings the words *queer*, *class*, and *exile* together. Rather than a relocation to the Oregon mountains, I want a redistribution of economic resources so that wherever we live—in the backwoods, the suburbs, or the city— there is enough to eat; warm, dry houses for everyone; true universal access to health care and education. I want queer activists to struggle against homophobic violence in rural areas with the same kind of tenacity and creativity we bring to the struggle in urban areas. I want rural queers, working-class queers, poor queers to be leaders in our communities, to shape the ways we will celebrate the fiftieth anniversary of Stonewall. I want each of us to be able to bring our queerness home. Only then will I be able to stop writing the words that ache.

Notes

1. In her brilliant essay "Whenever I Tell You the Language We Use Is a Class Issue, You Nod Your Head in Agreement—And Then You Open Your Mouth," about working-class culture and class oppression, Elliott maps out three definitions of the word *redneck*. Its denotation: "A member of the white rural laboring class." Its connotation: "A person who advocates a provincial, conservative, often bigoted sociopolitical attitude characteristic of a redneck." And lastly, its usage by progressives, including many lesbians and gay men: "1. Any person who is racist, violent, uneducated and stupid (as if they are the same thing), womon-hating, gay-bashing, X-tian fundy, etc. 2. Used as a synonym for every type of oppressive belief except classism" (*Lesbian Ethics*, 4:2).

2. *Sojourner: The Women's Forum*, June 1994.

Homophobic
Workers or Elitist
Queers?

JOANNA KADI

Things had not changed, and yet they had. I hopped out at the last stop on the Bloor line westbound and hurriedly followed the "Kiss 'n' Ride"[1] signs to the cars waiting to pick up passengers. Uncle Joe occupied the driver's seat of the big old red station wagon. All familiar. But four years had passed since I'd spent a Sunday afternoon this way. And now two pairs of feet walked quickly toward the wagon. I was bringing my lover home to meet Uncle Joe and Aunt Chuck, their four kids and partners and grandchildren.

Uncle Joe kissed and hugged Jan and me, then whisked us to the house, where he pulled in the driveway and laid on the horn. Aunt Chuck kissed and hugged us over and over. The cat ran away. I exclaimed over the kitchen; they'd knocked out a wall to make it bigger. "We spend all our time in here anyway," Uncle Joe told Jan. And indeed, my overwhelming memory is of wonderful Sundays spent sitting around that same table in a smaller kitchen and eating and eating and eating and feeling happy. Now, as then, plates crammed with olives, hot peppers, fresh veggies, dips, and bread covered the table. These "snacks" would keep us going until "dinner" began, loose categories since the eating continued all afternoon.

Jan handled herself well, letting Aunt Chuck trip over herself in her haste to bring food and beer. As various cousins arrived on the scene, Jan answered questions from all sides. Where did you grow up? What do you do? What's your cat's name? Where do your brothers live? When did your mother die? For the brief fifteen-minute pause between chowing down on olives and bread ("Eat! Eat! You haven't touched a thing!") and sitting down to the "real" dinner, Jan and I left the group to see Aunt Chuck's flowers at the front of the house. But we couldn't linger because Uncle Joe bellowed at the top of his lungs for my girlfriend: "Jan! Jan! Where are you? Charlotte, I need you to take a picture of me and Jan!"

I recall that day and revel in the feeling of being at home and being loved. Then I consider the enormity and appalling nature of classism in the queer movement.[2] For years I've listened to sweeping, elitist generalizations about the homophobic working class, to middle- and upper-class queers telling me that the liberal tolerance exhibited by their parents is the best we can expect when bringing our lovers home, to speeches and articles extolling lies about backward "rednecks" who hate queers. Through it all, I tried to hold on to what I know in my bones about working-class people. But what I heard had an impact. For days before our Sunday gathering I felt anxious. Maybe I was wrong in assuming that when I took Jan home to meet these folks, she'd be overwhelmed with love and attention, unquestioningly taken in. Had my years away sugarcoated the reality? Was their love really so strong?

I hadn't sugarcoated anything. I also hadn't put together all the pieces about classism in the queer movement, including the different working-class responses to queers, and the depth, impact, and history of the lie that working-class people are more homophobic than rich people.

A small aside to anyone reading this essay who's not queer. My observations about classism in the queer movement apply equally to other social-change movements, whether environmental, feminist, solidarity, peace. Don't hesitate to analyze your groups with these critiques.

⁓✂⁓

Working-class people's responses to queers vary widely. Some people are radically supportive, some are mildly supportive, some don't care much one way or the other, some hate queers viciously and say so to our faces, some stand outside queer bars with base-ball bats.

These responses parallel those of the middle and upper classes. Among these groups, some are radically supportive, some mildly supportive, some liberally tolerant, some hate queers viciously and say so. The most homophobic usually don't carry weapons; they've got other ways of maiming and killing us that don't involve anything as "dirty" as physical assault.[3]

Through friends, I've met radically supportive, upper-middle-class parents and radically supportive working-class parents. Visiting my aunt and uncle solidified my impression of the differences between these groups. Upper-middle-class parents talked openly about queer family members and participated in political work through groups like P-FLAG (Parents and Friends of Lesbians and Gays). Working-class parents didn't join groups, wear buttons, or talk about homophobia to neighbors. Their acceptance of queer family members felt almost casual, as did their integration of queer family members and lovers. They didn't seem the least bit sur-prised by the presence of queers in the family, and thus didn't make a fuss. I want to explore two issues here: this casual re-sponse to the presence of queer family members and the intense love working-class queers get from supportive family members.

First, why aren't working-class people surprised about queers in the family? Maybe working-class people have a better handle on reality. But I'm also intrigued by the word "queer" and possible associations between class identity and sexual identity.

I'm strongly attached to the word "queer" and find it more ap-propriate than any other for describing my identity. I first read this word as a teenager, where "queer" described girls who refused to obey strict gender codes. This came through in Louisa May Alcott's descriptions of Jo in *Little Women* and in Lucy Maud Mont-gomery's portrayal of Valancy in *The Blue Castle*. Today the word "queer" captures not only my sexual identity but my class identity as well. It accurately positions me on the margins of the class hier-archy, without any chance of being "normal," that is, middle-class. And the in-your-face power of this word speaks to the pride I ex-perience from my class identity, in strong contrast to the shame I felt growing up.

Figuring out my "queer" working-class identity helped me understand radical acceptance from working-class people. If contented working-class people share a gut feeling of queerness, it's not a total shock when a son comes out as gay. His sexual identity fits with our experiences as "queer" in relation to rich people. My aunt didn't freak out when I said, "I'm a lesbian. I live with my lover." She immediately asked if Jan treats me well and if she takes care of me. When I reassured her, she said, "That's wonderful." End of discussion.[4]

This lack of surprise over queer family members connects to the kind of love these working-class families feel for each other and their acceptance of queer family members. This love invariably feels deeper than what I've perceived in middle- and upper-middle-class families.

Within working-class families where members love and respect each other (and I'm *not* saying this describes all working-class families), caring for kin is linked to a deep distrust of "the system"—the capitalist system that exploits us and benefits the rich.[5] Our love for each other is tempered and steeled by our exploitation and our need to stick together. We're all we have, so we must stay connected.

Love among working-class people is further differentiated from love among rich people because working-class people can express deep love that springs from honest, unguarded, and clearly expressed emotions, the kind I've rarely seen in well-off families. Let me clarify this point so I don't reinforce stereotypes. When not vilified, working-class people are often romanticized in particular ways. Don't you recognize us? Warm folk who know how to laugh, cry, and love with abandon, homey folk with hearts of gold who can teach repressed rich people to find happiness in the simple joys of everyday living—walking a dog, sitting on a front porch, enjoying a sunset. Countless books and movies portray these touching little scenarios.

Such romanticized, essentialized versions of working-class life offer rich people a night of cheap entertainment, a few tender tears and crumpled lace handkerchiefs, and a reinforcement of the comforting belief that working-class people aren't scary, angry, threatening, or intelligent. *And* these depictions carry a grain of truth. Working-class people express feelings more than rich people do, know how to laugh, cry, and love with abandon, find happiness in everyday life. And not because of anything innate, biological, or essential. These tendencies clearly illustrate the workings of the class system. As working-class people, we haven't been socialized into grim, restrictive sets of manners, social codes, and behaviors. We don't have to act politely and formally, don't have to dole out emotions and feelings carefully and precisely, little bits at a time. Middle- and upper-class people do. The richer they are, the more intense the process. Constraining atmospheres of middle- and upper-class homes reflect this training, which begins early in life.

Working-class people receive little or none of this particular brand of socialization. This doesn't mean we're all emotionally healthy and vibrant, able to express deep, authentic feelings. But there's more possibility for this to arise.

While experiencing the pleasure of deep love and radical acceptance from some family members, I've also gone through the anticipated displeasure of vicious queer hatred from other family members, most notably my parents. The night I broke my big news, they said it all. "You're sick. You ought to be locked up in a mental hospital." They expressed disappointment that I was past the age where they could commit me. And clearly my new lifestyle would leave me not only lonely, but impoverished. "You'll die penniless in the gutter," my mother informed me.[6] Their disgust wouldn't allow them to even *think* about lesbian sex. Mixed with disgust was pity, followed by anger; they warned me to stay away from my niece, their only grandchild. They wrapped up the whole session with a grand concession: "We won't disown you. But don't ever talk about this again."

Now, homophobia can be tracked to many places—the christian church, fear of sexuality, gendered hierarchies. But what about my parents positioning themselves at the opposite end of the "Queer Response" spectrum from my aunt and uncle? Is the only difference that some of us believe what we're taught? I think not. Class comes into play here.

Working-class homophobes like my parents carry a lot of bitterness, which stems in large part from capitalist oppression. They don't accept their lot in life. They want more money, more stuff, and more status. Yet they don't agitate for change; they sit with other like-minded working-class people in resentful anger over the little they've been allowed to acquire.

This bitterness pops up when these people react to "difference,"[7] which they despise and fear in the family, society, themselves. Back to my parents. My father, a dark-skinned Arab, hates being set apart from white norms. He and my mother hate being set apart from middle-class norms and have no desire to experience "queerness" in relation to those norms. They'd rather make it in the system established by rich people; they'd love to assimilate and be welcomed into the fold. At the same time that they hate rich people, they want to be liked by them and to be like them. My parents can't embrace their queerness; they're doing everything possible to escape it. So it makes sense that they let loose with homophobic condemnation when I come out and embrace one particular form of queerness.

I'm convinced one reason for working-class homophobia is this bitterness, this burning desire to fit in with what's "normal." This factor also helps explain homophobia among the rich. Plenty of wealthy people share my parents' reactions. While some hide their feelings behind a mask of politeness, others express outrageous hatred of queers from a context of bitterness and fear—fear of difference, of not making it, of not living up to the high standards set for them. Alienated and disappointed, they're trying, probably harder than working-class people, to prove their normality and their worth. Queer children interfere with this plan. Then there's another problem. If they admit that sexual difference is not only possible but acceptable, they may have to perceive other differences as acceptable. Then what happens to their belief in superior status?

Similarities come to the foreground when explaining why homophobia exists in different classes, but only one class is classified outright as the most homophobic. Working-class/working-poor people claim the dubious honor of being dubbed more homophobic (and more racist, and more sexist) than rich people. This holds true in mainstream society, queer organizations, and other progressive movements.

Middle-class and upper-middle-class queers respond with boring predictability when I claim my working-class identity. They assume I can't be out, either in my family or my working-class neighborhood, because of unchecked and assaultive homophobia rampant in these arenas. When I contradict them, they either look at me with awe for my bravery or ask, in hushed tones, just how badly everything went. Although I enjoy giving these people an elaborate, lengthy recital of my aunt and uncle's treatment of Jan and me, underneath I'm angry and concerned. Why is this idea so prevalent? How did it get started? Who benefits?

With the passage of time and greater "successes," the capitalist system has sharpened its ability to spread misinformation and foster class and race divisions. Lies about backward, unenlightened poor people have been around forever and a day. This ensures our status as Other and our availability for drudge work at shit wages.

The advent of the Black Civil Rights movement reinforced this idea. While articulate, radical working-class activists from all racial/ethnic groups participated in this movement, they're not the ones well remembered four decades later. Americans do remember the white, southern, working-class men and women who spoke against desegregation, sneered at "niggers," and didn't mince words about their hatred. Why do we remember? Because the media highlighted them, over and over and over again. The media provided ample TV time, airplay, and newspaper photos.

These racist interviewees spoke clearly and to the point, in true working-class fashion. They had no reason to hide their thoughts and feelings, nothing to gain from lying. Nor had they spent years honing verbal skills that would allow them to cover up their real feelings and present a reasonable, caring, and polite facade to the world.

Meanwhile, back at the ranch, the media simply ignored white people with the power to devise, reinforce, and carry out brutally racist practices. After all, ownership has its privileges! The few times camera lights shone toward rich white people, they manipulated language, smiled, wore nice clothes, and said their university or state or business *wanted* equality; they just hoped it would happen the right way.

The ruling class emerged from this battle looking a whole lot better than working-class white people. Through subsequent decades, rich people have continued to bask in the glow of the winners'-circle lights, as progressive middle-class people consistently cast working-class people unfavorably. Consider environmental movements of the 1970s and 1980s. I vividly remember activists targeting Newfoundland fishermen who clubbed baby seals to death. An ardent supporter of animal liberation and a long-time vegetarian, I hated what happened to the seals. Just as much as I hated what happened to the fishermen. Having visited Newfoundland and seen the poverty, I had no quarrel with the fishermen. Why didn't activists challenge the people who had the power to change the situation?[8]

This problematic politic reinforced a viewpoint traditionally fostered by the ruling class–that of stupid, unenlightened, backward workers. Now middle-class activists reinforced and strengthened this belief. In the peace movement, activists denounced workers for taking jobs at munitions plants. In the environmental movement, activists denounced selfish loggers for not caring about the spotted owl. I rarely heard owners criticized and called to account.

These profound and sad examples resulted from community organizing without an integrated analysis of oppression, in particular without a class analysis. Through the 1960s, 1970s, and 1980s, incomplete analyses and problematic actions by progressive, middle-class activists supported the ruling class and offered new fodder in the war against working-class and working-poor people. The media, owned by the ruling class, happily took notes about selfish loggers and offered prominent airtime. Corporate owners sat complacently behind the scenes. As usual. Although I have no direct contact with these people, I assume they appreciated the classist and anti-environmental ideas verbalized time and again over the airwaves. I assume they appreciated reinforcement of the image of the backward, expendable, stupid laborer.

So many benefits to the ruling class! First, class divisions are heightened and reinforced. Second, focus is directed away from the harmful, retrograde, and oppressive ideas of the ruling class and toward workers. Third, organizers act as unthinking accomplices to the ruling class. Fourth, the grim reality of who has the power to keep homophobia, racism, and classism securely in place is obscured, as it has been for a long time.

In examining this point, I'm not saying working-class people are empty mouthpieces who can't think for ourselves; we're quite capable of devising our own homophobic ideas. I do want to articulate the difference between our homophobia and the homophobia of the rich. Truck drivers and garbagemen don't determine social policies. We don't make laws and decide what's acceptable and what's not. Wealthy people hold that power. They don't wait for us outside queer bars to beat us up; that's a working-class response for sure. But wealthy people do occupy judges' benches and presidents' offices and corporate boardrooms, and devise policies that ensure our children will be stolen, our relationships outlawed, our jobs taken, our partners denied health insurance. The queer movement must clearly name the powerful homophobes and strategize how to go after them.

I'm saddened, but not surprised, that the queer movement hasn't steered clear of this pitfall of middle-class progressive movements. Every step of the way it has swallowed the lie hook, line, and sinker. Belief about the homophobic working class sits firmly ensconced in political action and theory. A right-wing, homophobic response emerges as the only possible and authentic working-class response to queerness, a portrayal with several harmful ramifications. First, angry working-class and working-poor queers. And rightfully so. Classism permeates every level of the queer movement. How much can a social-change movement achieve when wrought with classist arrogance?

Second, over the past decades the queer movement has lost the chance to build ties and links with a natural ally—working-class and working-poor people. When I first came out, I couldn't understand why queer activists didn't attend union meetings and join picket lines. What better place to build bridges and engage in solidarity work? Then I realized classism prevents queer activists, leaders, and organizers from even considering the idea.

Third, poor people and queers are linked in critical ways. Extensive crossover exists between these groups. Lots of queers are firmly situated in working-class and working-poor communities, and 10 percent of this group outnumbers 10 percent from the middle and upper classes. Don't disguise reality by configuring us as the minority.[9] Also, queers and poor people share common agendas. Central concerns of working-class/working-poor people have recently been taken on by AIDS activists—nationalized health care and protection from unemployment. Another common struggle stems from restrictive definitions of the "family" that not only cast queers as sick and Other, but also attach that label to single mothers, common-law heterosexual partners, extended families, and various other conglomerations of people that end up living together under working-class roofs.

To date, however, the queer movement has focused on building alliances with rich people. No one has explicitly drafted this strategy; it happens because middle- and upper-class leadership steers toward people and institutions they know. With current assimilationist attitudes, it's even worse. When I flew to D.C. for the 1993 Queer March on Washington, I thought I would throw up if I heard one more TV interview with an earnest, middle-class queer explaining, "We're just like everyone else. This march will prove that." For the phrase "everyone else," read middle-class, white, monogamous, heterosexual couple. Don't read poor, Chicana, single mom.

Over the years I've been told, explicitly and implicitly, that liberal tolerance offered by rich people is the best queers can hope for. This needs analyzing, since it's a reaction that doesn't cut across class lines—that is, liberal tolerance only shows up in certain places. I'm happy to report I've never spotted the veneer of polite acceptance in working-class company, although it's rampant among the rich. Everyone's smiling, perhaps with a tinge of artificiality, and no one says anything nasty, but it's a far cry from being loved, welcomed, or integrated as a matter of course. It means I'm *tolerated*—that is, allowed to sit in the same room as people who know they rank above me. Is this really the best we can hope for? I refuse to accept that. While sitting in proper living rooms, I'm sizzling. I refuse to settle for condescending, patronizing tolerance from people who, underneath bland smiles and small talk, think much the same as my parents.

Liberal tolerance angers and irritates me, and I'm thankful it's not part of any working-class reality I've ever encountered. I can't deal with uptight rich folks who won't say shit when they step in it, who won't say queer when we fill up their living rooms. In the same way that working-class African Americans who grew up in the South and now live in the North have told me they prefer the more overt racism of the South, I deal better with working-class homophobes than with middle- or upper-class patronizingly tolerant homophobes. With the working-class person, I know where I stand, when to run, and when to talk. Someone who says to my face, "You're sick," might listen while I explain why I'm not. I can't argue with a person who *thinks* I'm sick and politely offers me tea, but I can engage with an honest factory worker. Change is never guaranteed, but in some cases it happens when we talk one on one about our sexuality. I predict it will happen even more if/when our actions as a movement prove we understand and care about the same bread-and-butter issues.

Working-class and working-poor queers who found each other in urban centers in the 1950s and 1960s ran the gamut from kiki to drag kings and queens to butch-femme couples to bull dykes. They toughed it out on the streets and did the best they could to resist extreme brutality and social scorn. But these folks weren't accorded leadership roles, let alone respect, in the larger movements for queer liberation that formed in the 1970s and 1980s. Sometimes they couldn't get in the door. When they did manage to, they didn't have a powerful role in shaping the movement, and neither did younger working-class queers. Instead, middle-class and upper-middle-class queers shaped the strategies and actions of the past three decades. I'm disturbed by the push for alliance with the corporate boardroom and not the union hall, by the invisibility of working-class queers, by a refusal to take class seriously.

I want the same things from the queer movement that I want from other social-change movements: a clear agenda, an inclusive definition of the group in question, an integrated analysis of all oppressions, a focus on coalition-building.

First, I want the queer movement to articulate a clear agenda of ending heterosexist/homophobic oppression, of integrating and welcoming all queers into the movement, of supporting liberation movements for women/disabled people/people of color/working-class and working-poor people. I want non-disabled queers at disability rights rallies stating support and a willingness to go to bat. I want non-union-member queers on picket lines. I wait for the day when we reap the benefits of solidarity work, and straight folks in wheelchairs and heterosexual welfare mothers speak at our demos and advocate on our behalf.

Second, I want a queer movement with a clear policy defining queer people and welcoming anyone who self-identifies as queer. While this seems so basic it's not worth mentioning, in reality it's critically important because so many queers have been left out of the movement's stated and unstated definitions. Bisexuals and transgender/transsexual people experience routine exclusion, as do queers of color, queers in wheelchairs, and working-poor/working-class queers.[10] The queer movement needs to clearly articulate who we are, state that anyone who self-identifies as queer is welcome, and then—here's the tough part—not freak out when the drag queens and kings, the trannies, and the high femmes arrive in full force. Or in full drag, which may be even scarier.

Third, the queer movement needs an integrated analysis of all oppressions. For queers to focus only on homophobia and heterosexism, without understanding racism, classism, imperialism, sexism, and ableism, is morally wrong and politically dangerous. This type of shallow analysis ignores the presence of queers living with more than one oppression, indirectly supports other oppressions through complicit silence, situates our struggle outside of other liberation movements, feeds isolation, and cuts us off from the power of connecting with others in struggle.

Fourth, while I always support coalition-building, it's especially important during this particular time, when overt right-wing individuals and groups continue to gain political power. Coalition-building displays an understanding of the connected strands of all oppressions and firmly situates queers within the context of the struggle for social justice. It affirms the identity of queers who belong to more than one oppressed group and allows us to do what we need to do—for example, connect our struggle to end racism with our struggle to end heterosexism. And coalition-building, which directly challenges divide-and-conquer strategies, presents a fiercer challenge to the powers that be than a single-issue campaign ever could.

~~~

The night after that sunlit day at Aunt Chuck and Uncle Joe's, Jan and I hung out with various cousins. Sitting in a room thick with smoke from cigarettes and joints, I tried to explain what my aunt and uncle's response meant, what it felt like to have my partner so accepted and welcomed and pulled tight into the heart of this family I love.

My cousins pursed their lips and frowned. They didn't understand me and kept saying: "Of course that happened. Why wouldn't it? This is your family. We care about you."

I gave up trying to explain, because I understood. *What else would we do?* I wondered how many anti-homophobia workshops rich people would have to attend before understanding, in their bones, the utter truth and simplicity and casualness of that understanding: *what else would we do?*

Notes

1. This is an area at certain Toronto subway stops where people in cars can park and wait for subway riders.

2. I use the term "queer movement" as a shorthand in this piece to describe the various queer political organizations in the United States at this point in time. I know there are different movements and communities, and in some ways it's inappropriate to lump them together, but in other ways it's not. I also know that while working-poor and working-class queers are active in these organizations, their structure and leadership are middle- and upper-middle-class. Classism is apparently a low priority in these groups at this time.

3. The violent homophobia of some privileged young men on college campuses offers an exception to prove that rule.

4. It's difficult to say how Arab culture fits into my aunt's response. While openness and tolerance have always been important values in the Arab world, this hasn't always crossed over into the responses of Arab Canadians and Arab Americans whose family members come out as queer. I plan to explore this issue in later essays.

5. When I use the word "rich" in this essay, I'm using it in the way most working-class people I know use it—anyone middle-class and up is rich, anyone working-class and down is poor. In some ways these two

categories are not subtle enough for all the nuances around class; one thing they do is hide my privilege of being working-class but not working-poor. On the other hand, I find "rich" and "poor" powerful, provocative, and appropriate categories. Middle-class people, who could choose to realize they are also being duped by rich people and decide they would be better off aligning themselves with working-class and working-poor people, continually align themselves with the rich. Thus, including middle-class people in the "rich" group is appropriate. So to the middle-class queers reading this—when I use the word "rich," I mean you.

6. This comment does make sense, in terms of my mother's gut knowledge of how class and gender oppression work together. One of the hardest things I had to face when I came out was knowing that when I left my middle-class husband, I'd be poor, and would probably stay that way the rest of my life.

7. I'm putting this problematic word in quotation marks to signify my concern. Even using this word can reinforce the social belief that carefully fostered race, class, and gender divisions are natural.

8. Thanks to Jan Binder for helping me articulate this point.

9. Privileged groups love to insist they're the majority, especially around race. Although as people of color, we're clearly the majority in terms of world population, the term "minority group" is continually used to describe us. Does this semantic distortion allow oppressors to feel less frightened about hordes of poor, dark people that massively outnumber them and have reason to despise them?

10. This is no different from people of color who don't know what to do with halfbreeds, or feminists who don't know what to do with members of transgender communities.

Intellectual Desire

ALLAN BÉRUBÉ

I n 1992 I was invited to present one of two keynote addresses at *La Ville en Rose: Le premier colloque Québécois d'études lesbiennes et gaies*–the First Québec Lesbian and Gay Studies Conference–held in Montréal that November. Nicole Brossard, the lesbian-feminist *Québécoise* poet, novelist, and essayist, presented the other address. We were paired up as speakers for a reason. The conference organizers were both anglophone and francophone, and their goal was to create an event that brought together lesbian and gay studies in Canada's two official languages. The conference was held at two locations: Concordia University in the predominantly English-speaking West End and *L'Université du Québec à Montréal* in the predominantly French-speaking East End (near *Le Village*–the gay center of the city). Nicole Brossard presented her address in French and I presented mine in English; both were simultaneously translated into the other language.

I was invited because, since the late 1970s, I've written and spoken about lesbian, gay, and bisexual social and political history, especially in my book *Coming Out Under Fire: The History of Gay Men and Women in World War II*. But I was also invited because I'm an anglophone Franco-American independent historian of Québec ancestry who could try to speak across some bounda-

ries—between Franco-American and French-Canadian, anglophone
and francophone, United States and Canada, the university and the
"community," literary studies and the social sciences. My audience
included people in all these categories, but I especially wanted to
speak to those intellectuals at the conference who, like myself,
were from working-class backgrounds or were in their family's first
generation to go to college. (Québec's modern, secular, public
colleges date only from the Quiet Revolution in the 1960s.) I also
wanted to use this occasion to see if I could weave together apparently separate strands of my own life—my white Franco-American
ethnicity, my class migration, my homosexuality, and my intellec-
tualism—and identify the desires that surround and sometimes
connect them. And I wanted to do this without hiding the romantic,
even sentimental, longing to go home that this first visit to Montréal
had aroused in me.

What follows is a revised version of what I said.[1]

<hr/>

When I accepted the invitation to address you at this first Québec
lesbian and gay studies conference, I knew that I was being offered
a chance to return to what novelist and essayist Salman Rushdie
has called an "imaginary homeland."[2] "My Québec" is the place my
ancestors came from but to which I've never traveled except in
my imagination. The thought of such a homecoming forced me to
look across the distances I've traveled and the boundaries I've
crossed to get here. How did I—a Franco-American kid raised rural
and working-class in New England, whose earlier family history
included no self-identified intellectuals or homosexuals—learn to
become this new thing: a gay community-based historian who lives
in a gay "ghetto" in San Francisco? I'm not going to answer this question with the happy-ending narrative of a coming-out story. Instead, I
want to describe how both my homosexual and intellectual desires
have moved me across class boundaries and how this movement
places me within a long tradition of ethnic migration and assimilation.
And I want to show how I use history to calm my anxieties about living in the borderlands where I've ended up, one of which is the
world of lesbian and gay intellectuals.

At the core of my anxiety about being a gay intellectual is a
dilemma: Books, ideas, and a college scholarship provided the

class escape route that gave me the resources to come out with pride as a gay man. But the middle-class educational and gay worlds I entered haven't helped me overcome the shame of having escaped my Franco-American working-class origins by doing intellectual work. When class, race, and ethnicity are not part of that work, studying with other gay and lesbian intellectuals can actually increase my anxiety. I worry that I'll pass as something I'm not. Or I worry that I'll fall into wearing my class origins as a badge of courage rather than using them to improve our thinking.

Class escape stories tell what happens when you get out of the class you grew up in and enter one of higher status. They reveal unresolved conflicts about what one has lost and gained. They expose the anguish of leaving a home you can't return to, while not belonging where you've ended up. These dislocations deepen what have been called the "hidden injuries of class."[3] Many of us from poor or working-class backgrounds experience these injuries when we are the first generation to go to college, as I was, even if we drop out before graduating, as I did, from class panic, lack of money, and unfulfilled homosexual desires. The injury is the belief that we've deserted our people by going away to serve our more desirable benefactors, who would use us for their ends and seduce us into abandoning our own.

My gay and intellectual journeys across ethnic and class lines have too often felt like a desertion. Yet my own migration patterns—going to college, coming out, moving West—continue a tradition in which at least four generations of my family also migrated across boundaries between nations, languages, cultures, and classes, leaving them unsure of where they belonged. Never undertaken lightly, our migrations put us in serious conflict with structures of power that were not our own. We used old strategies to survive and even invented new ones, some of which worked while others boomeranged, threatening our safety and well-being. The injuries I've sustained along the way have been, to use James Baldwin's words, the price of my ticket out,[4] just as there was a heavy price for the escape routes my family took before me.

My family's itinerary followed a larger map of French migration around North America—what Franco-American scholars have called a "tortured geography." Imagine trying to connect the dots of the many disconnected French worlds (past and present) just inside the United States: Woonsocket, Rhode Island; Manchester, New Hampshire; Lowell, Massachusetts; Lewiston, Maine; Lafayette, Louisiana; Frenchtown, Montana; Wildwood, New Jersey; Hollywood, Florida; Kankakee, Illinois; Ste. Genevieve, Missouri. They form a far-flung archipelago connected only by what has been called "fragile alliances spanning distant and disparate communities."[5] Not only is our French North American geography tortured, but so are the names that we have called ourselves or were hurled at us: Frenchy, Frog, Creole, Acadien, Métis, Franco, Coonass, Lard-Eater, Dumb Frenchman. "They say that you are a *Québécois*," observed Jean Morisset, a Franco-American geographer, "that others are *Fransaskois*, *Martiniquais*, Cajun, Canuck, *Haïtien*, *Franco-Tenois*, French-Cree..."[6] My generation in the United States grew up calling ourselves "French-Canadian," but people always asked us, "Where in Canada were you born?" We now call ourselves "Franco-American," but people ask us, "From where in France?" or make jokes about canned spaghetti. No common name fits.

"We bear the names of the itineraries we have traveled and the rivers we have navigated," explains Morisset, the geographer. My Uncle Larry—from the French "Laurent," he'd remind us, not from the English "Lawrence"—was named after the great river, the St. Laurent, the lifeline of Québec. Our French North American names, life stories, and writings are the living records of wherever our explorations, expulsions, and migrations have taken us—along great rivers and lakes, from our conquest of native peoples to our defeat and colonization by the English, even to losing a sense of ourselves and our history. Displacement and invisibility often characterize us. The Acadians became the Cajuns after the English forcibly deported them from the maritime provinces to the English colonies and then to Louisiana in the 1700s. Jack Kerouac made his itinerary his life work when he wrote *On the Road* after leaving his native Frenchtown in Lowell, Massachusetts. Our anglicized American names hide their Franco origins: White (LeBlanc), Greenwood (Boisvert), Fisher (Fourcier). Our writers describe us as a people with "a fractured culture, a culture that emerges in little bursts, a culture in which those to whom it belongs barely recognize themselves."[7] Or we are "a people in the process of becoming an endangered species, suffering from loss of memory."[8] Or we are "a people who have traditionally had nothing to say, who have been too far down the social ladder and too weighted with frustrations to make works of art."[9] Or as "an America that knows no name."[10] Or as no longer a people at all.

Silenced, forgotten, lost, sold, abandoned, translated into English, absorbed, deported, or conquered, still often poor or working-class, keeping to ourselves, staying out of sight, on the move. And ashamed of ourselves. "Where does our incredible sense of shame come from?" asks the geographer,[11] as if shame itself were a river you could see cutting across our internalized French maps of North America.

The history of working-class Francos trying to survive in a fiercely Anglo North America in so many ways resonates with the emotional history of homos trying to survive in a fiercely hetero world. It was only a matter of time before I'd see and feel these connections between class, ethnicity, and sexuality, and then use my intellect to make sense of them. My own life's itineraries—coming out across sexualities, becoming a working-class intellectual in middle-class worlds, moving to California—all distanced me from my Franco-American family of origin. Yet it is our common history of migration that I and my Franco ancestors share most profoundly—crossing borders generation after generation for more than three centuries on this continent as we searched for ways to survive, creating new selves in the process.

More than a hundred years ago, in the 1870s and 1880s, my great-grandparents left Trois-Rivières and Saint Pascal in Québec to live and work in the United States. This was not a pleasure trip. They moved because the small farms they were allowed to own could no longer support their large families. They were part of a huge exodus that lasted until the 1920s in which hundreds of thousands of French-Canadians moved south to find jobs during New England's industrial boom. They were lured away from Québec by mill owners' agents sent north across the border to recruit cheap manual labor for the mills that grew up all along New England's great rivers: the Connecticut, Merrimack, Penobscot, and Androscoggin.

My ancestors, the Bérubés, LeBlancs, Fleurys, and Boisverts, moved from Québec to Aldenville, a village between Holyoke and Chicopee, Massachusetts, on the Connecticut River. For three generations, the women and girls worked in the nearby textile mills, or as domestic workers in middle-class Yankee homes, or as mothers and homemakers in their large Catholic families. The men and boys worked as manual laborers in the surrounding brickyards, paper mills, and machine shops. Both envied and derided by folks back home in Québec and despised at the bottom of the white ethnic hierarchy in New England, these immigrants were of two minds about being in the United States. Fearful of losing their culture in a hostile Yankee land, they were fortified by their nearness to Québec. While many did go back home to visit their families, most stayed in their new *Québec d'en Bas* (Québec Down Below). There they took the strategies of *la survivance* they had developed in Québec against English domination—defending church, language, and family—and adapted them to this new country. In Aldenville they formed a *P'tit Canada* (Little Canada), as their "cousins" did in nearly every other industrial city in New England. Their little Frenchtown reconstructed the institutions of French Québec as barricades against assimilation in the United States—barricades against the English language, Protestantism, and the dominant Irish Catholic Church hierarchy. In Aldenville, three generations of my family lived totally French lives and kept French-Canadian customs at home, in church, at the parish schools, in the shops, and on the porches and backyards of their tenement "blocks." Their vision for these Little Canadas was to create something new—a particular way to remain French in the United States, to be American in French. "You are Americans," wrote Jacques Ducharme, a novelist from Holyoke, trying to articulate this vision to those Francos who were adopting English as their language, "*mais nous, nous sommes Américains.*"[12]

The limited Anglo imagination attacked this Franco refusal to assimilate by challenging their whiteness. Yankees called these French-Canadian immigrants in New England *les chinois de l'est*—"the Chinese of the East"—comparing the self-contained French-towns to the Chinatowns on the West Coast.[13] "It is said that there are more French-Canadians in New England than there are in

Canada," complained a *New York Times* editorial a century ago. "It is next to impossible to penetrate this mass of protected and se-cluded humanity with modern ideas....No other people," the *Times* went on, "except the Indians, are so persistent in repeating themselves. Where they halt they stay, and where they stay they multiply and cover the earth."[14] These French-Canadian migrants had not yet securely been granted the privileges of whiteness in the United States. Well into the twentieth century, public school teachers ordered Franco-American students to "speak white" when they were overheard talking to each other in their French mother tongue.[15] Such racist forms of ethnic shaming, when com-bined with the promise of white race privilege because of their European ancestry (despite their own Native American/First Na-tion ancestors), intensified the desperation of these Franco immi-grants to achieve and then defend their own American whiteness.[16]

In the 1930s, my grandparents and their six children were forced to leave Aldenville because of the Great Depression. Unable to support themselves on factory wages alone, they reversed ear-lier Franco-American migration patterns and moved from the city back to a farm in a rural Yankee town fifteen miles away. There, they survived by raising and hunting their own food, while the women made the Franco rural dishes that I grew up on as a child: our homemade maple syrup poured over snow, stewed tomatoes and fresh corn on the cob, *sauce blanche* (flour, milk, and hard-boiled eggs poured over bread or potatoes), wild venison and pheas-ant, and *tourtières*—Christmas meat pies. Isolated from their *P'tit Canada* as their parents had been isolated from Québec, they found themselves surrounded by Yankee farmers, attending mass at an unfriendly Irish Catholic church, and having to speak English while shopping in town. Although all six children had gone to the French parish school, L'École Sainte Jeanne D'Arc, in Aldenville, my father, the youngest, now had to attend the town's English-speaking public high school, where his Yankee teachers failed him in French, his mother tongue, because he did not speak it properly.

My family, unable to defend themselves with the community resources they'd had in Aldenville, devised other strategies to get out from under the social stigma of being a French minority in a

Yankee town. One strategy was to tell racist jokes to bond with others in their all-white but now ethnically mixed worlds. They were trying to ease the pain of being called "Dumb Frenchmen" by stigmatizing those who had been excluded from their whiteness. Another strategy was to "marry up" into Irish, Italian, and even Protestant Yankee families, and to raise my generation as the first to grow up speaking English. Learning to forget French was slow and painful in our family, as each generation was taught that our "lousy" French was not worth speaking. As a gay man I now make a living speaking and writing in English because my family was shamed into silencing their French. At first my aunts and uncles survived by staying close to home—my father and uncle built houses on the family farm—but eventually most of them moved away, even to other states. Slowly, they abandoned their traditional strategies of *la survivance*—the trinity of large family, Catholic Church, and French language—in order to survive as their world changed around them.

This bilingual, ethnically mixed extended family was the rural working-class world into which I was born in 1946. I was the seventh grandchild, but the first with both a French mother, Lorraine Tétreault, and a French father, Ronald Bérubé. Even in the 1950s I grew up feeling in my family an almost magnetic pull back to Aldenville, a place I'd never been. On Sundays after Mass, my grandmother, my *mé-mère*, would prepare a big dinner and, still wearing her Sunday dress under her apron, would sit on the front porch waiting for company to arrive from Aldenville with gossip and lively French conversation. When company did come, which was often, I caught glimpses of how full of vitality their *P'tit Canada* had been. And after they went home, I saw *Mé-mère's* melancholy pining as she was lost in the memories of a place she'd never wanted to leave.

It's still difficult for me to say the word *mé-mère* in public. It was a private Franco-American family word spoken only at home, not found in French dictionaries, that we always translated as "grandmother" when speaking to outsiders. It was one of a small category of words so charged with power they had to be said in hushed tones, with shame or reverence, or never at all. As Catholics, we had to bow our heads when we said "Jesus." By the second grade, I knew that the casual use of the word "nigger" marked our family as low-class, ignorant, and prejudiced. "Fuck" was dirty and obscene. The French language as we spoke it was like these words—a mark of shame, difference, or ignorance. "Homosexual" fit right in. When I first read this word in books, I had to make a deliberate decision to actually speak it aloud. When I did (to myself), it felt like the other words had felt in my mouth—my voice held back in a whisper, tongue and lips not quite completing each sound within it. This word, "homosexual," exposed more about me than I wanted anyone to know—even a priest. Growing up Franco, but ashamed to speak our French, gave me the practice I needed in not saying this word that was so often on the tip of my tongue.

As much as my father loved the farm, which had been his mother's prison, he had to leave it to give his own family the nice things and secure life he wanted for us. Being the first child in the family to escape assembly-line factory work, my father had earned a radio operator's license in night school and had gotten work in broadcasting, achieving the minor status that came with this skilled blue-collar job. But in 1950, when I was three, my mother died in childbirth, a too-common fate among Franco-American women. Their bodies, and those of their many babies who died at birth, were the casualties of yet another line of Franco self-defense, a part of *la survivance* called the "revenge of the cradle"—making large families so they wouldn't die out as a people. *Mé-mère* and *Pé-père* took me in. My father went to Manhattan for two years, where he found new opportunities in early television broadcasting and married a working-class, Polish-American Catholic woman from Brooklyn.

My just-married parents moved us all into a tiny house trailer, a cramped eight-by-thirty-six-foot space that eventually held a family of six. For years we moved around, unhitching our mobile home in blue-collar trailer parks named "Sunnyside" in Connecticut and "Sunset" in New Jersey. They were trying to save money to buy a real house and acquire the security, comfort, and leisure time that was their vision of a better life—a vision they acquired from reading *Better Homes and Gardens*, the bible for postwar migrants into the expanding middle class.

It was during grade school, when we lived in a trailer park in Bayonne, a multiracial blue-collar town in New Jersey, that my desires for other boys awakened, but were never fulfilled. I was drawn to boys whom I fantasized as my brothers (I was the oldest child with three younger sisters). From the start, my erotic desire for "brotherness" was shaped by class. The moments I felt it strongest was when I was in other boys' homes—something my parents strictly prohibited. I visited a schoolmate who lived on a wooden barge docked nearby on Newark Bay, and felt an erotic charge of sympathy for him in his poverty. A boy in another trailer park took me inside his trailer when his parents were at work. When we peed together in his tiny bathroom I wanted to pee with him again as brothers. And when I visited a schoolmate who lived up the street in a house—a real building with rooms, doors, and an upstairs—I fantasized that I lived there with him, sharing a bedroom and being able to close the door. Eroticizing other boys, up, down, and across these working-class hierarchies, entering their homes and imagining being alone there with them when I had no privacy at home, wanting them close to me forever as my brothers—these were desires that only later in college did I dare to name "homosexual."

An intellectual desire was awakened in me as well. I knew no one, other than my teachers, who had gone to college or who made a living working with ideas. Yet in the *Encyclopædia Britannica,* which my parents bought on credit from a door-to-door salesman who worked the trailer park, and in the collection of classical music records they bought in weekly installments at the supermarket and played on a hi-fi my father had built from a do-it-yourself kit, I envisioned a different world, full of poetry, literature, great music, philosophy, and art.

As my desire to find that world grew, I began to imagine the escape routes that might get me there. One of these pointed inward as I tried to create that world on my own. I became a bookworm who didn't like sports—that particular kind of male sissy who is teased in his working-class family for putting on airs by burying himself in books—the "smart one" who thinks he is no longer "one of us." With so many of us packed into this little trailer, it was hard to write or even read much. But each summer, when we went back to stay with my *mé-mère* and *pé-père* on the family farm, I found the solitude to read books and write poetry. I returned to the trailer with memories and dreams of going back to the farm that kept my imagination alive. My moving back and forth between the trailer park and the farm taught me early on that I could survive a difficult present by reminiscing about the past and dreaming about the future. This survival strategy has shaped my imagination ever since. It has infused my writing with a sentimental nostalgia that's still hard to overcome, but also with a utopian idealism that keeps me going through hard times.

I also imagined escape routes that pointed outward. I built a radio and every night I would hide under the covers wearing my father's klunky World War II headphones, searching the dial for the distant crackle of the classical music station, WQXR, from New York City. College was as far on the intellectual horizon as my limited vision could reach—a place where people like me could talk about art, literature, and ideas. My parents warned me over and over that if I wanted to go to college I'd have to win a scholarship because they didn't have the money to send me. In my nightly prayers I asked God to let us move to a town with good schools and to let me win a scholarship. And I became a student obsessed with reading and studying—no straight A's, no scholarship; no college education, no exit.

At the same time, I saw in my father what I might become if I couldn't escape by going to college. Although he was brilliant at making the most out of being trapped, my father's ingenuity couldn't rescue him from the working-class traps themselves. A cautious, self-effacing, honest man and a meticulous worker terrified of getting caught making mistakes, my father's life was shaped by the ethnic and class shame that came with living in "their" worlds, being forced to speak "their" languages. He spent his life behind the scenes, running the machinery that broadcast other people's voices and faces to television sets across North America. His need to justify his existence by satisfying his bosses, and his sacrificing himself through hard work to make our lives better, slowly killed him with a lifetime of stomach ulcers and finally cancer. I knew that the same traps could kill me, too—unless I got out.

For two years—my first years in high school, from 1960 until 1962—my parents' middle-class dream did come true. They bought a new, four-bedroom, colonial-style house in a New Jersey suburb and decorated it with new colonial furniture and new wall-to-wall carpeting, and even bought a new Plymouth station wagon to put in our two-car garage. They finally had a better home *and* garden. For the first time, I could proudly bring a friend over to my house for dinner. And I got my own bedroom and the good school I'd prayed for.

Our modern, suburban, 99-percent-white high school placed me in college-track classes, segregated from the vocational-track students. I'd felt lucky to be let into their honors classes, but I was always on guard, never quite sure I belonged in their world, afraid that it was only a matter of time before they would discover their mistake and send me "down" to the vocational track. But I held my own with a desperately good academic performance and a compulsion to join any extracurricular activity that would look great on a scholarship application form.

The crisis came in my sophomore year when my father was offered a low-level management position at work, which he turned down, he said, because he didn't want the responsibility of supervising other workers. But there was more to his refusal than class panic over becoming "one of them." The distance he had traveled—away from his French working-class family, their farm, and the land—was now so far from where he'd started that he began to lose the ground beneath his feet. He wanted to go home. My parents sold their dream house and bought the Massachusetts family farm, where my dad had grown up, from my *pé-père*, who continued to live with us there after my *mé-mère* died. My dad found a job at a local television station in Springfield for half his former wages and, after his union lost a critical strike, his income steadily declined.

My prospects for college now looked grim. The public high school in this mill town rarely sent anyone to a "good" university. My mother tells me that I cried for days at the thought of not going to college (I've blocked out all memory of this). I was rescued by the local, third-rate private boys' academy, which accepted me as a day-student "townie." Every morning and afternoon I hitched a ride between the farm and town on the public grade school bus, humiliated to be sitting there, a teenage bookworm dressed up in a sports jacket and tie, surrounded by screaming farm kids who must have thought I had dropped in from Mars. Luckily, I was rescued again, this time by a young, friendly, and handsome American history teacher (whom I had a crush on). With his guidance and connections, he helped me win a rare senior-year scholarship to a prestigious college preparatory boarding school fifty miles away.

I was about to enter an elite world my parents knew little about, while their income was rapidly falling. The class divide between me and my family was growing wider and deeper.

I arrived at prep school with a mixture of fear and awe, feeling as if I had been invited into the homes of the rich. This was the world that could give me the escape and the culture I wanted, yet it made me acutely aware of my "lower" class background. I earned my keep by washing dishes, setting tables, and serving students in the dining room, I performed well in classes, and I even wrote poetry and a play about my alienation that won a *Reader's Digest* creative writing award. During summer session, when I worked in the school's kitchen to earn money for college, I was housed with five other scholarship boys[17] in the basement of the same dormitory I'd lived in as a student. But now a locked door separated us from the well-to-do students upstairs. As workers, we were forbidden to visit or even talk to the students. But during time off from our fourteen-hour work day, we were graciously allowed to attend their general lectures, which that year were about the history of utopian socialism!

Here I was, a Franco-American, raised in a French family, learning French for the first time from Protestant, English-speaking teachers in this upper-class Yankee school—nice teachers who agreed that I was wise not to have learned "bad" French at home. This was proper Parisian French they taught me—"French from France," as Franco-Americans called it in English—a language my *mé-mère* used to love to hear spoken, as she loved touching fine Parisian lace, and as I enjoyed art and poetry—beautiful things that the well-to-do took for granted and that we could only dream about with envy.

This all-male Protestant school was nearly all white, and rumor was that it had quotas for no more than twenty-five Catholics and twenty-five Jews. It was here that I stopped going to Mass and left the Catholic Church, opening a door toward someday acting on my homosexual desires without having to confess my sins to a priest. I became intrigued with liberal Protestantism and especially my Protestant classmates—young white men who seemed so confident and in control, who looked good and knew how to dress in good clothes, and whose school had been so generous to let me in, for which I felt too much gratitude.

I knew that their attractive prep school world wasn't really mine—I was their guest. Yet I no longer belonged at home, either. When my parents came to visit me, I was stunned to see them through the eyes of a different class. Despite my homesickness for them, I was embarrassed by what was now their old station wagon, their sturdy rather than tasteful clothes, and the down-to-earth way they talked. Who was I becoming? And where was I going?

My desire to belong in an intellectual world—which in this school taught us to take whiteness, upper-class privilege, and maleness for granted—aroused a new but secret and often sexual desire for these smart, well-to-do, articulate men. I wanted to have them, I wanted to be them, and I wanted to be wanted by them. And so my homosexual desires began to split into two directions. They moved horizontally, toward working-class men like myself and the scholarship boys I worked with in the kitchen. Since childhood, I had eroticized such boys as brothers, and now I associated them with my past and my family. My homo desires also moved up vertically, toward my "betters," who seemed to have what I lacked, and who I believed had the authority to give me self-respect, verify my respectability, and offer me another escape route into a better, more secure future.

This class split in my homosexual desires continued to structure my lover relationships for years. In the 1980s I decided to stop having any middle-class boyfriends for a while. I partnered only with men who were raised working-class so I could begin to step outside and examine the dynamics of my cross-class desires. Yet I wondered how much my new relationships with working-class men were also shaped by my having moved as a guest into middle-class worlds. Was my desire for working-class guys now an expression of a middle-class sexual attraction to the "other," an attraction absorbed from my "betters"? Or was it an expression of an erotic, romantic longing to come home? Or was it both—a hybrid mix of same-class and cross-class desires?

I graduated from prep school in 1964 with honors and won a work-study scholarship to the University of Chicago as an English major. My class was still nearly all white (98 percent), but now only two-thirds rather than 100 percent male. During the economic boom of the 1960s, the gratitude and indebtedness I and too many other poor or working-class students felt for winning scholarships to private colleges reflected our desperation to scramble through these temporarily open doors.[18] Our scholarships were attempts by our elite benefactors not only to be generous but also to mine us for what they often condescendingly praised us for—our "freshness" and "vitality," our "passion" and "original thinking"—and then to train us and even trap us with loans and enormous debts into serving their institutions. We usually made their lives richer rather than enriching those of our own people, whose sacrifices had gotten us as far as they could. This is how the mill owners had mined Québec and the *P'tits Canadas* for the cheap manual labor of my family years before, and how my European ancestors had mined the native peoples of North America for their resources, land, and culture.

My parents and *Pé-père* were of two minds about where my college education was taking me. They wanted me to "better" myself. But they didn't want me to become a "stuffed shirt"—to think or act as if I were better than they were. I knew these were the risks—that I might betray them by abandoning them in their difficult lives while fulfilling their dreams of self-improvement and escape. This is a core dilemma that many working-class intellectuals often face by ourselves: By pursuing our intellectual desires, we risk becoming like our own and our parents' class "enemies"— those who would rescue us only to use us for their ends, while looking down on those they left behind.

I tried to figure out how to resolve this class dilemma and still keep up with the demands of a hyper-academic college curriculum. Convinced that I had nothing intelligent to say compared to the articulate students around me, I never spoke a word in any of my courses. Then, in 1968, I faced more serious crises, all in April.

One crisis involved riots and police repression: explosions of grief, anger, and fear after the assassination of Dr. Martin Luther King, Jr., followed by the declaration of martial law in Chicago and the closing of our campus in a citywide curfew. Another crisis was set off when, a week after the riots, I said "I have a homosexual problem" to the man I was in love with and had to deal with the consequences on my own. As my grades plummeted in the wake of these and other incidents, and the university punished me by changing my scholarship to a loan, I faced a new class panic as well: I didn't know how I was ever going to pay back the debts. I dropped out. Like my father who had panicked in the suburbs, I felt the ground disappearing beneath my feet and wanted to go back home. But home wasn't where I could come out. So I moved to Boston.

College, and bull-sessions with students I hung out with after I dropped out, taught me two new languages. One was the shop talk of intellectual work—educated talk that either made you feel smart or stupid, depending on how you performed and who you were. The other language was political. At its best, it gave us a way to analyze systems of oppression and take action, although usually from a white, middle-class perspective, rather than from the perspective of a scholarship student. At its worst, it was show-off talk about talk itself, as if talk alone were the same as action. I wanted to learn how to use both these new languages because they let me understand and discuss ideas I needed. But they also conflicted with a native language I had learned at home—a language that spoke through action and held a deep mistrust of educated talk that doesn't come through when times get tough. And now that I'd dropped out of school with big debts and no money, my times were getting tough.

One of the things I used my educated languages for was to come out. By 1970 I'd read psychology and sociology articles and some gay liberation literature, and I'd gone to Student Homophile League meetings at MIT. I'd learned how to talk politically and intellectually about my own and other people's homosexuality. But when I finally went home to come out to my parents, I ended up re-opening old wounds of class rupture between us. They accepted my being gay. But they heard me describing my homosexuality in the language of those more powerful and more educated than they were and saw my homosexuality as one more indication that I had entered elite worlds that were changing me beyond recognition. Through me they saw "gay" as college-educated—and I couldn't deny it, since, in my middle-class worlds, that's what I had learned, too. Yet I was trying to appropriate that educated language (such as "homophobia" and "sexual orientation") so that its words would become "ours" as well. I wanted these ideas to belong to me, to my family, and even to my class of origin, so we could use them to make *our* lives better, too.

In 1973 I discovered a gay community when I visited San Francisco for the first time. I saved some money and moved there a year later. Living in a gay male hippie commune in the Haight-Ashbury district, I saw other gay men settling in the more affluent Castro district, building a gay neighborhood that was called both a "Mecca" and a "ghetto." As Aldenville had been created by French-Canadian immigrants a century earlier out of their memories of Québec, "the Castro" was being created out of new dreams by "sexual migrants."[19] Uprooted from my own class and ethnic backgrounds, and attracted by the openness of gay life in San Francisco, I was a sexual migrant, too. I was intrigued by the ability of these mostly white gay men in the Castro to build a new identity, their own gay politics, and their own neighborhood. I wanted passionately to belong in that gay community. These men were constructing what I grew up so aware of losing—an extended family and an almost-ethnic community with a culture and language all its own. In their neighborhood, gay could be ordinary. I hung out in the Castro a lot. In 1979 I worked with others to create our own activist/intellectual version of community, the San Francisco Lesbian and Gay History Project—a study group that became the home base for my work as a gay historian for more than ten years.

These attempts at community-building, and the broader lesbian and gay movement, helped me transform my gay shame into gay pride, and gave me the support I needed to make a living as a "community-based" gay historian. But I hadn't overcome the shame from my own class escape, ethnic erasure, and white-skin privilege. Gay pride showed me this was possible, but it was only a metaphor for the specific work on class, ethnicity, and race I had yet to do.

The ideas of gay community, gay politics, and gay studies were built partly by white, middle-class-identified, college-educated gay men around a belief that homosexuality could and should stand alone as the organizing principle for our lives and work—as if our homosexualities had not been significantly shaped by our race, gender, and class. Many lesbians and people of color told us that much of what we created with the resources we had—money, education, connections, professional skills—reproduced the race and gender hierarchies of the larger society. What I experienced most directly as a white gay man with little money and no college degree was how the gay community reproduced class hierarchies. There were many gay restaurants, disco parties, conferences, resorts, and bathhouses I couldn't afford. And I didn't have the income to live in the Castro.

It's a mistaken idea that gay community or gay activism or gay studies can stand alone as "gay." They all were made possible by past civil rights, ethnic, class, and women's struggles, and by those who enjoyed many forms of institutionalized power and privilege. The white, male, and middle-class separation of "gay" from these other struggles and histories is one of the many predictable outcomes of a larger process of Americanization that I know too well from my family's class and ethnic history. The newcomer's desire to fully belong—as American, or white, or middle-class, or college-educated, or gay—tempts many of us to join others in scrambling up ladders beyond, and even on the backs of, those on the lower rungs. Moving closer to the top, we're encouraged to believe we got there on our own. We're taught to forget those on the bottom, or regretfully leave them behind, or romanticize them, or look down on them with pity or disdain, or study them to get Ph.D.s. In my life, I find myself both on the higher and lower rungs of many ladders.[20] I've climbed up through access to a privileged and systematically exclusive private education—fractured and interrupted as it was. At the same time, I've endured the painful injuries of class, and of ethnic and sexual shame. The hurt is what drove me so passionately toward creating a supportive gay life and community; the privileges gave me the resources to do it. So long as we white, educated gay men in queer studies do not investigate, then incorporate into our work, the class, race, and gender structures that shape our own intellectual pursuits—keeping our histories buried as if they were something "not gay" or "not intellectual"—I will never be able to think that our work is "real," as my mother would say, or relevant to the lives of those we have left behind or left out.

In the last few years I've been doing a community-based history of the Marine Cooks and Stewards Union—a left-wing, multiracial maritime union on the West Coast that included lots of openly gay, working-class men. I've created a slide show about them that I take to union halls, labor conferences, and community colleges, as well as to private universities. I was inspired to do this work by a former member of the union now in his late seventies, a gay Franco-American whose family name was anglicized from Blais to Blair when his relatives crossed the Canadian border to live in Minnesota at the turn of the century.

My interest in the queer, multiracial, working-class history of this union is part of the magnetic pull back to the past that haunts me as it has haunted at least four generations of my family. It's expressed in my intellectual desire to bridge the distances I've traveled that still make me feel so dislocated in the present, and to search the past for answers, solutions, maps, and useful strategies that might make things better for those still in my class of origin. For my father, the pull back was the homesickness that made him return to the family farm. From that farm, my *mé-mère* longed for her French community in Aldenville. There, her parents looked back toward their homes in Québec. My gay history work, paradoxically, grows out of my desire to break this chain of longing, so that I can finally arrive here, now, in this place in North America, as I am and as we are, fully belonging, with all the disconnected fragments of my life finally put together into an integrated, dignified whole. This utopian vision of the future mirrors the most romantic visions of lost, imaginary homelands.

My desire to realize this dream of wholeness at first drew me to Catholicism, then to having a college education, then to embracing the identity politics of gay liberation, then to going West, then to "reclaiming" my ethnic roots. But none of these could ever make my dream come true.

I'm learning from others in similar situations to accept and constructively use the distances and dislocation, the double vision and two-mindedness, and the homosexual desires up, down, and across class lines. This is where I've ended up as a gay, working-class intellectual and as a Franco-American, too. The "America in between" the geographer Morisset names as the Franco's location on this continent is also my home base as a gay writer and historian.[21]

I do my work now in the borderlands between social classes, between the university and the community, between heterosexual and homosexual, between educated speech and down-to-earth talk, between Franco-American and Québécois, between my family and the gay community, between the past and the present. This is a land where I make visits home, then leave again; a land where I maintain long-distance relationships and enjoy one-night stands; where, without a B.A., I teach in an elite university, then enter a maximum security prison because the men inside asked me to talk to them about gay history; where I am my family's historian because they know I've published gay history; and where on my bedroom wall I hang my *mé-mère*'s rosary beads next to my Tom of Finland leatherman print. These temporarily bridged distances and unexpected combinations have become a workshop in which it seems possible to make the gay, intellectual, working-class, and Franco-American parts of myself reinforce each other, rather than split me apart.

What I've tried to do in this talk is to describe one particular white gay man's history from the inside in a way that focuses on class, ethnic, and educational migration, rather than on coming out. But the danger in describing a working-class life from the inside is the temptation to frame one's narrative within a "rhetoric of hardship"—a storytelling strategy that tries to mitigate class oppression by appealing to the sympathy and generosity of the more fortunate. This rhetorical strategy is very seductive because it reshapes working-class lives into stories of courageous struggle against impossible odds. It may be the working-class equivalent of using the coming-out story as an appeal for heterosexual understanding and acceptance. But the class hardship narrative only reinforces class hierarchies in the telling. Even as it makes visible and validates the lives of working-class people, and evokes sympathy from middle-class listeners, it reduces us to either victims or heroes. Our lives become satisfying dramas of suffering that end in inspiring victory or poignant tragedy.[22] I've tried to resist this temptation, and to use the stuff of my life to understand a much larger historical process: how class and racialized ethnic histories shape our languages, our sexual desires and relationships, our psychologies, our writings, and our intellectualities.

I want to speak for a minute to those of you who were taught that intellectual work belonged to your "betters," not to you. Whenever we've entered middle-class worlds, especially those of "higher" education, many of us have had to pass, and still pass, as one of "them"; we've been invited in as guests or we've even trespassed without invitation. The risks of this cross-class movement are great. *Class passing* forces us to erase our own history. It makes us afraid that someone will find out the truth about us and kick us out. Being treated as a *guest*—as a scholarship student in college, as a member of the "community" invited to attend an academic conference, or as a scholar without a degree asked to give a university lecture or keynote address—seems to demand our gratitude and indebtedness in return. Guest status can make us afraid of being disinvited, expelled, or humiliated if we say or do the wrong thing. *Class trespassing*, the deliberate violation of class boundaries—going where we are not wanted, bringing up class when we are not asked—can get us caught and punished, then sent back to where we came from.

While I can now proudly call myself gay without feeling the shame I once knew, it's still not easy to call myself an intellectual without feeling like an impostor. But none of us can do our best work until we believe that the life of the mind really does belong to us, from the pleasures of theoretical analysis and brilliant insights to the way an idea can save lives. When we who are independent scholars, or the first generation to go to college, or avid readers and writers, do claim our intellectualities as our own, we become a force to be reckoned with. Among our most valuable resources are the abilities to see the familiar in new ways, to question privileged assumptions, and even to use our intellects to dismantle the powerful systems that cause the class injuries we know too well.

Coming here to this conference, I am completing a circle of migration that my great-grandparents began when they left Québec over a century ago. I now see that their escape route was not destined to be a one-way trip for our family. They left hoping that factory work in the United States would help them survive as French Catholic families. I've come back because I'm gay and intellectual and Franco-American—and I wanted to see what happens if I connect these three parts of my life. I'm awed when I realize that my great-grandparents could never have imagined my being here with all of you today, creating with each other something new in North America: a *Québécois* way of doing lesbian, gay, and bisexual studies, which is a project I want and need to be a part of.

After visiting Montréal for the first time these last two weeks, I'm pleased to discover that this place, including this conference, is not the sentimental Québec of my imaginary homeland, not "My Own Private Québec." You are full of more contradictions than I could ever have imagined from so great a distance. Because of that, you make me feel a little more at home.

Notes

1. Earlier versions of this essay were presented as a keynote address at *La Ville en Rose: Le premier colloque Québécois d'études lesbiennes et gaies* (The First Québec Lesbian and Gay Studies Conference), Montréal, November 1992; on the panel "Writing Working Class" at the 1992 OutWrite Lesbian and Gay Writers Conference in San Francisco; and at the Summer 1994 Crossing Boundaries lecture series at Portland State University in Oregon. An earlier version was also published in *GLQ: A Journal of Lesbian and Gay Studies* 3 (1996). I wish to thank Smoky Cormier, Jeffrey Escoffier, Lisa Kahaleole Chang Hall, David Halperin, Ross Higgins, Jonathan Ned Katz, Robert Mercer, Peter Nardi, Susan Raffo, Gayle Rubin, Robert Schwartzwald, Bill Walker, Tom Waugh, and many other friends and family members, including my sister Annette Bérubé and my mother, Florence Bérubé, whose encouragement, conversations, reading of drafts or memories helped solidify my ideas, clarify my writing, and correct inaccuracies. My thinking and writing in this talk were also inspired by the work of Dorothy Allison, James Baldwin, Amber Hollibaugh, bell hooks, Audre Lorde, Biddy Martin, Cherríe Moraga, Minnie Bruce Pratt, Richard Rodriguez, David Plante, Steven Riel, Mab Segrest, Barbara Smith, and Carolyn Kay Steedman. I had also read special "class" issues of the following periodicals: "Call It Class: A Three-Part Supplement

on Class in Lesbian/Gay Communities," *Gay Community News*, 21-27 January, 28 January-3 February, and 4-10 February 1990; *Lesbian Ethics* 4, no. 2 (Spring 1991); "Lesbians & Class," *Sinister Wisdom* 45 (Winter 1991/92); "Making Our Lives Visible: Poor and Working-Class Women Speak Out," *Bridges: A Journal for Jewish Feminists and Our Friends* 3:1 (Spring/Summer 1992).

2. Salman Rushdie, *Imaginary Homelands: Essays and Criticism 1981-1991* (New York: Penguin, 1992).

3. Richard Sennett and Jonathan Cobb, *The Hidden Injuries of Class* (New York: Knopf, 1972).

4. James Baldwin, *The Price of the Ticket: Collected Nonfiction 1948-1985* (New York: St. Martin's, 1985).

5. Eric Waddell and Dean R. Louder, "The Search for Home in America," in *French America: Mobility, Identity, and Minority Experiences Across the Continent*, ed. Dean R. Louder and Eric Waddell, trans. Franklin Phillip (Baton Rouge: Louisiana State University Press, 1993), pp. 348-50.

6. Jean Morisset, "An America That Knows No Name," in Louder and Waddell, p. 340.

7. René Daniel Dubois, "October 1990," in *Boundaries of Identity: A Québec Reader*, ed. William Dodge (Toronto: Lester Publishing, 1992), p. 69.

8. Dubois, p. 71.

9. David Homel, "The Way They Talk in *Broke City*," in Dodge, p. 87.

10. Morisset, p. 337.

11. Morisset, pp. 339, 346.

12. "But we are *Américains*." "Jacques Ducharme," in Rosaire Dion-Levesque, *Silhouettes Franco-Américaines* (Manchester, NH: Publications de l'Association Canado-américain, 1957), pp. 261-64; Jacques Ducharme, *The Shadows of the Trees: The Story of French Canadians in New England* (New York: Harper, 1943).

13. Normand Lafleur, *Les Chinois de l'Est* (Ottawa: Parles Editions Leméac, 1981).

14. "The French-Canadians in New England," editorial, *New York Times*, 6 June 1892, p. 4.

15. Royal Ford, "Cultural Resolution: Franco Americans struggle to preserve their heritage," *Boston Globe*, 28 October 1994, pp. 1, 16.

16. There is a small but growing body of literature on the history of American whiteness. See, for example, Toni Morrison, *Playing in the Dark: Whiteness and the Literary Imagination* (New York: Vintage, 1992); David Roediger, *The Wages of Whiteness: Race and the Making of the American Working Class* (New York: Verso, 1991); and *Toward the Abolition of Whiteness* (New York: Verso, 1994).

17. I first read about the "scholarship boy" in Richard Rodriguez, *Hunger of Memory: An Autobiography* (New York: Bantam, 1982), Chapter 2, "The Achievement of Desire," pp. 41-73; Rodriguez describes reading about the scholarship boy in Richard Hoggart, *The Uses of Literacy: Aspects of Working-Class Life with Special Reference to Publica-*

tions and Entertainment (1957; reprint, New York: Oxford University Press, 1970), pp. 238-49.

18. On the situation of working-class male scholarship students from this generation who became academics, see Jake Ryan and Charles Sackrey, *Strangers in Paradise: Academics from the Working Class* (Boston: South End Press, 1984).

19. On sexual migration, see Gayle Rubin, "Thinking Sex: Notes for a Radical Theory of the Politics of Sexuality," in *Pleasure and Danger: Exploring Female Sexuality*, ed. Carole Vance (Boston: Routledge & Kegan Paul, 1984), p. 286.

20. I wish to thank Lisa Kahaleole Chang Hall for our conversations about looking both up and down the hierarchies of power in which we are located. See Lisa Kahaleole Chang Hall, "Compromising Positions," in *Beyond a Dream Deferred: Multicultural Education and the Politics of Excellence,* ed. Becky W. Thompson and Sangeeta Tyagi (Minneapolis: University of Minnesota Press, 1993), p. 170.

21. Morisset, quoted in Louder and Waddell, p. 348.

22. On working-class storytelling strategies within and across class hierarchies, see, for example, "Working/Women/Writing," in *Sex, Class, and Culture*, ed. Lillian S. Robinson (Bloomington: Indiana University Press, 1978), pp. 223-53; Karen Olson and Linda Shopes, "Crossing Boundaries, Building Bridges: Doing Oral History among Working-Class Women and Men," in *Women's Words: The Feminist Practice of Oral History*, ed. Sherna Berger Gluck and Daphne Patai (New York: Routledge, 1991), pp. 189-204; and Pamela Fox, *Class Fictions: Shame and Resistance in the British Working-Class Novel, 1890-1945* (Durham, NC: Duke University Press, 1994).

Life in
the Passing Lane
Exposing the Class Closet

VICTORIA A. BROWNWORTH

I am a writer. As a writer, I am often asked the question: What class are you?

I am a lesbian. As a lesbian, I am often asked the question: What class are you?

I avoid these questions nearly as often as I am asked them because the answer is not simple. The answer is, as is often the case with writers, complex. The answer is a story. If this were a story about gender identity, then I would be transgendered. But since this is a story about class, and this is America, I cannot be transclassed. I would say, however, that for most of my life I have suffered from class dysphoria.

The answer is, then, a story. But like a tale about gender, it is about how I am one thing in the body of another—how I am one class, and yet another. It is, in a way, a coming-out story. But it is also a story about outing. Because, like gender identity and sexual identity, class identity is not just about self but about those who created and shaped and informed that identity, whatever it may be. In coming out of the class closet, you out the people who put you there—your family.

As I said, this is a story. It is, in some respects, a story about a story. It is about the language of class identity and where we learn that language.

I am a writer and a lesbian. I became a writer through being a reader because it was through reading that I learned the importance of language and learned that nothing affected me more than the power of language.

I also became a lesbian through being a reader because the very first lesbians I ever met (who knew that they were lesbians) were on the pages of books. These lesbians I met taught me the language of lesbianism, just like books had taught me the language of being a storyteller, a writer.

I would say, then, that I am a writer and a lesbian because I am a reader. I spoke early (nine months) and I read early (three). I became a reader because my parents were readers. I grew up in a house filled with books. Everyone in my house felt close to books, if not to each other. Everyone in my house felt close to language, if only on the printed page. Everyone in my house was a storyteller.

Reading was both reward and punishment in my house growing up. Television watching was eschewed, rationed, censored, denigrated. *Read*, my mother would command, and I would, gladly. Reading was an escape, a lifeline, a life.

My parents were more than readers. They were intellectuals. My father was an artist and failed writer from a family of artists and artisans. His family were the first photographers in Philadelphia. A great-great uncle invented the fire escape. (There are wonderful metaphors for my family life in these achievements.) My mother was a linguist who came from a family of linguists, scientists, mathematicians, and writers. There is a Nobel Prize-winning linguist on her side of the family, some famous scientists and mathematicians, a great-great uncle who wrote *'Twas the Night Before Christmas*. My father went to an Ivy League university, my mother to a Seven Sisters college. They were brilliant, they were intellectuals, they were physically beautiful, they were political leftists. They were what F. Scott Fitzgerald called "the beautiful and damned."

We lived in what Tennessee Williams refined for the stage: genteel poverty. This meant that my mother owned things like Limoges and Havilland china and Waterford crystal and real silverware, all of which had been passed down through her family for generations. We had a piano and some beautiful pieces of furniture (also inherited) over a hundred years old. And we had hundreds of books.

These things–my parents' seeming background of intellectual promise, the accoutrements of an upper-middle-class life–were what characterized my life. I was told about these things over and over again as a child. This was my legacy, this was the story I was told, this was the class I was taught I belonged to. My upper-middle-class birthright. That was the story.

These facts about my parents' background and their personal history are important. If they weren't so vital, they would not have been told to my sister and me time after time, they would not have become the subplot in my parents' class story. But these facts are also important because they are the markers, the physical abstracts of our lives (my life). These were the markers that said we could be of one class while living in another. These were the markers that said we weren't pretending, we really were who we said we were. We could be of the upper class while having the means of the lower class. *Genteel poverty*, it is euphemistically called. These markers set us apart from the other kind of poverty, the kind that was not genteel. These artifacts of gentility, of upper-classness, set us apart from our cousins in poverty, the *dirt poor*. We didn't *look* poor, we didn't *act* poor. And in my parents' version of their class story, that meant we *weren't* poor.

Genteel poverty has its own rules and definitions, its own lines and demarcations. I learned, for example, that everything you own is old. There is the handful of antiques, and there are the clothes from thrift stores. There is the smattering of inherited books with leather bindings and faded gold-leaf titles, and there are the books that come from flea markets and church rummage sales.

Everything in a life of genteel poverty is passed down from somewhere else. Nothing is fresh or new, nothing is ever yours *first*, yours alone. Everything *smells* of someplace else. The bed you sleep in smells like your grandfather's lilac hair tonic. The clothes you wear smell like someone else's sweat, someone else's embedded perfume, someone else's disinfectant that is supposed to kill the smell of someone else's life in your clothes.

The physicality of this life informed everything else. There is, for example, no difference between dirt-poor food and genteel poverty food. It all revolves around powdered milk, white bread, canned mushroom soup, peas, and Jell-O. It revolves around how four people can be fed on scant money for one. It is food that never smells good or tastes good but is merely, at best, filling.

I learned about telephones, too. That when the phone rings, it is someone you don't want to talk to, someone to avoid. I learned that the phone never rings at dinnertime in homes where bills are paid on time. That a bill collector's voice has a different tone to it from that of a family friend or a business associate of your father. That sometimes you just have to let the phone ring until it stops, even if you're home.

These were the incidental elements to my parents' story about our lives that it took years to decode. What I learned from our genteel poverty set me apart, but also taught me that looks can be deceiving. I was not surprised as I grew up, then, to realize I was a lesbian—an outsider in the straight world. My life of genteel poverty had prepared me to be an outsider—I was, in a sense, born to it. But just as I didn't "look" poor, I didn't, to the straight world, "look" lesbian. Because what a life of genteel poverty teaches you, first and foremost, is how to "pass," to look like the others.

Stories are the mainstay, the foundation of a life led in genteel poverty, so it was natural that my parents would be both readers and storytellers, would raise me to be intimate with language, if not with people. Would turn me into a storyteller, too. Had I truly been born into an upper-middle-class family, as opposed to a family *passing* for upper-middle-class, I might not be a writer. I might not even be a reader. I probably would not be a lesbian. And I most certainly would not be an intellectual. It was the effort to understand the subtext of my parents' story that led me into my intellectual lesbian writer's life.

I never understood as a young child that we were poor, that we had no money, that my parents' lives were about appearances, not actualities. My sister and I were too young to understand about passing, too young to understand the reality of our storytelling lives. What *was* and what we *saw* were as different as those two words; the letters are the same, but the transposition defines the context.

My mother had a closet full of clothes, most of which I never saw her wear. She owned at least (to my memory) thirty pairs of high-heeled shoes to go with her dresses and suits (this was the sixties, and women of my mother's mythic class did not wear pants outside the home). It was important that my mother had these clothes, even though she rarely wore them. But like the clothes themselves, the story behind them was hidden, unrevealed, closeted.

I was in high school before I understood that there were shoes and clothes that weren't like my mother's: shoes that did not have a big black crayon mark (25¢) scrawled on the instep; dresses and suits that smelled of sizing, not mothballs or stale sweat. I was in high school before I realized that there were clothes that didn't have big laundry marks on the labels, tears under the arm, moth holes that would need invisible mending on a sleeve or a hem. That there were new clothes with tags attached, new clothes your mother hadn't made the night before for Easter, Christmas, or the school recital.

Genteel poverty is a sham, of course. It's an invention of language, a reconfiguration of words, that diabolical truism—the honest lie.

My parents had grown up poor during the Depression. My father's family was nearly penniless, often going without food, fearful of landing on the streets. My grandmother took in washing, my grandfather counted cars; no one had money for photographs during the Depression. There was oilcloth on the table and waxed paper covering broken windows. There was no money for anything better, anything new.

My mother's family lived in genteel poverty. My grandfather lost his job and his money in the Florida land-boom collapse. My grandmother wore her one good suit for years, day in and day out. At night she rinsed out her blouse, by day she pretended that her suit was one of many. They lived in a housing project until my grandfather was laid off from his new job. Then they became the poor relations living a hideous shadow life in the spare room of my grandmother's brother's house.

My parents were both scholarship students, scaling their way out of poverty into the Ivy League and the Seven Sisters. I think of this as a point of pride: their brilliance, their creativity, their hard work propelled them into these schools on their merits, not on their money. But for them the scholarships were a source of pain, not pride. My father feigned indifference to this aspect of his life, but my mother despised it, telling story after story of humiliations at the hands of her wealthy classmates. The closet full of thrift-store items—the myriad dresses, the silk shoes in every color—these were her response to going off to Northampton with one skirt, two blouses, two sweaters, and a cloth coat, all handmade by my grandmother. My mother went to thrift stores and looked for the "good" labels, the fine fabrics. By the time I was seven I knew how to find an Evan Picone suit or a real cashmere sweater among the racks and racks of other people's cast-offs.

My mother taught me all about passing.

My father was less discreet in his reaction to being poor. He hated authority and had been thrown in the brig numerous times while in the Navy. He yearned always for a big house and a new car, for his pretty wife and pretty daughters to be well dressed and charming. He wanted everything new, no matter how cheap or flimsy, no matter how it didn't meet the standards of upper-middle-class aspirations. A used car that looked flashy. A new suit in a too-bright plaid. A big house in a bad neighborhood. A pretty wife and daughters dressed in someone else's old clothes.

My father taught me blood will tell.

I was the oldest child born too soon into this poverty-stricken rage of my parents. My mother searching for a dollar's worth of quality clothes in the thrift store, my father drinking to blur the edges of the reality of his life. My mother telling me the stories of her life, her china, her furniture. My mother telling me the stories of the right clothes, the right inflection, the right grammar, the right manners, the right knowledge of these things would allow me entrée into any world, *into any class*. My father telling me stories about his life, his travels around the world in the Navy, his artistic dreams, and his poverty-bound reality. His hopes for my future. His belief that although language couldn't save him, it could save me.

My parents' class rage is in my blood. So is their dishonesty. They implied—even as they described the poverty they came from—that their lives were different, *now*. They implied, even as they knew it to be a lie, that language was power, that language could transcend class. That the right grammar, the right inflection, the right ideas, the right configuration of the wrong words could alter class reality. That *passing* was the same as *being*.

As I have gotten older, I have come to understand what my parents were doing: They were passing, and they taught me and my sister to pass. In fact, they taught us so well that I only began to realize I was passing very recently. (My sister still doesn't realize it, even as she lives in a suburban neighborhood and buys her "good" clothes and those of her children at the thrift store.)

I have been living life in the class passing lane for years, replicating that life of genteel poverty that I grew up in. Talking middle-class but living on the fine line between poverty and working class. Living in white working-class or poor black neighborhoods. Making half or a third or a quarter of what my friends make in salary. Trying to imitate a middle-class life even as I know I have never actually lived one. Setting the table—my parents' dining-room table—with my grandmother's china, my mother's tablecloth.

Unlike those of my mother (and my sister), all my clothes are new; I cannot step over the threshold of a thrift shop without gagging from the smell. Unlike my father, what is new in my life is "quality": my clothes are few, but they're in the classic styles and fabrics my mother taught me class was made from. There are no indelible laundry markings in anything I own. Like my grandmother, my one good suit could see me through ten years of Depression.

The *things* of my childhood are in my house now. The china, the silverware, the glass. There are photographs, too, of my parents in their prime. "Scott and Zelda," my lover calls them, after the Fitzgeralds. Their photos are the iconography of their expert passing: They look beautiful, smart—and rich.

Sociologists say poverty is passed down from generation to generation. So too is genteel poverty.

My grandparents passed the lie and how to make it work on to my parents, who passed it on to me. Now I am supposed to be living their lie, telling their stories, reinventing a life in which the poverty of powdered milk and bean dinners never existed, only the good china and the real silverware.

It is the language of poverty that both creates the lie and makes it work. Subtlety is the hallmark of the language of passing—you learn it is about *presentation*—how you eat, how you speak, how you dress, how you sit, whether you write thank-you notes or not. Passing is how you present yourself, not who you are. But it is still, beneath the subterfuges, a lie, and one that, ultimately, cannot work. Someone, even if it is only yourself, knows it isn't true.

I saw this immediately as a lesbian. At fourteen I knew that although I could easily pass for straight, passing for straight wasn't good for me, passing for straight was a *lie* about who I was at my core. But I handled coming out like a girl of good breeding, like a rich girl, like a girl with no worries and nothing to lose. I did not come out as some fugitive from the wrong side of the class tracks, but with the *élan* of *noblesse oblige*.

It never occurred to me to live life in the sexual identity closet, but I have lived for decades in a class closet. When my father was told by my high school principal that his fifteen-year-old daughter was a lesbian and about to be expelled, he said to me: "But you're pretty, and boys like you."

This should have been a clue about the realities of my passing life, yet it wasn't. There, in those words of my father, lies the truth of the tremendous importance appearances played in my parents' lives. *But you're pretty, and boys like you.* My appearance didn't fit my father's reality. He wasn't asking me to pass, to pretend to be straight, but he was explaining how it could be done, how my appearance of passing had fooled him, and therefore could fool others.

But because I was busy passing for upper-middle-class, as my parents had raised me, it didn't occur to me to try and pass for straight. I thought I could do what I wanted, I thought I could make my own rules, I thought I could just go ahead and be out, and even though next to no one was out then, except in San Francisco and Greenwich Village, I believed it was the way to be. And I believed, because I believed my parents' lie, that I had the privilege to do so.

But the reality is, there is no privilege in a life that is a lie. There is no privilege in a life of genteel poverty. There is only reality in constant conflict with the *story* of that reality. (This would be the beautiful clothes in the closet with the tears, moth holes, laundry markings, and sweat stains.)

Over the years my parents' upwardly mobile middle-class friends drifted away, embarrassed, I believe, by the reality of our situation. Some stories don't sustain themselves over time. My parents had been born outsiders and they remained that way. And their class lie about their lives couldn't obscure the truth. Now the poverty they live in has no shred of gentility—it is awful, grinding, ugly. As vivid and indelible as all those laundry marker prices written into our thrift-store clothes.

I often ask myself why my parents' lives were such failures, why they so missed the mark of their potential. It seems too simple to say my father drank, my mother became afraid to go out of the house. I constantly worry—am I like them, could I become them? My lover assures me I cannot. I pay my bills. I work hard. I am older now than they were when their lives began to collapse from the weight of their class lie, their pretense that they could defy class and, in doing so, defeat their own class history of being *dirt poor* with their reinvented class history, their belief that the right education, the right books, the right stories, and the right affect are enough to transcend class markers.

I have begun to call myself, shuddering as I do so, working-class, because in doing this I am acknowledging that I am no longer attempting to pass for what I am not and have never been. I *am* working-class now, but I have come to realize this is not a step down from the class I once was, the mythic class of my childhood, but rather a step up from the real class I was born into.

I am trying to establish what my grandmother called "pride of place," trying to see where I am—poor but comfortable, no longer grasping, not quite bitter—as a good thing. Trying to give up the language of passing.

I am a lover of Southern fiction, regional writing, and I have come to realize that it is because these stories mirror my life, echo my life. Writers like Truman Capote, Flannery O'Connor, and Tennessee Williams crafted stories with characters much like my family—people living on the edge of a nightmare, people living within the confines of their own tiny, carefully constructed fantasy. These writers are the doyens of the genre of genteel poverty, of class passing. My family is there, in some small Southern town, yearning, aching for that new ball gown thirty years ago or wishing they'd married for money instead of love or just eking out a living amid the old furniture, the mended lace curtains, the same starchy food night after night.

My mother is like Amanda Wingfield or Blanche DuBois, living her life from a vantage point before I was born. My father is like the handsome boy in a failed marriage and failed life, a character in William Inge's *Picnic* or *Splendor in the Grass*. Past the point where suicide is a graceful exit, trying hard not to make so much of life look like marking time.

My parents are outside their own lives, outsiders in their generation, outsiders in their class, because they never knew where they belonged, always yearning to move up, move out, move away, even as they—like Br'er Rabbit and the Tar Baby—found themselves stuck fast.

I am trying to write a new text for myself, to break away now from the hold my parents' storytelling has had on me, break away from the mythic hold of their desperate desire for an upper-class life, rewrite the story of my childhood as it was rather than as they tried to make it seem. In revising their tale of rags to would-be riches, I am coming to understand that class passing is simply life lived in a different closet, learning that class identity is as fundamental and inalterable as sexual identity.

The most terrible aspect of the lie of passing is that there can never be acceptance—either from oneself or from others. The lie is always in the way, the lie always obscures intimacy and possibility. My parents could not compete with their friends who were actually living an upper-middle-class life because they did not have access to the money or things that make that life a reality. We could only pass effectively out among strangers or at home among ourselves. Otherwise the lie was revealed. And as the lie was uncovered again and again, my father drank more, my mother hid inside our house. And all of us read, as if immersing ourselves in someone else's stories and limiting our interaction with each other would sustain the fiction that we were all something we so obviously were not.

Acceptance of one's own class identity, like acceptance of one's sexual identity, is—despite what those who decry the use of labels insist—freeing. Rather than limiting one to what the label (lesbian, working-class) states, it expands the realm of personal experience. Knowing who and what you are answers the most basic need: self-knowledge.

My life is no longer patterned on the subterfuge of my parents' class fears. My life is neither invention nor reinvention—no false starts toward belonging to a class or a lifestyle or even a sexual orientation that places me on the other side of a window or fence, looking out onto what my life could or even should be. My own class consciousness has superseded that of my parents; where theirs drove them to hide and lie and craft a story that matched their desire, mine has led me to explore the damage created by class passing, life lived in the class closet, as well as the societal prejudices that make passing acceptable, even desirable.

In defining my own identity, some answers are easier than others to give. I have always been a lesbian, always been a writer. Have I always been working class? No. My parents' legacy to me is that I have spent half my life in class dysphoria, transclassed between being poor and being upper-middle-class, living the reality of one class while being taught the language of another.

Like sexual orientation, class is defined first by society—one may, for example, like girls, but if the world outside says this is wrong or bad, it will take you longer to come to terms with your lesbianism. It will also take longer to come to terms with an undesirable class status. In the process of deconstructing and decoding my own class story I have learned this basic truth: Society rewards passing. And passing is viable because it perpetuates social separations—among different classes, races, religions, sexual orientations. When we succumb to the seduction of passing, we accept soci-

ety's view that our sexual orientation, race, or class is not acceptable to the majority or mainstream, that who we are is less than
who we pretend to be.

For my parents, passing was always more seductive than being
who they were, yet I am convinced that if they had acknowledged
that truth, instead of working so hard at the lie, their lives would
have been far better, that self-acceptance would have allowed
them some level of personal contentment, despite their understandable rage. Instead, their anger grew as their ability to maintain
the lie slipped away. And the class ground they gained in college
disintegrated, their potential lost in the endless struggle to pass.

It seems a simple lesson, even trite. But passing never works;
the lie always distances you from those who aren't party to it. Society
may reward the lie, may even demand it, but the passing person is
always punished for passing—either by being caught in the lie or by
believing it. Every closet is a prison, whether it is a construct of sex
or class. Passing kills; it annihilates who we are. And keeps us from
who we could be.

The Bath Story

MICHIYO FUKAYA

Y ou have to understand that I'm not trying to present myself as a victim: "poor little me see what my roommate is doing to me." As if I were helpless. Just the same this is a genuine problem in communication between us, my roommate and me. A little background might be helpful; Lydia, you know I grew up poor but I never went into much detail on it. Yeah, I know you care but that stuff never seemed relevant before. As being poor relates to bathing, my sisters and I took a bath once a week. I suppose that sounds bad; we did wash up every day so it wasn't as if we didn't. It's just that we had this hot water tank that ran out of hot water if you did dishes, a load of clothes, and took a bath. And a family with six people in it uses a lot of water that way. You can't let the dishes go cuz there is too many from one meal. They have to be done. So my sister and I took baths together when we were small.

Then there's clothes. Clothes from six people: Dad, Mom, my two brothers, my sister, and me. Mom worked and Dad worked and they couldn't spend their time doing laundry: my sister and I did it. Mom used to make us wear one outfit two or three times to save on laundry. That meant I had to be careful of my clothes, not get them too dirty and all. Besides which, we didn't have enough clothes to change every day.

So that was my past around bathing and clothes. As to the house, we had to keep it picked up and clean at all times. Every weekend, Mom was a stickler that we had to do a top-to-bottom job on the house: dusting, vacuuming, laundry, mopping and waxing floors, clean the bathroom and all. I'm saying this to show I'm not in the habit of being dirty or anything like that.

I'm older now, and I still have those habits. I have more clothes, not fancy, just plain old clothes, but I can change more often now. Sometimes I forget and wear an outfit two or three days running, not so it's filthy, just so it might be a little wilted. And living alone and oh, another thing, I have a bad sense of smell so if something is all sweaty I don't always pay attention unless I can see or feel that it's sweaty. That causes problems with my roommate because she grew up not rich but well-to-do and in her circle I guess people don't wear clothes like I did because they had more clothes and could change more often. So she told me about that and about my bathing. I guess she's literally trying to clean my act up.

So when I went to college, I used to shave under my arms, shave my legs, use deodorant and brush my teeth every morning. Well, I soon left off shaving in college and I always hated using deodorant so I stopped that, too. You see, I didn't realize that I could get raunchy without it.

Deodorant hurt me and made me break out so why use it? To me, brushing my teeth meant cleaning them so they don't decay. I found out dentists say that brushing at night is the best time if you brush once a day. So I did that: brushed once a day at night. School was busy and I had eight o'clock classes a lot; sometimes all I could do was pull on my clothes, pick up my books, and run to class.

I lived alone after school; you know that story, single working woman rents room or apartment from someone. Sometimes I would be so tired that I wouldn't wash up, and doing heavy physical work doesn't help that situation. Or I would not eat cuz I was so tired. My roommate is an office worker so she doesn't work up as much sweat as I do and her sense of smell is real keen. So she started leaning on me to do things more her way. And it makes sense in a way but sometimes... I even use deodorant without breaking out, I don't shave my arms and legs and I guess I broke out with deodorant because I didn't put it on right. Of course, living alone I had no one to comment on or reflect back to me how others saw me as opposed to how I see myself.

I brush my teeth twice a day. At night, because dentists say to, and in the morning because my roomie says my breath smells. Lydia, I wish things were more equal class-wise between my roomie and me. I feel oppressed cuz to her, people do things one way, period. But being from the streets, I'm more emotional and I know lots of ways people do things. I could never afford to be immaculate, and she could, in terms of money and time.

I never had extra of either and I still don't. When I tried to tell her this stuff, she got all huffy like I was trying to get out of hearing what she was saying. It's more like I didn't want her to think I was dirty and that resources were limited for me and mine. I got her point but mine went by the board. There's a kind of class arrogance about things like that but I like her and all. It's funny; her upsets are crises; mine are dramatics. So I need to stand up for my rights, don't you think?

Notes from the
Working Class

JANE VANDERBOSCH

R eader: I don't know who you are, but you need to know
what's coming. A three-part take on class: the first part's rage,
the second part's mind, and the third is where I try—but do not
succeed—to integrate it all. The structure of the paper is very much
like the chronology of my life: for the first twenty years, I emotionally absorbed (and then repressed) what I was experiencing. In the
second twenty years, I intellectualized it all. And now, in this latest
portion of my life, I am trying to bring the parts of myself together.

That said, I suspect this paper will be as hard to read as it was
to write. I can only ask that you, like the listeners to stories of
those in recovery, take what you need and simply discard the rest.

One final note: I must reiterate before you start that the emotional
and physical violence that I describe is not intrinsic to the working
class. Rather, it's a (dys)function of American culture itself—and
occurs in nearly all families, middle- and upper-class as well.

Part One

I grew up working-class in New York City. Into a family that never
heard of Leonard Bernstein. That never realized he was gay. A fam-

ily that didn't know anyone who went to Key West or Fire Island for the summer. Who didn't *want* to know anyone who did.

I grew up in a family that went to Mass every morning. That considered it a sin to cheat or steal. But that lied just about every day of the week.

Oh, we didn't call it lying. We didn't even call it not telling the truth. We just did it—left out the most important part of the story, or the one bit of information that might explain the nutziness in our lives.

For example, we lied about something as innocuous as the rent. We said it was a "great deal." What we didn't say was that it was cheap because we lived with my grandparents. Three of them. And my "maiden" aunt. Nine of us stuffed into a two-bedroom apartment.

We also lied about the extent of my father's drinking. About the fights. The welts from the cat-o'-nine-tails. About the gambling: the horses, cards, numbers, the Dodgers versus the Yankees in the Series. The number of fleas on the dog.

We lied about Mom's suicide attempts. And Dad's loans.

We even fibbed a bit about why we were sent to Catholic schools. It wasn't just for a "good education." That wasn't the reason my mother marched to Open School Day every year and told Sister Miriam Agnes or Sister John Thomas that they had her permission to "beat the shit outta Janie if she gives you any trouble."

Even with tuition, Catholic school was cheaper. Because we wore uniforms, we didn't have to buy clothes. (I had one uniform, one set of "play clothes," and a hand-me-down dress for church on Sunday. The dress had belonged to my cousin Marie, two years older and three sizes bigger.)

I *loved* wearing the uniform, though. Thick blue serge; the blouses so starched they blistered the back of my neck. The bow tie best of all. I'd clip it on every morning and feel... well, rich. Like my clothes were expensive. Elegant. Like I was Janie Vanderbosch turned into Gloria Vanderbilt by throwing on some clothes.

So we lied. Barbara, Joseph, and me. To protect my mother's sanity and my father's ego. So that Mrs. Walker or Mrs. Brennan wouldn't know that Dad was off on a binge. That the gas bill wasn't paid. That we had elbow macaroni in tomato soup for a week.

We lied because we would have all gone crazy if we had sat around one day and told each other the truth:

"Hey, did you hear Mom and Dad last night? Screaming about money again?"

"Yeah. But it wasn't as loud as last time. And she didn't beat us when he walked out the door."

"C'mon, it's not that bad. She doesn't hit us all the time."

We may not have told each other the truth, but that didn't mean we didn't know what it was. One summer afternoon, the oldest of the Gregory boys across the street had his leg broken by his father. I remember watching the ambulance turn the corner and thinking, "I wish I were going. I wish they were taking me away."

For years, *years*, I talked about "the Gregory boy." Until it became a joke. Janie and the Gregory boy. But it was simple: not knowing how to explain my own pain, I could easily latch on to his.

I could feel his fear. Of being taken away from his father, of being beaten again for having been beaten.

But I never saw him again. We moved to another neighborhood, and everybody—from Mom and Dad on down—had lots more lying to do. Small lies, like the one about why I didn't get a bicycle ("You were bad, and Santa only brings bikes if you're good"). Big ones: my father admitting after his second anniversary in A.A. (complete with an ice-cream cake with a big "Two Years!" on top) that he'd been drinking the whole time. The whole damn time.

Mom's specialty was: "We're just as good as anybody else. No better and no worse. And don't you ever forget it." So *why* was she saying it, if we were so wonderful? I mean, if it was so evident, why did it have to be repeated every day? (Did you ever hear of Mrs. Vanderbilt sitting little Gloria down and telling her she was just as good as the Rockefellers?)

Secrets, denial, and more lies. Big and little, mortal and venial. Making it hard to know when it was okay to lie. Like the time the guy from Con Edison came to shut off the electricity. My mother saying, "Jane, tell him I'm not home. That you can't let anybody in." "But, Mom, that's a lie." "Shut up and do it, before I get the stick."

So I open the door a crack. "My mom's not here, and she says I can't let anybody in." He repeats his announcement. I repeat mine. We stare at each other. I try to look skinny. He leaves.

For weeks I try to figure out (without asking my mother) why it was okay to lie to the Con Ed guy. I try to imagine us freezing to death, all our stuff piled on the curb. Or the neck bones going bad in the refrigerator, resulting in more macaroni and soup. While I don't quite get the subtleties, the gist of the message is clear. Sometimes, it's a sin to tell the truth.

Years pass. I pass. First for smart. Then educated. And then middle-class. I get farther and farther from who I am. From the tough but marshmallow kid I know myself to be. From the skinny kid lying to Con Ed.

I get one degree after another. I pretend I'm proud of my family; they pretend they're proud of me. I deny the past; my family denies the present. (Me: physical abuse and depression. Them: their over-educated, radical queer.)

But the past keeps erupting into the present, the present into the past. I get a Ph.D. Nobody in my family shows up. How can they celebrate the biggest day of my life when it's not a wedding?

I move to Madison, Wisconsin, to do a postdoctoral fellowship in Women's Studies. I start drinking in earnest again. Doing the weed. Tumbling into the deepest depression in more than ten years.

Madison is therapy heaven. I wind up talking for the first time in years to a therapist who's working-class. A sixty-five-year-old working-class dyke. I talk about the beatings. The screaming. The Gregory boy.

And one day in February, I start talking about the incest. My mother, my father, my mother's dad. The years of depression, the whole hee-haw gang.

Within two years, I'm doing therapy, twelve-step groups, and tofu. I've stopped the drinking, the alcohol, the three packs a day. I've broken up with the latest two-week affair that's been going on for eight months. I'm finally alone.

More years pass. I can drink every once in a while. I can even walk into bars—pick a bar, any bar—but now it's more than my stomach that churns. Because I'm just not comfortable around bar dykes.

They're like my family. The snot-nosed, wise-ass butches, an-gling for a fight. They're my mom, waiting to jump my father. After a binge. After three months on Skid Row.

And the femmes are Barbara, Joseph, and I. Tippy-toeing around. Trying to be quiet, trying to please. The big versus the little. The moms and dads versus the kids.

Butches and femmes don't have to be queer.

That's what I think when I'm trying not to analyze my adult-hood. (My childhood's been picked over fine, thank you.) It's the part of working-class I don't even *want* to remember. With its aura of violence, its aura of pain. I can taste it. Like blood. Feel it like a bruise or a welt. (When my mother whipped us with the cat-o'-nine-tails, she made sure it was a place that wouldn't show. The thighs, the butt, the lower back.)

It's the urge to oblivion. To get so wasted you can't remember the fight with your girlfriend or the last time you ripped out the phone. The fact that your job stinks, you hate yourself, and life—the big one—just sucks.

I can't stand being around them, the large women dressed in blacks and blues. Carrying their rage in a beer. Just waiting to slam their fists into a door or a girlfriend. Just dying, *dying*, to get out.

Well, I can't stand it. It's like walking back into hell.

Oh, I know it's not all the dykes in the bar. But enough. Enough that I want to run for the ambulance driving the Gregory boy away. It's the violence. And the violent sex. The kisses that end as bruises. The fingers ripping open what the mouths call a cunt.

It's my family in drag.

It's my mother forcing me to undress so she can beat the shit outta me. It's my father standing in the kitchen, shit-faced and call-ing me a whore.

So I want to run because I'm socialized into running. But I also want to run 'cause it's not safe. I don't remember it safe.

What was safe was the library. The St. Albans branch of the New York Public Library. No, not the lions on the stairs. This was a storefront in Queens. Filled with shelves that I can smell to this minute. Brown books. Green books. Books filled with old and calm.

So the library was safe. Not the bar. Not loud music. Not beer.

Which means I can't enjoy it: the pool tables, the leather crowd, the velvet art on the walls. I can't enjoy it because it's not a library. It's not quiet. It's where my family might go. So does that make me a snob? A middle-class wannabe? Or does it make me a lesbian in recovery? A smart dyke who didn't wanna die? Or—even deeper—does it make me all those things? And all at the same time: pissed and vulnerable, scared and confused. Does it make me disloyal? Turning my back on the class I was born into, the class I escaped. It's all so convoluted. This isn't street-ball, four to a side. No good guys to shoot the bad guys. No neat lines: working class/good, middle class/bad. No more scapegoats. (I once vowed—erroneously—that I would never forgive my parents. My father for climbing into my baby bed. My mother: well, for everything I couldn't pin on him.)

It's so damn hard to explain. Even now, I still feel the fear when I walk into a bar and half the dykes sound like my mother. Especially when they have pool cues in their hands. Or they're yanking on some other butch's jacket, pulling her closer, yelling, "Whaddya doin' with my girlfriend?"

The rage I feel when I see that dead, boozy glaze in a woman's eyes. Watch her stumble down some alley to her car.

It's like a support group I was in once. At a national Women's Studies conference. The theme of the conference that year was Racism and Feminism. All us little feminists were separated by class and told to deal with our racism.

There were eleven in our group. All working-class and, by some hunk of magic, all dykes.

At first we were pretty guarded. Mouthing platitudes we'd learned by rote. Till somebody got down in the dirt. Talked about her family. How they hated "spics." How she got out as fast as she could.

We looked at her; we looked at each other. Pretty soon, we were all in the dirt. How racist we knew we were. How ashamed. I remember saying how stupid I felt, identifying with the whites on TV instead of the blacks next door. How dumb it felt to be a foot soldier in the capitalist army and not even know I joined.

Imagine! To not know my job was to buffer the rich from the rest of the poor. How goddamn stupid can ya get?

There we were: eleven dykes. Our accents getting thicker by the minute. Swimming in tears. Baskets of pity, buckets of shame. Eleven "educated" lesbians finally telling the awful, shameful, stupid-ass truth of our lives.

So, if the bars are the worst, that conference was some of the best. The best of the working class. The best of *my* working class. Best, too, because it taught me that class goes both ways. I have to remember that, even now: it always goes both ways.

But the conference was four days long. Four days out of one lifetime.

And that's not the only thing: when it does go the other way, it ain't pretty. (It's *still* so hard to say ain't. Even here. Especially here. Because I'm trying to connect and disconnect all at the same time.)

Okay. To go back to "it ain't pretty." Like when I'm trying to ignore the shame or the rage. Or my every-once-in-a-while hatred of the rich. A hatred that made me want to shoot, string up, *demolish* a bunch of preppies in Harvard Square last year. To destroy them. For that air about them. That entitled air. That they had been born to inherit the earth.

It's all there: the careless way they hold their forks, wear their clothes, snap for the waitress (who used to be me). It brought out that "I wish I had a machine gun" feeling. That urge to blow their leisured heads right off.

So. Back to basics. I grew up in a working-class family. A dysfunctional working-class family. I have been trained by twenty-six years of education to speak middle-class, think middle-class, make love middle-class. In other words, to pass.

And, as I've learned from six bouts of recovery, passing is just another way to lie. To pretend to be something I ain't. But—and here comes the problem—what if that's also something I don't want to be? Like too tough to feel. Drunk out of my mind. Nasty.

It isn't that middle-class people aren't tough, drunk, or nasty. They are. But I don't associate the pain of my past with their version of hell. I associate it with my own. And my own is working-class. My own is me.

So, basics, part two. What came first: the association or the pain?

Or, in other words, how can I tell the difference between running a classist trip on myself and really escaping? The pain. The violence. The untreated rage.

The answer is: I can't. The classism's gonna leak into everything I think, feel, and do. It's going to affect how I analyze the past, how I experience the present.

It's going to undermine a vulnerability that I've worked a lifetime to learn. A vulnerability that lets me write—and rewrite—this essay with less and less snarl. Less and less need to string up my parents. To admit that I loved them all through the hate.

Because class issues aren't just in the head. Aren't just ideas to be chewed and swallowed. They're my mother and father. Barbara and Joseph. They're me, trying to walk into a dyke bar. Or writing an essay on class.

Part Two

It has not been easy to re-read this essay, even months later. Because I knew right away the power of the piece comes from its almost palpable fury, a rage big enough to suck in the stars. And as soon as I knew it, I felt ashamed.

Ashamed that I had been vulnerable, that I had "aired our dirty laundry in public." Ashamed that I had told the truth.

But I sensed something else: raw emotion—even well-expressed—is not enough. Something else was still required of me. At first, I wasn't sure what it was. A thoughtfulness that could extend the piece beyond the pain of a single life? Perhaps a willingness to pore over the wreckage of "my" class to examine how classism deforms us all?

In order to get past the rage, I had to examine points that seemed peripheral at first. Like how, disclaimers aside, I'd unintentionally managed to equate the *physicality* of the working class with physical violence. Because, even for me (thirty years later), the working class *embodies* physicality in its more dangerous aspects.

The same way women and people of color do—as in voracious cunts and black men waiting to beat a rich white man to death. As in too loud, too strong, too sexy, too much. As in work and sex.

Filthy work, sweaty sex; knifing your lover. It means using mouths and hands like hammers–to threaten, to dominate, and to maim.

It means savage and out of control.

That was my first realization: I'd stereotyped. Taken my own experience of family violence and generalized it as a characteristic of the working class. And I'd also particularized the resultant pain–made it sound as if the only people who suffer under the rules of class are the suckers at the bottom. Those who do the "dirty work" for others, the "beasts of burden" considered too dumb to feel.

Because–taking all this down to the next level of understanding, the next level of pain–that's the essence of what it means to be "working class." It isn't simply the work I do or how much I get paid. It isn't the extent of my status, wealth, or power. It's the knowledge that I *am* the bottom of the barrel. That my job is to feel inferior.

My life's work, then, is to *be* inferior; to be everyone else's "bottom line." So that those in the classes "above" me can feel better about themselves because they are–at the very least–superior to me, to my family, to my neighbors. To all those who inhabit my class.

Well, that helps explain the pain, the shame, and the rage of those suckers at the bottom of the heap, but what about the rest of the crowd? What about the troops in the middle?

I suspect that the middle class needs us–the stiffs at the bottom– to know who they are and where they stand. (Much the same way men need women.) The middle class needs a bunch of people to look at, to point to and say: "See, we're not like *them*. We're better. Not quite the top, but nowhere–nowhere–near the bottom."

The Politics of Otherness in yet another guise; the politics plays itself out in the "popular" view of the working class–folks who are a paycheck away from oppression. (Or, if not that, then folks wearing polyester instead of cotton or eating ice cream instead of sorbet. Folks who can always be accused of *not knowing*. Not knowing what's in; what's cool; what's healthy, wealthy, and wise.)

Having been educated into middle-class values, socialized to accept middle-class means, I have experienced some of the pain of what it means to be near but not in the center. Which is, ultimately, a place of inordinate anxiety. For there's no safety net between me and the bottom. Only my intelligence, my cunning, my mind. I have got to keep moving—get a foot up on the slobs at the bottom, always keep one eye on the folks at the top.

Which is incredibly stressful: to never relax, to have to work for every ounce of self-esteem I have.

Which I am never allowed to enjoy. There is no pleasure—or real leisure—associated with the middle class. It's about getting very little for a lot. It's all about being paid to be a buffer between the tiny number of truly wealthy people—i.e., those who don't have to work—and the millions who do. And who are defined, then, by what they are not.

From my perspective, that's the job, the gig, the *career* of the middle class. But what about the Vanderbilts and the Rockefellers? What about the rich?

Having never—for an instant—known what it's like to have something simply because I wanted it, or having it without worrying about where the money was coming from to pay for my slice of pleasure, I find it difficult to speculate about the truly rich. About those who live on their interest.

Fantasy helps, though. I imagine that the rich get an incredible perk out of being who they are, far beyond the joys of power or pleasure. *They get to be envied.* By everyone else. Those at the bottom, the middle, and the bottom of the top. By everybody, *everybody,* who isn't them.

They also get to worry that being envied, that being what is "devoutly to be wished" by everyone else, will cease the moment they lose their fortunes. Their money, their stocks, their diamonds, their looks. Whatever it is that makes them immune from the rest of us—crowded together in cities, isolated in small towns and on farms.

Whatever insulates them from what's ordinary in life.

Yeah, the rich get to be the desired, just as the working class get to be the despised. And the middle class gets to be just what it says: the middle—halfway between dreams of plenty and nightmares of want. (For again, the working class is defined by what it is not: not rich enough, not smart enough, not good enough...It is always defined by what it is not; it is an absence, an emptiness, a loss.)

Part Three

Another couple of months go by. Now I have two sections to read and remember. One that is emotionally explosive, the other almost calm—in a semi-detached, intellectual kind of way.

After going over both sections again and again, I get the message: it's not what I think of the words I've written. The message is this: what do they mean to *you*, reader? I mean—did they get you to think? Did they piss you off or lull you? Do you think I'm onto something or full of some kind of shit?

Say what?

Say: talk is cheap. Say: we can talk "about" class until the cows come home, but if we don't do three things, not a damn thing is gonna change.

And what, you ask, are they?

One, we have to talk *to* each other. The way we did in that support group. Eleven dykes spilling secrets; eleven dykes saying forbidden words: race words, class words, woman words, dirty words. Telling our stories. Crying and raging our pain. And then stopping, just at that precise moment. Stopping to think. Think it through. The shame. The fear—of not being heard, of being misunderstood. Of being too vulnerable. Too stupid. Too naive. Of getting stepped on, getting laughed at, getting hurt.

In other words, kicking up the suffering of a lifetime; thinking through the logic of our lies.

Which is tied up with the second thing we have to do: destroy our silence. Yours. Mine. Uncle Sam's. Break through the lies that *everyone* tells: "We're as good as they are." "We're better than those lazy Pollacks (or blacks or Jews or Hmong or. . .)." "We don't eat with our fingers." "They are too stupid to learn."

Because we're all polarized around a single issue. And believe that our pain (being despised, working to stay in place, being envied) is different. It isn't: that's the lie. *The pain is the same.* Not the feelings—they're not the same. But the pain.

So that's it: we are all in incredible pain around class. The same way we're in incredible pain around gender or race or homophobia. And we've been trained to think they're different pains, the same way we've been trained to think people from another class are a different species. That they can't know our pain; that we can't know theirs.

And as long as we believe that, as long as we act on those beliefs, dear reader, we are going to kick the shit out of one another. Or get the shit kicked out of us. And nothing *will* ever change.

Which leads to the third thing. A small thing. Tied up with "talk is cheap." We've got to act on our feelings, on our thoughts. Act on our values; "act out" the best of our beliefs. Not just take the lies we've been given. But take those lies and turn them around.

Act in ways that confront or at least challenge classism—our own and everyone else's—wherever it rears its ugly but honeyed little head. And not wait for the lesbian stevedore who's been maligned to do it. Or the gay teacher who's been ignored to do it. Or the Vanderbilt who hasn't a clue.

Because, in the end, it isn't gonna be some movement "out there" that will eliminate oppression. It won't be six groups based in Milwaukee turning the rest of us around. And it's not just gonna be some personal insight, some "movement within." It's got to be both: the stories that grow with each telling, the links that those stories connect. It's got to be us, doing it together—and not just in our heads. And not just in our hearts. And not just in the streets.

But all of us, inside and out. Doing it all the time.

Not Just Merely Queer

JUDITH K. WITHEROW

Don't I wish this were a story about closets and how you find your way out of them? The houses I grew up in didn't contain any closets. Instead of closets there were cut-down broomsticks wedged into the corner. This allowed you and anyone else to see what you did or didn't have. Nails were the other option used for the hanging of clothes. It wasn't like the walls were defaced. In fact, covering them with anything was an improvement. We did have a dirt-floor cellar, but "coming out" from that doesn't sound quite as elegant.

Summertime in the Appalachian Mountains is usually cool at night and warm-to-hot as the day wears on. It makes you want to spend the morning lying on the porch by the dog so that you can absorb and double the warmth. I know for sure that skinny kids who lack clothes and bedcovers need the sun more than others. Surely that is the explanation for the creation of the solar system.

On just such a morning, I was looking through a magazine while waiting for the thawout of my bones. It was a magazine some neighbor had given us, or maybe we found it while out trash picking. No matter. It contained pictures of famous people. I was about six years old then. One page had a picture of Eartha Kitt in a leopard-print, short, tight dress. Spellbinding is the only word to describe the moment. Forty-four years have not erased or faded the image of that picture.

That was my earliest memory of a deep and abiding love for another woman. I kept that picture until it was in shreds. Knowing me, I showed it to others while their reaction of shock floated silently away. Don't tell me children can't form deep attachments to someone other than their family or friends. My feelings were as genuine then as they are today.

Time has not lessened my early attraction to other women of color. Dinah Washington, Nina Simone, Billie Holiday, and Esther Phillips were just a few of the women who came into my heart via a big-city radio station. I'm sure my love for them grew out of the words they sang that echoed my own life. As a mixed-blood Native American girl growing up in an otherwise totally white area, I recognized others with the voices and rhythms to express my alienation. Separating class, culture, sexuality, and race is about as easy as untangling a grapevine.

When the far Right speaks of children being recruited by that ho-mo-sex-u-al conspiracy, they are not talking about me. Wouldn't I have noticed a stranger passing through the hollow? If you were to ask me, I'd have to truthfully say I was born this way. To paraphrase my mother, "you were always so different."

Yes, I was always so different. Throughout life I've had this attitude that clothes didn't matter much to me because I was denied the clothes I felt most comfortable in. As a child I knew how I wanted to dress, but I had no control over where my clothes came from. Nor did I have the knowledge or wardrobe to compete with other girls, straight or Queer. Like numerous other helpful items, that genetic piece of information along with the stylish clothes must have been given to someone else. There was sparse clothing money and even less understanding for a girl who only wanted to wear jeans and flannel shirts.

For someone who always thought they didn't care about clothes, the writing of this article has been a revelation that my life has always revolved around what I wore. As a young girl, when clothes were needed to conform with others, I could never rely on having them. Events that required special clothing were avoided by any excuse possible. Constant shame and pain caused me to vow that as an adult I wouldn't care how I dressed. (One exception to this vow was that no one would make me "dress like a girl.") The exact opposite is true. The reality is that the importance of clothes covers my life like Kudzu. This fact disturbs me. I didn't want ever to care so much about anything so painful in my life again. It takes and gives power to those who have even less understanding than I do. Why is it that your peers—the other classmates— think the demeaning remarks they make leave you unscarred? Do they honestly think your intelligence is as barren as your wardrobe? I don't even like to use the word "peers." It makes me feel like someone thinks I'm trying to pass for something I'm not.

I still only want to wear jeans and flannel shirts. But now I've learned how to "accessorize" them to my liking. It's amazing what you can do with belts, western hats, three earrings in each ear, a tattoo of a howling wolf with feathers that appear to float down my left arm, and all the Native American jewelry I once avoided. Anything racially suggestive was avoided. When you are mixed blood and Queer, you learn to hide that which makes you stand out. From an early age, I realized that people like to discriminate knowingly, so I developed a closet mentality. I've celebrated more than one coming out since asserting my true identity.

My manner of dress is my own. I'm told there are Queer fashion magazines. Given the choice, I'd bypass even the cover of one and read a gum wrapper. My partner tells me that the closest fashion concept I resemble is the Marlboro Man. Make that the Marlboro Woman if you have to make it anything.

When I entered the sixth grade in 1954, it was an entrance clothed in flannel shirts and jeans. If anyone had a problem with my manner of dress they didn't state it directly. Maybe happiness closed my eyes and ears to the outside world. Mother ordered them from a catalog. If we didn't need up-front cash, we sometimes got new outfits. Mother said she only did it to keep me out of my brother's clothes. Never mind that he was younger and the shirtsleeves struck me halfway up my arms, and the pants legs hit somewhere between knee and ankle. Whatever. They were of my choosing. The boys didn't mind. I outplayed most of them in sports and was always chosen for their team. Wearing a dress and sliding into home plate was not what I wanted to do. It curtailed my tree and rock climbing.

I'd like to think that Mother gave in on the clothing argument because she knew that the seventh grade was going to be particularly hard on me. She had to know that wearing dresses or skirts was going to just about kill me. If anyone knew hardship and what the lack of proper attire meant, she did. (She quit school in the eighth grade. Her one outfit was the top of a dress for a blouse and the bottom of a man's wool overcoat for a skirt.) The thought of my first day in the seventh grade can still make me cringe. No disrespect intended: I felt like I was in drag. That was not me in female attire. Wearing girls' clothes also attracted the boys' attention in a new way. They no longer wanted me to play on their team. It was the beginning of being treated like a sex object and having no understanding of what was happening.

My oldest sister was as happy as I was about Mom's decision. This signaled to her that the period of trying to dress us like twins was definitely over. Dressing like me was not something she had *ever* strived for. She was ultra-feminine, petite, and wanted nothing more than to fit in with the other girls.

When most of your clothes are second- or third-hand, it's a challenge to try dressing a couple of your kids as twins. The fact that no one discarded matching outfits in two different sizes didn't deter Mother. I have two theories on why she did this. One, she read a story in a women's magazine. To her, these trash mags were the true gospel on upping your class. Since we didn't have a television, and relatives and friends were of the same background, she used these magazines to raise us "correctly." Or, two, she thought if she could teach me to dress like my sister, I would learn to love it. Wrong. She would have had less trouble putting a dress on one of my brothers.

Twins? When you have children spilling out through the cracks in the wood shack walls, could anyone really think that duplicating us would impress anyone? We could have run around buck naked with our crotch hair on fire and gotten the same reaction.

My sixth-grade class picture remains something that I can still intimidate myself with. It was a concession! We all know the definition of that word. You do something loathsome in return for something you really want. To ensure the wearing of my new shirt and jeans on picture day, I submitted to my mother putting those hated, long finger curls in my hair. This was her Shirley Temple, "ain't my half-breed daughter something" phase. I couldn't even finger comb the curls out because I was getting my damn picture taken. It would have been proof that I didn't uphold my end of the bargain. Long hair, if not braided, should always be the way the wind tosses and teases it. The Spirits surely decree this to be true.

Someone entering puberty can feel and understand the meaning of not fitting in on several levels. Class, race, culture, and sexuality, combined with raging hormones, can magnify any flaw that you and society believe exists. Without a doubt, these were the most damaging years of my life.

Seventh grade saw the end of my wearing jeans to school. It was a rule punishable by suspension. The wearing of dresses or skirts remained a wretched task. My sister tried to help me set and tame my hair with curlers, but that seriously failed. Three of my female cousins who were in the same grade as I was also tried to help. They involved me in that female tribal rite of experimentation with makeup. Wanting to wear makeup and dress up seemed to come naturally to them. Their ability to apply makeup without the use of a mirror impressed me. It was almost as good as making a double play in baseball. I admired the skill part of it. But most of all I loved them for wanting to protect me and teach me another means of survival.

There were two major girl rules in our home. One, you couldn't date until you were sixteen years old. Two, you couldn't wear makeup of any kind. These rules just about killed my "champing at the bit" older sister. She could be just as determined as I was and didn't follow either "road to hell" threat. These rules were discarded for me. My parents wanted to turn their tomboy into a girl. Why didn't they discuss with me what they saw as a problem? No adult ever mentioned that the outrageously Queer things I did were not acceptable for a number of reasons. My sister still resents the double standard she thought existed during our upbringing. Does she still not get it? Her and most of the straight world, I guess.

In the eleventh grade I went to a barber shop and had my hair cut as short as possible. This would have been 1961. Sometimes what seems like a genuinely inspired idea doesn't quite turn out like you might expect. While the haircut seemed perfect and natural to me, others were appalled. The first day back at school, my male English teacher had me stand and said, "Look how beautiful Judith looks." He took the heat off and defied anyone to say differently. Given the choice, I would have preferred to remain invisible.

I'm fifty years old now and wear my hair in a braid. Mostly it's a cultural trait, but I just can't be bothered with hair fixing. Bothered? Bewildered is more like it.

Perhaps when you're as poor as we were no one gives a rat's casket about anything you do. Or they care way too much about things that are purely none of their business. I remember a visiting adult male family member saying, "It's true what they say. A hog always returns to its wallow." He was referring to the beat-down poverty of both my parents. No one contradicted him. Marrying someone poor no doubt contributed to his belief of superiority. To this day, forty-five years later, this man who married into our family has the attitude that we were put here to serve him. Once in a while I see my aunt stand up to him, but the moments are all too rare. This trap of subservience takes a lifetime of sidestepping. You get used to having your bones rolled like a pair of loaded dice that land any way the other person wants. It snares me more times than I care to admit.

My Cherokee dad thought everything I did was fine. He gloried in my "spunk" and encouraged me to participate in a variety of sports. He and I would sit up late every Friday night and listen to the boxing matches on the radio. On weekends we would listen to the Pittsburgh Pirates' baseball games. The rest of my family was not interested in sports of any kind. Dad gave me an everlasting love and understanding of competition. There isn't a sporting event I watch that my first thought isn't to call him for an inspired discussion. I'll always miss sharing this part of my life with him. R.I.P. "Striped Lizard," my father, the Golden Gloves boxer.

Mother didn't understand or care for sports. She was too worn out with everything else to take the time to sit and listen to most things on the radio. I remember her heating "sad" irons on the wood stove while doing our laundry and listening to the Stella Dallas soap opera blaring in the background. The "soaps" were another way she kept in touch with the outside world to help us blend. I believe it's why they remain popular. It fills a need for many women living in isolation.

God, how I hated wash day. It was an endless day of chopping wood and carrying two ten-quart buckets of water at a time. In addition, you had to keep the wood stove stoked for nonstop heating of water. There was fantasy and there was the reality of our life. The magazines and soap operas could only distract and teach you so much. You had to have a vivid imagination to survive what we did. I sincerely hope my mom inhabited as rich a fantasy world as I did. She only had shack after closetless shack to come out of. We could have shared a few survival techniques.

Unlike Mother, I didn't particularly care what the outside world thought about most subjects. While this wasn't always true, I did manage to cover my feelings better than her gentle, tender self could. Since my world revolved around adventure books, thanks to my father, my fantasy escape route was an easier one to navigate.

I cared most about the outside world when it affected a family member. If someone hurt or insulted my brothers or sisters, I whipped ass, no matter whether it was a boy or a girl. Telling my parents was not usually an option because they would question whether one of us had been doing something to deserve the treatment. It was their way of teaching self-censure. This belief never protected them, but they somehow thought it would work for us. It taught me a great deal about self-reliance. This Houdini atmosphere also enabled me to enter and leave invisible closets without so much as the sound of a feather falling.

There was and is a sense of loyalty that time, money, disagreements, or locality can't erase in our family. When your life consists of belly-touching-backbone hunger and culture and race discrimination, it creates a bond not understood by someone who hasn't survived the same experiences.

The fact that you live in poverty does not stop you from wanting, loving, or having children. Just the opposite is true. I have three adult sons and two grandchildren and wouldn't trade the parenting hardships for anything of a material or monetary nature.

In our immediate family, I was the only female who hunted, fished, and trapped regularly. (Because of numerous health problems, including multiple sclerosis and lupus, fishing is the only skill that I continue.) My knowledge is passed on to the younger ones so that our culture is not completely lost. They face added discrimination because of these practices. I'm well aware that many people harbor deep resentment where hunting and guns are concerned. It's a narrow and racist attitude that is applied without consideration to the Native American way of life. I deflect this ignorance and instill pride whenever possible. The increase of powwows is making my educational job easier. This past winter I had the sons get me two deer hides and the feathers from a wild turkey. It was a present for a "Fancy Dancer" friend to aid in the new outfit he is making. Thus swings open another closet door.

While growing up I fell in love with several friends. They never knew because it was my problem to deal with, and I couldn't bear the loss of their friendship. As a teenager I always chose girls who were totally out of my class. In adulthood I consciously "tried" to do the exact opposite. If I took the class card out of the deck, it would make the game more even.

It came as a shock and puzzlement when white women who had a great deal of money pursued me. To be truthful, it angered and caused me to lose respect for them. Couldn't they see all of the things wrong with me? If high school girls had the power to shake and break my heart untold times, what the hell were these women up to?

I attended no college or any other class since high school. My grammar must have been lacking because it got corrected on a regular basis. The lack of clothes sense I exhibited remained the same. An apt description of myself would have been untamed and untrained. This left me with the conclusion that my looks were all that was important.

One woman took me to her house and showed me all of her name-brand evening gowns and numerous fur coats. (Like I'd know a de la Renta from a blue-light special.) At the time it didn't occur to me that she was trying to impress me. I was taught that showing off your belongings was wrong. It also bored the crap out of me. Remember? I loathe dresses. Now there was a woman who had a lot of closets to come out of.

On another day spent with this woman, I needed to go by a friend's house to give her some rockfish. The fish were in a garbage bag. When I took them inside my friend said, "Gee, Judith, it must be nice riding around in a Porsche." All I could think of was, "So that's what a Porsche looks like." Now, I wonder what that woman must have thought of me putting a bag full of fish in her expensive car. What did I know? That's the way I would have carried them in my car. Those fish brought me as much pride as I'm sure her car did her.

Another woman wanted to buy me a car or put my name on her house. She said by doing this she "would have a hold on me." I never accepted expensive gifts because I didn't want to feel indebted. It had a feeling of slavery to it.

See, this is what puzzles me about the upper-class women I've been involved with. Where did this idea of holding someone with material possessions originate? Why not just give something because you want to? Trying to impress someone who is ignorant to the trappings of wealth will be very frustrating. I know if it's man-made it can be taken away in one way or another.

In 1975 I met my partner of twenty years. During this time I was also seeing a few other women. After a lifetime of living the way everyone else demanded, I decided some happiness of my own was due. It was a giant juggling act, but I pulled it off.

During this period I was also married and living way the hell out in the country. To say I was in a dangerous situation would be to put it mildly. My husband wanted nothing less than death for me. During one of his fits he fired six bullets at me. I didn't know until later that he had loaded the pistol with blanks. The amount of violence the boys were seeing gave me the courage to leave.

The next morning I moved in with Sue. I didn't take my children with me because it would have given him an added excuse to kill me. Being without the boys was a pain that nothing could lessen. Within a week he willingly gave the boys up. He only wanted them as a threat. When that didn't work, I received full custody.

Sue was, and is, everything I have always wanted in a partner. When we first met, she was a self-defense instructor and a cab driver. Her face was framed with "gone to hell" curly blond hair. She rode a motorcycle and had killer scars to show from hitting parked cars. Parked cars? I was impressed. I was wowed. I was wrong. Why couldn't it have been wintertime? All bundled up she would have been harder to classify. Make no mistake. I wanted someone from my own class background. There were many problems in my marriage, but classism wasn't one of them.

It was wrong to base my assumptions on Sue's class by the way she dressed or her sparsely furnished apartment. She was dressing down because she had the confidence to do it. What an alien idea! The discovery of her higher education and background came when it was too late to walk away.

Just recently, while discussing this article with Sue, I stated how much alike we were. "Jesus, Judith," she said. "We're almost nothing alike, except both being female. You live in a western hat, braid your hair, and are totally into your Native American culture. You have a worm ranch in our basement to grow food for the frogs you keep in your bedroom. Then there is the horned toad in another aquarium that only wants fed live food. During your last multiple sclerosis exacerbation, you went outside and killed a rat with your cane." I killed it because it was up inside the bird feeder eating the seeds and scaring the birds. "Your idea of a good time is taking your 9mm pistol to the range and shooting it. Your three grown sons think you are about the toughest thing going." OK. I get the message.

After our discussion, I gave what she said a lot of thought. She's right. We're very different women. Beyond our dress are our conflicts over money. Once you are poor, money loses most of the power I see it holds over the more affluent, including Sue. We struggle with budget and money issues. We've learned to compromise when class clashes occur.

Another disagreement centers around higher education. She has the luxury of calling it bullshit. I think she can do this because she is the one who has a couple of degrees.

Yes, we're very different women. But I shouldn't feel the need to be like anyone but myself. These are words that I'll probably always repeat to myself. Repeat but not quite believe.

I am different, but not alone in my difference. Over New Year's I was showing my friend Deb a really fancy flannel shirt. We share much of the same taste in clothes. I asked her, "Did you ever think you would see a flannel shirt with embroidered flowers on the shoulders that you would want to wear?" She assured me she hadn't. While we were busy looking in my closet, who should appear but Sue. She said that she never thought she would ever hear the two of us discussing clothes. See?

You bet she's right when she says that we are very different. Who has a closet full of dresses and skirts? Which one would rather wear tap shoes than boots? Guess which woman has a sparkly top hat, matching fairy wand, and a glitter-filled baton? Those of us in the know answered correctly. There is really no right or wrong answer. There is also the plea that others will keep an open mind regarding discrimination in all forms.

Not just merely Queer. I'm most sincerely Queer.

Class Struggles

MORGAN GRAYCE WILLOW

Recently I met for a potluck with a group of eight women writers, all of us lesbian or bisexual. We'd gathered in the sparely furnished apartment of one of us to celebrate each other, our work, and our remarkable abilities to survive. After we'd eaten a sumptuous meal, we congregated in the sunny, west-facing room that serves as one-part kitchen, one-part bedroom. I leaned against the oak woodwork that outlined what had once been a doorframe and listened to the group's banter and laughter. From my vantage point I could see the other women against the backdrop of an expansive view of the Lowry Hill area of Minneapolis. At one point, the hostess drew our attention to a homey mobile made from knives, forks, and spoons that she'd picked up at a craft fair many years before. She explained it was the one single thing she would never sell in the ongoing permutations of travel, home, and ownership demanded by the writing life we all shared.

Now, as I sit in my west-facing study in a troubled neighborhood further south in Minneapolis, the image of that mobile comes to mind as I struggle to write about class. The flatware in the mobile is certainly not sterling, or if it is, it's long since tarnished beyond recognition. Even old stainless, for that matter, takes on the look of pewter. Eventually there's no shine to it. The flatware itself is a simple, broad-handled design, the kind you'd save for use at camp after you've graduated to a nicer set for the table. It's serviceable, durable, basic—exactly like all the class qualities I absorbed growing up in the rural midwest.

I'm inspired by the mobile, a work of art made from plain materials. What I envy about that finished work is the center string that holds the whole thing together. On that string the mobile can move and clank in the early spring breeze. By contrast, this piece I'm trying to write has no central string, no fulcrum. Instead it resembles a handful of flatware tossed haphazardly on a rough-hewn kitchen table. The knives, forks, and spoons I'm contemplating lie in such a confused heap not because I have nothing to say about class, but for precisely the opposite reason. There is so much I want to say. So I start by pulling one fork from the pile, only to discover that it's tangled among knives and spoons. I try again, with the spoon, and end up in the same tangle. Each time I enter this unstructured heap, in search of that balancing place where the center string needs to be hung, I end up feeling as if I am the fork and my tines have been bent at incongruous angles. Finally, I step back and just look at the heap of metal.

I begin to understand a couple of reasons for the tangle. The first is inside my own head, where I discover that class is a difficult, taboo subject even between me and myself. Personally, the issue is fraught with rage, grief, and confusion. The second lies outside me, where the same taboo appears to extend throughout our many levels and varieties of communities. Publicly, the issue is fraught with rage, grief, and confusion. So we have avoided talking about it. So I find that I'm not stepping into a dialogue where someone has already sorted out the silverware for me. We're all starting with a heap of metal and trying to invent the wooden case in which the forks, spoons, and knives fit into their own velvet-lined slots. We're all going to have to approach this piece by piece.

Having decided that I'm probably not going to be able to replicate the mobile, or even build the case where all the pieces nestle in clean rows, I pull out one knife and one fork. These are the two that repeatedly show up as the structures supporting my internal and external silence about class. One is the question of definition. What class do I belong to? The other is the question of authority.

Whose word am I willing to accept on this or any other issue? What complicates the problem is that each of these questions is itself an issue of class. The questions and their answers loop and tangle in and around each other. Yet the sorting has to start somewhere.

I was born to an Iowa farm family. The family was large, the farm small. We had only a quarter-section of land, 160 acres, in the southeastern corner of Mitchell County. This land barely supported us.

Life on the farm revolves entirely around work. By its nature, farming is a day-by-day, twenty-four-hours-a-day kind of work. In addition, ours was a dairy farm. Every day, before six o'clock, both morning and evening, the cows had to be herded into the barn, stanchioned, milked, fed, and released. In between, the milk itself had to be processed for storage, the milking equipment cleaned and sterilized. Barns had to be cleaned of tons of manure. Feed and water had to be in steady supply. All of this had to go on irrespective of time of year, school and bus schedules. Plus, it had to wrap around planting time—those few narrow weeks in spring when the soil has warmed and dried enough to let you get in and out of the fields without being mired down in mud—and harvest—those comparable few weeks in the fall when the corn must be picked as soon as it's ripened and before the first blizzard. Plus two summer harvests of hay, late summer harvest of oats, early fall harvest of soybeans. And I haven't even mentioned the needs of other livestock: chickens with their daily round of egg-laying; hogs with their seasons of breeding and farrowing. None of these cycles conform to human cycles. All are subject to the vagaries of weather. We were certainly a class of people who worked.

Here is precisely where I slam into one of the two structures holding up my silence about class. The fork. Nasty, sharp, huge, and essential as a pitchfork, it's the problem of definition. I am of a class of people who work, but I am not precisely "working-class." Just where do I fit in?

"Class" seems, by its nature, to be an exclusionary term. I feel left out even as I begin considering what it means. The word comes from the Latin *classis*, which means one of the six divisions of the Roman people. According to the *Oxford English Dictionary*, Servius Tuilius devised these six "classes" for purposes of property and taxation. Even with a magnifying glass I find no hint in the fine print about why he chose six, and only six, divisions. By now we know that slaves were left out of those divisions, as were most women. Still, this is an improvement over Plato's *Republic*, in which there are only three class divisions: the ruling class, their aux-iliaries (the police-soldiers), and laborers. Plato ranked farmers with laborers, none of whom had any rights to govern in the Ideal State.

In my own experience, on those rare occasions when the topic of class has come up in conversation, the focus has always been on two divisions of American people: the "working class" and the "middle class." From time to time, I've heard references to the "up-per class," but few of the people I know have direct experience with that. So we drop it. Sometimes other terms, like the "under-class" and the "working poor," crop up. But for the most part, our speculations revolve around what it means to be "working-class" or "middle-class." In any of these conversations and any of these class terms, my own origins are simply left out.

We are an invisible class, we working farm folk. Although work is what we did, all the time, on that farm that barely supported us. We did not earn an hourly wage, a criterion that often helps de-fine the "working class." Nor did we belong to the class Marx and Engels called the petite bourgeoisie, for we were neither trades-men nor professionals. We managed a family business, true. Yet we couldn't quite fit into a contemporary notion of a white-collar management class, since we did not earn salaries. And, though we were entrepreneurs, we could hardly be described as members of the class owning the means of production. We owned the farm, to be sure, and we produced grains, meats, vegetables, and dairy products. But farm production has never fit Marx's tidy industrial model. We produced just enough to eat or sell, and thus hovered dangerously close to the subsistence level. We made virtually no profit. Besides, we didn't employ any workers. We, the family, were the workers.

For those of us in this unnamed class, our very survival was based on one thing only—work. Work as a way of life. We were born not as children, but as farmhands. Childhood meant being a not-yet-ripe laborer. Our role as children was not to play, but to learn about and prepare for work. Our apprenticeship began when we were able to walk. We became beasts of burden. Our first job was to carry objects to weary adults. Later, as our language evolved and we learned the names of things, we were ordered to "go get" this or that for a tired adult. "Go get the hammer." "Take the cookie to Daddy." Gradually, the complexity and responsibility of the jobs increased. We were told to guard the gate so the hogs couldn't get through. We were instructed to plant potatoes and onions in the garden. We were sent to the bean fields to pull up the "volunteer" corn that had seeded itself in unwanted places. We were given scythes and sent out to chop down thistles in the north pasture. We were sent, early spring and late fall, through the fields to "pick rock," which meant we gathered up stones and boulders that had worked their way up through the soil. If these were not cleared from the fields, they could break expensive plowshares. All in graduated degrees as our muscles matured us into the persistent, back-breaking labor that was to be our way of life.

The work started out relatively gender-neutral, but before long it became very clearly gender-defined. When we graduated from low-to-the-ground manual labor to the privilege of working with machinery, the division of labor was suddenly strict. Boys were trained to drive tractors, planters, cultivators, hay bailers, and combines. Girls were sent to the house and trained on brooms, dish pans, wash machines, and pie tins. In the milking barn, my brothers learned how to run the milkers; my sister and I were taught to scrub and sterilize them. Boys tilled the garden; girls canned the vegetables.

Perhaps, had there not been four boys before me, and I a girl— at long last a girl, someone to help our poor, worn-out mother— maybe I'd have been trained to do fieldwork. I might have learned to feel the power of those machines and the stubborn gratification of that land. I'll never know. But I do remember that when I said I wanted to work in the fields, I was told I wouldn't like it anyway, I was lucky to be a girl, to stay inside and have life easy. Subject closed.

It didn't look to me like such an easy life, that of a heterosexual farm wife. The men eventually did come in from the fields to tables laden with food, to clothes drying on the line, to kids bathed, fed, and burped. There were women on some of the farms around us who worked the fields, but most of my role models were house-wives. Thus the future that was presented to me was to grow up,

marry a farmer, and have a whole passel of kids. The only alternative to that fecund model of sexuality in which women both
worked and produced future workers were the nuns I saw in
church and school. They, of course, were celibate. And given the
choice between heterosexuality on those terms and asexuality, for
a long stretch I opted for the latter. There was no third alternative.
Of the few women and men from that community who remained
single, and may possibly have been lesbian or gay, most moved
away. It even seemed to me that to a Catholic as devout as my
mother, the notion of having a nun in the family would be welcome. I knew I wanted something different. But I remember her
response one day when I expressed the wish to become a nun.
She assured me that the nuns still had to do housework at the end
of the school day. Even choices about sexuality were somehow reduced to work.

Whatever our assigned roles on the farm were, my brothers,
sister, and I took them very seriously. We had to. We were told, repeatedly: "No work; no supper." This, of course, is true for the
class of farmers in a general way. If the work is not done, there is
no harvest; no grain, beef, or pork means no money, which means
no food. But for us as child members of the class of farming people, we learned the message on a personal level: "If I do not work,
I do not survive."

This is very different from the kind of shift work I think of in
connection with "working-class." When I was growing up, the
only people I knew who worked that way were "townies." My
introduction to the culture of wage labor came from reading *The
Jungle*, Upton Sinclair's novel about working conditions in Chicago's
stockyards and slaughterhouses. Later, I read about Mother Jones
and her union organizing activities in the coal mines of West
Virginia, silver mines of New Mexico, and even the iron mines in
northern Minnesota. The goal of all of this union organizing was to
set limits on how much labor the working class could be required
to do in reasonable exchange for a livable wage.

Later, in the 1970s, I participated in the United Farm Workers'
boycott of grapes and iceberg lettuce. Their struggles made me
think for the first time about agricultural workers as "workers" for
whom traditional union tactics might have some benefit. Even so,

organizing as a way to improve working conditions seemed irrelevant to my class, until the 1980s. Then, in highly controversial actions, the Farmers' Union organized tractorcades—thousands of farm tractors parading en masse to state capitals and on to Washington, D.C.—in protest of the steady erosion of farm subsidy programs. In other actions, dairy farmers dumped out tankloads of milk to protest declining milk prices. Still, most of the kinds of work limitations unions demand on behalf of the working class don't apply in agriculture. Eight-hour days. Five-day workweek. Time-and-a-half pay for overtime work. Paid vacations. Farming knows no such benefits or limits.

Again, it was the "townies," a separate class of people, who had weekends off and paid vacations. My Uncle Dale belonged to this class. He worked in a meat-packing plant in Mason City. Yet during the growing season he drove out to our farm almost every Sunday to do a little work. He would lend his hand during planting and harvest. In midsummer, he came out and cultivated the fields of corn. For him, however, this was ritual work, a way to stay connected to the farming lifestyle he'd grown up in alongside his brother, my dad. He would work a few hours, then come in for coffee and pie. Apparently he felt an emotional need to stay connected to the land and the farming life, but his life did not depend on it. And on those days when he could not come because he was called in to work overtime, he earned time-and-a-half. Whereas for us, planting and harvesting meant around-the-clock work—perhaps three, maximum four, hours of sleep—until the crop was in or out, depending upon which end of the year we were at.

For good or ill, these farm class values have thoroughly shaped my life. I've been off the farm for twenty-seven years, but I still cannot feel work shrunk down to the limits of a nine-to-five day. Somewhere, the belief that if I do not work, I do not deserve to eat, sticks. Whatever class this is, work is fundamental to it.

⁓

By now it seems clear that traditional class analysis doesn't apply to us farming folk. The voices of Marx and Engels, Upton Sinclair, labor historians, even Mother Jones, don't speak a truth we connect with. From this vacancy emerges the second structure holding up our silence about class. This, a sharp knife pulled from the tangle of disheveled metal, is the question of authority. Whose word do we accept? Whom do we believe?

In the prevailing folklore of rural Iowa there is no one as stubborn as a farmer. This stubbornness is often cited as the reason why farmers have so seldom—until the Farm Crisis of the 1980s—joined forces in collective action. Farmers, the lore goes, are simply too independent, too stubborn. They tend not to trust anyone's authority except their own. This makes sense. In a livelihood where survival depends directly on the forces of nature, the relationship between self and nature is primary. The real authorities are nature, experience, and the self.

My dad was a prime example of this stubbornness and skepticism about authority. Throughout his professional life as a farmer, the authority that fought most for his loyalty was the U.S. Department of Agriculture (USDA). In 1962, based on recommendations of a group of analysts called the Committee for Economic Development (CED), the USDA began devising policies and changing price support programs. The goal was to transform American agriculture from a small-scale family farm system to a vast industrialized system. The CED had concluded that if American agricultural commodities were to control world markets, the number of small family farms would have to be significantly reduced and the average acreage per existing farm radically increased. The CED believed that this would significantly boost production and generate surplus grain for export.

The following year, not long before I turned fourteen, the last of my seven brothers was born. My younger sister and I were responsible for raising him. We were living, at that time, on the farm in Mitchell County that had originally been purchased by my great-grandfather in 1890. Family records are incomplete, and family stories even more vague, but apparently sometime during the Great Depression there was a foreclosure, and the farm fell into the hands of bankers. When I was just a baby, my parents bought the same farm back. So Dad had been working that soil—and grumbling about its clay mud sinks—for a good thirteen years by this time. For as many generations back as anyone in the family knew, his people, all farmers, had been doing the same.

The struggle that year to get the crops in and out was no different from most. In good years, the operating debt could be reduced
somewhat. In bad years, the debt deepened. Dad didn't know
about the Committee for Economic Development as an entity. He
didn't need to. He had the ASCS office—the Agricultural Stabiliza-
tion and Conservation Service—and the Agricultural Extension
Service to contend with. These agencies were the policy imple-
mentation and propaganda arms of the USDA at the state and local
levels. They were giving out advice that would, in another twenty
years, bring about the results called for by the CED. In specific
terms, this meant dropping the practice of check planting, in
which corn rows were spaced widely and evenly apart and seeds
were dropped along a checking wire to measure out their dis-
bursement. The geometric configuration of fields planted in this
way (immortalized in the paintings of Grant Wood) made it appear
as though corn rows radiated out in diagonal lines from any given
point where you might happen to be standing. The horticultural
reason for this practice was to give the roots of corn plants plenty
of room to grow. It also left space for cultivators—very narrow-
bladed plowing machines—to pass through the fields two or three
times during the growing season and take out the weeds that competed with the corn for water and nutrients. What the ASCS was
urging instead was for farmers to plant corn rows closer together.
The official charge became to plant "fencerow to fencerow,"
leaving as little unplanted land as possible. And for weed control?
The ASCS encouraged farmers to use chemical herbicides. Meanwhile, the ASCS discouraged the ancient practice of yearly crop
rotation to replenish nutrients in spent soil. Instead, official policy
supported the use of chemical fertilizers, particularly anhydrous
ammonia, or liquid nitrogen, as we informally called it.

Dad's grumblings about those "damned government agents
coming in here and telling us how to farm our crops" grew gradually into full-blown rages. He might have been able to simply ignore them had their intrusion remained only advice, words
splashed across pamphlets or tossed out through loudspeakers
over the heads of farm families at the county fair. But the agents'
words were backed by government dollars in the form of subsidy
programs. Following ASCS policies meant checks in the bank. And

each payment was tied up in countless, indecipherable rules that were only understandable to farmers via the interpretation of the very agents, and their staffs, who were administering them. In addition, conditions of bank loans were designed to match the policies of the ASCS. Economic necessity forced Dad, and many farmers like him, to comply with policies that he knew to be in direct contradiction to the health of the soil and the safe practices of farming that had been handed down generation after generation, dating back to the Old Country. He used to rant, "They're trying to run us off our farms." At the time, no one believed him. History has proven him right.

Dad's specific focus of distrust was the government and its propaganda arm, the university, which had spawned the Agricultural Extension Service. But his questioning of authority extended to just about any medium. Though he himself never graduated from high school, he was a critical thinker and an avid newspaper reader. He often said, "Don't believe anything you read and only half of what you see." When we finally got television in our home, he warned about the dangers of advertising. I was young then. I thought he was crazy. At times I would have preferred that he be crazy rather than accept the reality of a world as treacherous as he made it out to be. Like the other kids around me, I wanted to accept the slick surface of things without question. But in each succeeding decade of my life, I came to value his once-crazy ranting as sage advice. Eventually, I inherited his distrust of authority. Both a world view and a habit, it served me well as I came of age during the Sexual Revolution, the war in Viet Nam, the Second Wave of feminism in the U.S., Stonewall, and the struggle for lesbian and gay rights. I had, essentially, a class-shaped predilection to question authority.

I used to think this had more to do with being a lesbian than with class. After all, irrespective of when we come out, lesbians grow up and live on the margins of society. From our vantage point off to the side, we have the opportunity, whether we like it or not, to see the culture from a different angle. Our position out on this edge always reminds me of the ancient Greek mathematician Archimedes, who is said to have invented the lever. Archimedes believed he could move the entire earth with his new invention. All he needed was his lever, a fulcrum to balance it on, and a platform off to the side of the earth. As lesbians divested of heterosexual privilege we are, in a sense, thrust out on such a platform. From here it's much easier to see the lie in the voice of authority.

It was Dorothy Allison who helped me bring this skepticism of authority back to my class roots. In an article entitled "To Tell the Truth" in *Ms.* (July/August 1994) she wrote: "I went to college in the early seventies, and I had the great good fortune of being there at a time when other working-class kids were also confronting a world in which we were barely acknowledged, and certainly not welcomed. That experience spurred in me, as in many of us, an outrage and determination that questioned accepted barriers of authority, validation, rightness."

I started college a little earlier than she, the late sixties. After dropping out and wandering the country with the flood of other nomads and hippies, it was the late seventies by the time I returned and finished. Like Allison, I was one of those kids who could not have gone but for a combination of scholarships and National Direct Student Loans (NDSL), one of those basic building blocks in Lyndon Johnson's Great Society.

The seething current of rage I experienced started back home, however, before I left for college. To get the NDSL my parents were required to fill out an endless battery of forms called the Parents' Confidential Financial Statement. They had to document every penny of their liabilities and assets to prove that their daughter would not be able to get a college education without the beneficence of the federal government. My father adamantly refused to do this.

From my vantage point now, I understand why. Fed up to his chin hairs with federal programs, wearied by the tedium of forms from the ASCS office, the bank, and the IRS (who always breathed heavily down farmers' necks), he was hard put to document his farm business failures in yet another format. However, what he said at the time was: "You don't need to go to college. You'll just get married anyway."

That hurt. Even though I had by then given up on the idea of the nunnery, I had secretly vowed never to marry. This was not the third alternative I really sought, and eventually found—to live my life as a lesbian. But at that time, it was an alternative. It was also my own private sacrilege, that I intended to violate the cultural expectations of our Catholic, rural farm community. Now Dad had spoken precisely what I feared my only option to be if I did not get away to college. I flew into a rage.

I've mentioned that he had not graduated from high school. Mom had. I did have one brother who was then going to college on the G.I. Bill. But here I was, a first-generation daughter presuming the right to a college education. And it meant Dad would have to parade his worth (which he read as worthlessness) one more time on paper to be scrutinized by government bureaucrats. This was, at first, too much for him. His class shame welled up and compelled him to deny me what my class shame demanded I must have.

In truth, he really did want me to go to college. He was a thinking man, mostly self-educated, but a visionary. He knew I was smart, and he liked, some of the time, that I would argue back with him. He wanted a different future for me. And a part of him wanted me to get the education he never had and then use it to challenge the things that were wrong in the world, the conditions that kept both of us stuck in a despised and invisible class. We stormed at each other for a while, our rages equally matched. Eventually, he relented. He filled out the forms just in the nick of time before the application deadline. He agreed to bow one more time to the dictates of an authority he despised to gain me some leverage on a future.

Off I went, my suitcase chock-full of class tension, high expectations, and not nearly enough sweater sets. It was a small, midwestern, liberal arts college. We were required to wear skirts and stockings to dinner. We had to be in the dorm by ten o'clock. We were required to attend faculty teas and convocations. The rules on campus were rigid. Meanwhile, off campus, the Viet Nam War steadily escalated. The young men around me were deciding what to do with their draft cards. Martin Luther King, Jr., was assassinated in the spring, and Robert Kennedy in early summer. By the next fall we were smuggling booze and dope into our dorm rooms. And the course work, with the exception of the honors humanities series I was in, was dull and irrelevant. I'd hoped to turn myself over to an authority I could trust, my father's old enemy, the academy. Without realizing it, I'd bought into the middle-class notion that knowledge could make me free. Instead, the conflict between those voices of authority and what I was experiencing in a world at undeclared war proved to be too much. I left the academy.

Years later, when my own inner voice of authority had gained strength, I did return to the academy and take a couple of degrees. But I used my sharply honed class sensibility to help me discern what to accept. True to my father's dictum, I didn't believe anything I read, which made me an excellent philosophy student. While occasionally I wish I were not haunted by doubt verging on cynicism, most of the time I am grateful that my first reaction is to question what I am told, what I read, and what I see. As a lesbian, my life depends on it.

This is not a full place setting, one fork, one knife. Not even for a farm table, much less a formal, seven-course dinner. But these are the basics. This is what we lesbian/bisexual writers had at our potluck: forks and knives for everyone. Spoons enough to share, if need be. Only the mobile, the completed work of art, hanging in the window and clanking in the breeze, had a full set that evening.

For myself, this serves as a beginning of the untangling of my own issues around class. I understand more than I did when I started out. Hopefully, for us queer people as a class this is a step in the sorting, measuring, and balancing we need to do together to understand what class means for us.

origin

AKLILU DUNLAP

i come from industry, instinct, ingenuity.
from she, who wove miracles out of strewn clutter—
a matriarch strong as sandalwood, warm as steel.
from he, the well of patience and affection,
who sees the poet in the statesman,
and the man in the state.

i come from goodwill, garage sales, salvation armies.
from paper-plate kites, makeshift bikes;
pants too big, shoes too small.
i come from oscar meyer bologna, jaw breakers,
salt-water taffy, and flintstone vitamins.

i come from empty bayer bottles.
from honor rolls, student government, and weekends alone
with a mirror hiding no detail the scalpel can't correct.
from solitary corners, closed doors,
and pursed lips mouthing "nigger," "faggot."

from loud whispers, averted eyes,
and snickers spilling over cupped hands.

i come from relaxers and sun-shy tans.
from shaun cassidy aspirations and houseboy resignations.
from the arms of dusty pages and lips of frayed edges. from
     the ravage
of heathcliffs in the moors, the club-footed stagger of master
     philip; from
pecola's bluest eyes and darkest secrets. from the toils of
     friday, the curiosity
of george, and the self-emancipation of ramona the pest.

i come from r & b, scat, gregorian chant.
from the voice of oppression: aretha, nina, billie;
and the hand of defiance: sojourner, martin; thurgood, anita.
from the hearts of divas, the salt of banshees,
the foot of kings, and the shrill of pansies.

i come from closets, veneers, silence—invisibility.
from dark corners harboring secret affections,
unnamed passions, the love few recognize.
from glossy faces, spurious sighs, and insipid smiles;
from hope, determination, even occasional desperation.

i come from abandoned prayers. from community, coalition,
     cooperation.
from boycotts, silent protests, picket signs, and candlelight
     marches that
torch the night streets with rage and conviction.
from bold visionaries and meek giants, whose tired eyes caress
     the dark
before resigning to the promises of change.

Spirit and Passion

CARMEN VAZQUEZ

I continue to search for passion in my reason, to understand my journey, to understand why I move and leave the ones I love only to miss and seek them again, to come back to the same place that is now different because she wears a new perfume and there is in her a new yearning. I was looking for the yearning.

Yearning belongs to the spirit. Spirit is what we can't know yet about ourselves. Spirit lives in the impossibly sweet smell of honeysuckle in summer heat. Spirit brings a white rose blooming on a cold November day. Spirit soars on salted ocean air and stays in my lover's hair. Spirit imagines the sinews of her back and thighs for me when she isn't here. Spirit saunters with me and Marcie over the Brooklyn Bridge, and from its highest point we see Manhattan, glittering phallic splendor of lights and steel, rising in triumph before us. Spirit is what I hope for and dream about. Spirit is what I lose myself for and in.

The trouble is, when a lesbian speaks of spirit, she is suspect. This is because it used to be that lesbians and people like us were not named, our presence invisible, our yearning forbidden, our spirit denied. We were She-devils and witches, warlocks and mad-

121

men. When we dared embrace our desire, we were no more than silent snow whispering down frosted lamplights outside my window, every flake visible in a midnight moment that is beautiful because it will never come again, not the same way, not the same snowflakes, not the same lamplight. But we never dared dream of morning. The flakes died on the ground.

The modern lesbian, gay, bisexual, and transgender movement misses this point. We forget how we were once unnamed and how young we are, how few are the years we have had to reflect on our experience, and how unique a gift we are to the collective human spirit. We forget that it is lesbians and gay men who have embraced the pleasure of sexual desire and the power of love freely chosen without the justification of reproduction. We forget that over and over again we have created family and community among ourselves without acknowledgment from the state or institutional religion. We forget that it is lesbians and gay men who have refused to submit to the sexual constrictions of gender.

This is what I know: Sexuality is not simply what we do, it is who we are. Morality defines behavior as good or bad depending on a set of values commonly shared among a people. Our society has invented morality as a shield against passion and greed and lawlessness. We have woven stories and myths of what is decent and necessary for the preservation of the common good and the betterment of humanity. Morality changes because humanity evolves, and our evolution is not ever a linear forward progression. If it were, the excess of political and social power we have termed fascism would not have happened sixty years ago. It would not still threaten us today.

But sexuality is not a function of morality. Sexuality is an expression of passion and spirit, as unique to each of us as the snowflakes outside my window. As an expression of self, it cannot be good or bad. It can be delicious or boorish, but it cannot be good or bad. Christian right-wing ideologues are lying when they paint us as evil, and they know it. They know that what is forbidden is not desire but its satisfaction. They know that a culture that has become completely eroticized thrives on appetite. They know you can wear Calvin Klein's Escape, but you can't escape Calvin Klein—

cannot avoid the constant bombardment of images designed to keep us in a constant state of desire.

We keep muddling our response because, in our haste to become "accepted" by mainstream culture, we think we have to downplay our desire. We think spirit must be placed outside our passion. We are wrong. Our passion is our spirit. We can name and give voice to what the Right accepts as commercial necessity but denies as immoral—the pleasure of desire divorced from reproduction. It is our gift to humanity.

The Catholic Church was the home of my spirit for a long time in my life, but it wasn't my first home. My first home was in Vega Alta, Puerto Rico. It was a country home, high up in hills filled with the sweetness of *azucenas* and oranges and mangoes. I lived in a house built on wood beams with a porch all around that saved me from the flaming sun of noon. I used to sleep underneath that porch in the afternoons and breathe in the coolness of the earth. At night, I sat in my grandmother's lap on her rocker, overwhelmed by her softness and the talcum that smelled of roses on her neck. When the silver moon rose big as the sun just beyond my reach before I went to sleep, I used to think that big moon was Los Nueva Yores, where my mother and father had gone to make a new life and be rich and have *electricidad* and a car.

That's how I first got to be lonely. My mother left me to go to New York to make money and be with my father, and I got to stay with Pepita and Nito, my grandparents. I would get up in the still night-wet, cool morning that was just turning blue-gray to get milk from the cow with my Uncle Hernan, when the coqui had quit their "*coqui coqui coqui*" shrill and the birds weren't singing. It was *callaito, callao*. It was very, very still *en la mañanita* when I went for the milk from that cow. She had no name. She was just a cow.

I was sitting on the kitchen porch one of those wet mornings waiting for my Uncle Hernan to pick me up so we could get the milk from the cow when I saw my grandma Pepita. I called her Mami. I saw Mami Pepita's room. I could see Mami Pepita and Nito in the room, in there in the bed under the mosquito net. It was all a white light, except under the mosquito net were shadows. But it was them. They were fighting, I knew it. I saw them in their shadows, and then I heard Mami Pepita screaming, and I saw Nito's arm go up, a huge tree shadow on that mosquito net, and then the tree arm came crashing down on Mami Pepita's face, came up and down and up and down again, smashing her screaming whimpers into the bed. I saw her and heard her cry out once more, and then she was just a flat shadow on the bed, and then Nito screamed real hard, so hard I thought he was dying and killing Mami Pepita. But he wasn't because I saw him come out of the bedroom and smoke a cigarette on the porch.

Now the blue-gray light was getting lighter, and I could hardly breathe in my crouch on the porch, but I knew I was crying because I could feel the hot on my face, but I didn't dare move. I just stayed like that for a long time. I missed my mother, my Mami Carmin, very much. Then Hernan came to get me so we could get milk from the cow. I wanted to tell him about Nito hurting Pepita, but nothing came out of my mouth. I didn't know what to say to him. There was only dryness in my mouth. Then all of my body hurt, and I cried like my baby cousin, sobbing and screaming with no words. Hernan held me until I could tell him that Mami Pepita wouldn't hold me on the porch anymore at night. He hushed and stroked me and told me that wasn't true. Then he took me to milk the cow and when we were done we took the warm milk to the kitchen for Mami Pepita to make *café* like she always did, but she wasn't there. Hernan took me to her room, where we found her, crying. She took me in the bed with her, and I stayed there next to her until the sun rose hot. Then she asked me to bring her slippers, and we went to the kitchen.

This is a memory of misogyny and violence, of lush beauty and innocence. I have other memories of mothers wailing, beating dirt and devil spirits out of threadbare clothes down by the river shore on rocks smoothed and bleached by decades of wash days. I have memories of soft soap water and wrinkled hands that fingered rosary beads, dug out *yautias* from the earth, and soothed the fevered sweating foreheads of little children and grown men. The mothers said to me: "It is the flesh, not the spirit that will die. Oh, Jesus, save her from the evil of the flesh." I watched the mothers lift white lace veils over their old heads with the parched skin of their hands. I watched the cracked and yellowed fingernails on their bent fingers make the sign of the cross. I watched those hands, trembling, light a row of candles to the holy Virgin Mary who crushed the snake and brought forth our salvation, the Word incarnate, Jesus, son of God. I prayed I would not be evil. But I didn't know what evil meant. I understood *la carne*, the flesh, my body. I prayed my body would not be evil.

The strain of social discourse that insists on the "immorality of homosexuality" is actually an old voice that condemns all sexuality not related to procreation. The separation of pleasure, sexual desire, and its satisfaction from reproduction, however, is well over a hundred years old. Why then, does the voice of the religious right and their insistence on moralizing sexuality hold such sway? Why does a secular democratic government allow such blatantly religious viewpoints to remain or become social policy or law? Why is sexuality as morality, a religious minority point of view, so powerfully the voice of the State? The answer is not a moral one. It is political and economic. Sexuality as a tool for power and control is older than the concepts of homosexuality or heterosexuality. It is older than the United States itself. If you can control a people sexually, you can control them absolutely. You can declare a war on drugs while letting the streets fill with crack and heroin. You can sell a woman ten shades of Revlon lipstick and then tell her what to do with her body when the sexy lady gets pregnant. You can condemn pornography and wink at Navy men "buying" women at their ports of call.

In our individual and personal lives, political and religious strings on our desire are not what we first remember. My first memory of sensuality is the soft sheen of black that was my mother's hair as she brushed it, stroke after stroke, in the blue and amber haze of a lamp fueled by kerosene. I was three. My first memory of desire was Judy, the German girl on Fifth Street in New York whose new perm I mocked as I walked by her, but whom I wanted to be near, sit near, touch in the private place when we played in the backyard under the fire escape. I was six. My first memory of ecstasy was in St. Joseph's Church on Morningside and 125th Street in Harlem, New York, when, in the midst of incense and the chanting of a choir and the longing for what God might be, I sat transfixed and unmoving on a church pew, lost in a never-ending stream of stars in the blackness of the universe. I was eight.

The sensuality, desire, and spirit life of the child are those of the woman. Their essence has not changed. Only my consciousness of them and my will to seek them over and over again are different.

Why, then, are my sensuality, desire, and spirit at the center of a national debate? Am I that important to the economy of this nation? To the nation's security? Do I affect the rate of crime? Will there be more homeless people if I am allowed to live freely? Will the air be less clean? Will more fish die in the rivers? Will more husbands rape their wives?

There are no answers to my questions because the questions are unrelated to the truth of why Mr. Buchanan and Mr. Sheldon and Mr. Robertson and Mr. Gingrich and all the other Mr.'s and their Mrs.'s are so determined to bring the full force of the state to bear on my body. There is one kind of state-sanctioned sexuality and one only: heterosexual sex in marriage for the purpose of procreation. There is one kind of state-sanctioned family wrought into the consciousness of each and every one of us: father, mother, the offspring of both, and their blood kin. In the United States, those images have historically been what is called "white." It is almost impossible to think of a "traditional American" family and not conjure this image. This Christian social construct as the ideal (it has never been the only reality for rural and urban poor people) represents a social contract that the state enforces in the interests of "traditional values," a poorly disguised code for "white" people with enough economic and social clout to influence and control the workings of government and its considerable force.

I mix up my childhood memories with the politics of queer oppression because, despite our numerous protests to the contrary, I believe there is such a thing as a "Gay" sensibility, forged in the contradiction of growing up gay and with our feet on the ground, with a job and a roof over our heads, with some semblance of trying to live without fear, and with some shred of pride in the midst of hatred and violence and the spewing of "abomination" and "immoral" and "child molesters" that makes us want to run as far as possible from the truth of who we are even when we're at the front of the Gay Rights March.

The modern lesbian and gay movement is ill-equipped to defend itself because it insists on denying the very difference that might help us understand the essence of our historic origins as a self-identified group and the basis for our oppression and continued persecution: our sexuality. Our experience of a different sexuality informs our sense of self, our spirit and passion, our art, our view of the world, our creation of family and community, and above all, our perpetual status as outsiders in a Christian state. Our sexuality and the shape of our desire are also informed by our race, our class histories and present economic circumstances, and our status as citizens or noncitizens.

The heterosexual nuclear family is the ideal we are all socialized to aspire to. Some of us believe we should be like that or that we should at least be granted the benefits and protections accorded to people who are like that. Well, yes, we should be accorded the rights and benefits accorded to heterosexuals. But we should have those rights because we breathe. We have a right to health care and shelter and equal opportunity for an education and to work; we have a right to love—because we exist. Our relationship to another human being and the form of our desire, the expression of our love and spirit, cannot and must not be reason to bestow or deny anyone the rights and benefits of living in a democracy.

I have been a lesbian and gay rights activist for the last eighteen years. Despite the racism of so many of my colleagues and because of the generosity of so many, I have been able to hold on to the different threads that I have woven into what I call my self, my identity—my Puerto Rican self, my butch self, my socialist self. In this historic moment of right-wing political ascendance, however, I am profoundly saddened by the barrenness of spirit, by the emptiness of "gay speak" that refuses over and over again to listen and give credence to the voices within our own movement and to the many, many people outside our movement whose experiences might allow us to understand what being treated as though you had no soul feels like. Among the most clipped and nonsensical of the "gay speak" jargon I hear is the *we are just like everybody else* soundbite we love to mouth on talk shows and at the first hint of controversy.

What does that mean? Which "everybody else"?

I think "everybody" in gay speak is meant to have us believe that we will be free if we just act "normal," if we can prove to the abstract "everybody" that is America that we are just the same as they are. Gay folks who want to be part of the "everybody" desperately claim that we are not messy, not poor, not addicted, not shot through our hearts or brains by random gunfire, not promiscuous or "obsessed by sex," not into leather or sex roles of any kind, not making a living with our bodies, not traveling on Greyhound buses to the underbellies of U.S. cities or to dusty towns without hope.

No. "Everybody" in gay speak is actually Norman Rockwell. The middle- and upper-class distortions that are the requisite public image of the modern lesbian and gay movement preclude any genuine reflection on the nature of queerness as something that, when freely expressed, can only be considered social rebellion against prescribed state sexuality, appropriate male and female gender roles, and the prevailing legal and dominant social definition of family. You can't be queer and like "everybody" else, because heterosexuality is to other expressions of sexuality what whiteness is to "race." It is the normative standard against which everything else is "other." The heterosexual standard needs no definition of its own, and it bestows upon those that adhere to it legal protections and social privileges denied the rest of us.

I am without borders, at least without the "normal" ones. I know what they are. I can't live within them. I never have. I have wanted to be great. Not good. Great. Better than good. Better than myself yesterday or even this morning. I get up, like everybody, and repeat routines, rituals of comfort. I put on the water and milk to heat for coffee. I feed the kitties. I turn on *The Today Show* and smile at Katie and Bryant and the snake line of people waiting their turn to wave hello to America in the morning. When the milk is done and the coffee and sugar are in it and stirred to perfect sweetness, I smoke my first Export "A" and then think about this day, the letters and memos and phone calls, the words to tell Marcie I need and love her, my sister's baffled life and disease I can't understand because every few months it's a different one or a compounded one. I wonder if my brother is still working. I feel my body waking up to caffeine and nicotine *(I know it's bad)* and myself spreading around the middle of me for lack of the exercise I don't do once again.

All the while I am putting on my Calvin Klein briefs and my white tab-collar shirt and Urban Canvas tie and my Roma Uomo scent, I know I am butch. I put on the coat and scarf and close the door behind me, leaving the kitties to jazz. I walk down the stairs and pick up the *New York Times* from the stoop on my brownstone on Henry Street. For a moment, I will feel like everybody else in Brooklyn. But I won't be. I will be my butch self smiling good morning to the old Italian man standing in front of the brownstone two houses down, his shoulders bent and eyes watering from the cold air under his black cap, with smoke rising blue from his morning cigarette. I watch him adjust to my tie and my Roma Uomo scent, smiling my good morning back to me in his discomfort and the odd pleasure of experiencing a woman greeting him man to man. I love the moment with him and walk on.

The parameters of "normal" fall apart every morning for millions of queers in the United States. This is true whether we drive buses or march into law firms or city halls or enter medical practices or answer the phones or sweep the entryways to our community centers or organize unions. Individual and collective liberation requires that we understand and consciously be who we are as much of the time as we can stand. It also requires that we be conscious of who else is standing there with us and who won't fall back in fear when "normal" falls apart.

Upper-class aspirations—or the promise of their comfort—require a dulling of that consciousness, a thwarting of the desire to be great by being exactly who you are. In addition to what you earn or own, "class" has also come to mean acting white and straight and pretentious regardless of your skin color or your language or what's underneath your skin in the explosions of desire and tenderness and fury and fear that we call sex.

None of this should be construed as an assault on the middle class or the United States or things American. I am, in fact, more of a patriot than the new or old Republicans. I actually believe in the Constitution. I hold out for the promise, still to be realized, of equality and freedom for all people living in this land. I do not, however,

believe individual freedom or equality of opportunity are attainable
for people of color or lesbians and gay men without radical change
in the values, family definitions, and economic systems we live under. My detractors would say we have achieved those changes.
They would be lying or ignoring history. With the significant exception of the constitutional amendments that enfranchised Black
men and, later, women, there have been no radical and sustained
changes in the values, family definitions, and economic systems of
the U.S. since the end of slavery.

I haven't ever believed that we could leapfrog from the
anonymity of the "love that dared not speak its name" or the
pathologizing of homosexuality without the legal strategies and
cultural adaptations that would make it possible for us to be heard
and seen by people who have been well trained in how to loathe
and fear us. Seeking common ground is a tactical necessity in the
struggle for civil rights, and it would be foolish to argue against it.
What I have tried to argue for a very long time is that those tactical
and strategic efforts alone would not be sufficient to undo the fundamental character of heterosexism and racism and sexism in our
society. I have tried to argue that the racism, sexism, and lack of
class analysis internal to our movement leaves us ill-prepared to defend ourselves against the erosion of whatever civil rights we may
have carved out for ourselves when the backlash comes. Well, the
backlash is here in all its fury and, for the most part, mainstream
queers still think I'm a cuckoo lefty who just doesn't get the "reality" of what it takes to create political change in the United States.
I'm left to wonder, am I really off-base here? Is my language truly
inaccessible or excessively Left and archaic? Or have I missed a
crucial piece of the organizing puzzle?

All of the above could be true. I think what is most true is that I
have missed a crucial piece of the organizing puzzle. *There is a
Left to this movement, and there is a Right.* We have different
goals and different processes. An understanding of class and class
privilege and their relationship to any system of oppression is the
only bridge we queers have to build on in our efforts to forge relationships of solidarity and respect with other oppressed people.
Drop the class piece, and we have no basis for understanding the
wedge created by the right wing (both internal and external to our

movement) between us and communities of color. We have no basis for understanding the welfare war or the immigrant war or the teenage pregnancy war or the reproductive rights war. And, by and large, we have dropped the class piece.

Sometimes, *we are the Right.* Until some of us are willing to make that distinction, our ability to cohere a progressive lesbian, gay, bisexual, and transgender agenda capable of working with other progressive movements in this country will be extremely limited. We need a class analysis that can illuminate the role and persistence of heterosexuality in western, advanced-capitalist culture, and the emergence of homosexual identity, culture, and community as a logical response to the changing exigencies of the family. Because that analysis is not going to come from the Right in our movement, we also need an identified Left in our movement.

It will be pointed out, correctly, that such an analysis already exists in the work of people like Barbara Smith and Mab Segrest and John D'Emilio and many, many others in our movement. What exists as queer left theory, however, remains that—queer left theory. We are challenged by how to make such theory an organizing principle. We are challenged by how to make our theory make sense and become a point of unity with people who completely repudiate the Right because they know their lives depend on their ability to resist the Right and its political ascendance. We are challenged by the terrible confusion of trying to simultaneously create and defend a relatively new identity in a culture and economic system that is very good at absorbing social unrest and political dissent and eventually turning them into marketable commodities. We are challenged by our unwillingness or inability to let our sexuality and desire be at the very center of our popular movement— even if we are of the Left. We say people just can't handle that, the sex thing. We make it too rarefied a field of thought and political resistance for poor folk and colored folk to take kindly to. We buy the race and class lie that poor and colored folk are too unsophisticated to hear the truth of who we are and love us that way. When we have tried, we have never been turned away, not if we were honest.

In a society that exalts enforced heterosexuality, queer liberation is not possible without prolonged cultural struggle (in educational systems, media, and the arts) to change the value assigned to "traditional" male and female roles and to change sex into something human beings engage in for pleasure and spiritual communion rather than for procreation only. In a society that values economic profit above the individual and communal needs of its citizens, a queer "mainstreaming" strategy leaves those of us who happen to be female, of color, working-class, or poor still knocking on the door of a freedom that can't be realized without a conscious redistribution of wealth—something that requires the political muscle and sinew of a broad-based political movement and party that don't exist yet.

This is not theory. This is my life.

My full participation in a democratic society should not require that I wear a dress, act white, fuck a man, or remain mute in the face of the obscene redistribution of wealth upward that is leaving one U.S. working-class community after another feeling hopeless, alienated, and furious. But, in fact, such are the requirements for accommodation and success if you are female in the United States. I have no use for an accommodation requiring me to jettison the spirit and passion of my ancestors or the liberation of spirit I can only experience when I am free to love and desire as I choose. A lesbian and gay movement strategically focused on assimilation into the status quo leaves huge pieces of my soul in prison. It isn't enough.

I believe we need a broader audience for alliance. I believe we need to speak with and touch the people who have been left adrift by current economic policies: with African Americans who still live under the burden of a slave-era-imposed sexuality as sexual "predatory" males and "promiscuous" females; with Latinos who can't find work above the minimum wage even when jobs are *available,* but get plenty of fanfare as "hot and sexy" people whose homelands we should vacation in; with Asian Pacific Islander people whose relatives are sold to G.I.s every day for sex.

We needn't bother with engaging Newt Gingrich or Bob Dole or even Bill Clinton in a dialogue about whether we are born gay or choose it. They don't care.

Rather, the dialogue we should engage in is with other people who know what it is to have their lives threatened and their homes burned and their livelihood denied because of who they are. The fact that who we are is ultimately tied to our erotic desire for people of our own gender changes none of the circumstances or experiences of bigotry; it changes none of the feelings of it. We need to learn to speak the truth of that experience to the majority of people who can actually understand it. We need to find ways of speaking to poor and working-class Americans because that's who the majority of us are connected to by blood, by class, and by spirit.

If we are serious about creating a broader audience for alliance, the dialogue we must engage in with our sisters and brothers of color, the dialogue we must engage in with organized labor and unorganized civil service workers, college students, and the people in welfare waiting rooms, is about the truth of who we are, the whole truth. The sex part and the race part and the class part and the gender part.

The dialogue about racism in the United States must be about more than whether or not we will use offensive language; it must also be about how together, white people and people of color, we will end the subjugation by political and economic force of white people over people of color. So, too, must the dialogue be about more than whether we were born gay or chose it and how we are alike or unlike everybody else. The dialogue must instead be about how we will choose to be subject and object in our sexual lives, how we will be free.

In our hurry to win legal and legislative battles, we must not forsake the spirit in us that keeps longing for a freedom that laws alone can never give us. The language and image, the strategies and tactics, the song and spirit of our movement should have more in common with the people still working to end racism and economic injustice in our country than with those espousing the notion that thirty years of affirmative action have somehow given African Americans and other people of color in this country "equal" opportunity. It should, because, like ours, these are struggles for dignity and hope, for the right to choose where we live and whom we love, for the right to choose work commensurate with our capacities—not our color or our gender or our sexual orientation or our bank statement.

The challenge of realizing liberation for lesbian, gay, bisexual, and transgendered people requires that we look beyond the next election. It is a challenge to transform ourselves and our society, to claim our passion as our spirit, to reclaim the Left and, in the process, to reclaim our souls.

Snowflakes don't really die when they fall on the ground. They melt and evaporate and come back to us again in a spring rain or a summer storm. So do we return in the life of two-spirit people, in the men and women who fought fascism in a military that rejected them and still does, in the life of UPS drivers who press their uniforms every day and come out just a little at a time, in the lives of African Americans who stood up to the dogs and water hoses and gunfire for racial equality even as their ministers railed against the abomination of homosexuality. We return in the lives of young queers today who demand and deserve a life of joy and dignity in an intergenerational community. We will return until we are free.

Windows & Water Towers

B.MICHAEL HUNTER
& JOHN ALBERT MANZON-SANTOS

For the last six years, our relationship, perhaps like any other, has been in search of anchorage. We have learned how commitment, trust, and, yes, intimacy, can ebb and flow over time. What grounds us is when we attempt to break our familiar Catholic patterns of silence, especially when it feels most risky. In this case, we hope that our talking through issues together (and sharing them via a transcribed dialogue)—seams and all—will demonstrate some of the ways in which we struggle to understand how class is braided with other factors in our relationship.

BERT: When I was growing up in Woodrow Wilson Houses in East Harlem, my family went through periods where we seemed to have everything we needed and other times when we had to go on food stamps. The most important thing was to avoid being on welfare. Food stamps meant that someone in the family still worked, and you just needed a little help. But welfare meant that your parents couldn't "make it," and that was not okay. So one indicator of your class situation was whether or not you had a job, and there was a shame factor attached if you had to rely on help from the government. It wasn't until I went to college that my parameters that defined someone's class status were expanded to include where you live, what you own, how exposed you are to the world, even how you act in social settings.

JOHN: For me, someone's socioeconomic class is measured by their access to resources—not just money, but other resources like housing, employment, nutrition, health care, mobility, public-sector decision-making, and education. So, for example, even though I grew up working-class and wasn't wealthy like the majority of the other college students, I know my Ivy League university degree affords me broader access to middle-class opportunities, like what kind of jobs I could have, what quality of healthcare providers I'd look for, how possible I'd think it was to travel or re-locate, where I lived, etc. And meeting students who grew up poorer than me gave me some sense of perspective and helped me gauge where I fit in this landscape relative to all these class mark-ers. I don't think I and my brother and sisters grew up with any conscious class identity, though I assumed that immigrant status meant being poor or working-class. Like when my family lived in Army housing, you could see the hierarchy pretty clearly. The sol-diers who wore green camouflage uniforms lived in barracks, en-listed men like my father lived with their families in row housing, and the "big brass" generals that my father cooked for lived in gigan-tic, free-standing houses. Actually, figuring out *our* living situation kicked up a lot of issues.

B: In 1988, when I moved into the apartment at 528 East 11th Street, the rent was $325 a month, a good deal for two bedrooms in the Lower East Side of Manhattan, even with no sink in the bath-room. At first it seemed like a really family-oriented building, quiet and safe. But a police raid uncovered a large amount of cash, drugs, and a number of firearms, including two AK-47s, in the apartment across the hall from mine. Our landlord's solution to de-ter other alleged drug dealers from working out of the building was to disable the intercom system and remove the front door to the street. It was like that for eight months. There was no collec-tive outcry from the thirty-three apartments, but the situation gen-erated enough attention that a local newspaper listed 528 as one of the top ten worst buildings in Manhattan . . .

J: . . . which *I* didn't know before I moved in! That entire first year living together at 528, I don't think I ever felt safe going from the corner of East 11th Street/Avenue A to the front door—less because of the drugs, more because I thought I'd be "fag-bashed" or else mugged or harassed because I'm Asian. Even though it's also true that sometimes people don't fuck with me because they think I know kung fu or something. But over time I think people started to get used to us as a couple. I even became friendly with some of the neighbors. In a way, the drug dealers who were always on the block kept an eye on everything that went down, a kind of neighborhood patrol! I mean, they're businesspeople after all, so if you don't get in their way, they'll leave you alone.

528 was a decent size for two (and big enough for nine houseguests during Stonewall!), and I was certainly fine with splitting a $400 rent. I was also conscious of me-as-gentrifier, especially as I was sure people perceived me as one of the outsider Asian and/or Queer artist-types who flocked to the surrounding East Village.

B: I did have guilt about gentrifying the neighborhood, but in a lot of ways, because of my race, my sexuality, and my perceived class background, I was excluded from a lot of other moderate-income housing. On some level I tried to absolve some of my guilt by joining the local Community Board and chairing the Human Resources Committee, where we had N.I.M.B.Y. (Not in My Back-yard) debates around AIDS housing facilities, women's transitional housing (from prison back to the community), and other social service agencies in the neighborhood. I even sat on their Lesbian/Gay Community Task Force to sensitize the police.

J: I think we could've lived there longer than we anticipated. We did paint the walls and make other improvements here and there. Then I received a windfall from that legal settlement, which started us thinking about moving and the possibility of a pretty dramatic change, quality-of-life-wise. Like an elevator would help. Some of it had to do with the fact that your relatives, especially your mom and aunts and grandmother, aren't able to negotiate stairs. Then there's the weekly schlepping up and down of groceries, laundry, and garbage. I don't think we talked about it much at that point, but your being HIV-positive entered into it, specifically what it'd mean for either of us to have some potentially debilitating illness. So we started thinking about stuff like having more space, a washer/dryer in the building, a sink in the bathroom, *and* the possibility of leaving behind our pets (i.e., the roaches).

B: John, *you're* the one who brought the roaches when you moved in. Because that's when we got more into the habit of eating in, since I *always* ate out when I lived alone!

J: You know, for my parents it was a dream come true to buy a house after my father retired from the Army, but prior to this legal settlement, I never imagined, nor did I have any aspirations about buying or owning anything. The culture of it all made me feel uncomfortable, partly because real estate has such a rep for being a discriminatory sector, partly because I didn't want to deal with tax planning and all that. I also didn't want a doorperson, which promotes some sort of urban gated-community dynamic. And as two men, we maybe didn't need the assumed level of security that a doorperson would provide. Then when we thought of *where* to live in New York, pickin's seemed slim. As an interracial couple, there are few neighborhoods where we would feel comfortable as individuals and together.

B: As a Black man, I had no intention of living in any of the Asian enclaves like Chinatown and dealing with stares or hostility from others. And as a Manhattanite, born and raised, living in any other borough seemed too remote.

J: Harlem, or even Fort Green, wouldn't prove much more welcoming to me . . .

B: . . . because people would think you were working in the markets.

J: There are also the gay-concentrated neighborhoods like Greenwich Village and the Upper West Side, but there're too many white people per capita for my comfort level, especially after spending all those years in predominantly rich, white private schools.

B: After looking at half a dozen lofts and apartments with doormen in view, we walked into the one place the realtor was reluctant to show us—her descriptive word was "funky." When we walked into this 1,500-square-foot corner loft it had two things that were high on our list—space and natural sunlight, which poured through five-by-seven foot windows on two sides.

J: You know there'd be very few places we would both fall in love with, as different as I think our aesthetic senses are. But for the first few months—and once in a while even now—I felt very strange being in such a huge, spacious living arrangement. I definitely associate large living spaces with the rich kids I went to school with and the kinds of houses they lived in. On some level, I also didn't feel like I *deserved* to occupy so much living area or to access the kind of stability that you get from not throwing rent down a hole every month. It also felt strange since owning this home wasn't part of my value system or something I worked for and saved for over time. But like you said, this new home is "full of possibilities," and the process of buying the loft, especially in its raw condition, has moved us as a couple to look more at life-planning and focus on our needs, something I don't think either of us have done a very good job of doing up until recently.

I dig the roof, too, and you can see both the Empire State Building and the World Trade Center Twin Towers *and* how every building in Manhattan over five stories has a cedar-wood water tower like on a *West Side Story* set or something, which you never see walking around on street level. We got the washer/dryer that we share with the three other couples on the floor, but we did give up the family atmosphere that 528 had with seniors and baby carriages and little kids running around and playing in the street.

B: It's definitely not a residential neighborhood. The street's bustling between the hours of 8 a.m. and 6 p.m., when only commercial parking like the loading/unloading of UPS trucks is allowed. Then there are the import/export businesses dealing in fashion, furs, toys, and sundries, the motorcycle-repair guy working on the sidewalk, but the street really shuts down in the evening, and it's not too safe for single women who visit. The area's zoned for light industrial, full of converted manufacturing facilities, garment sweatshops (like the one across from our bedroom window), printing presses, photography studios, and we're on the perimeter of all these communities: the new Korea Town, Gay Chelsea below West 23rd Street, the Garment District, the Flower District, where wholesale vendors sell cut flowers and potted plants. And in a two-block radius there are five weekend antique flea markets. However, real estate brokers of course promote the neighborhood as the "new SoHo" (New York's premier artists' colony), which is slowly becoming more residential—the building we live in, anyway.

J: I have mixed feelings living so close to Chelsea. I generally feel ambivalent, at times hostile, when walking down Seventh or Eighth Avenue, two of Chelsea's main arteries, and I never do it alone, if I can help it. All these uniformed, gay male soldiers at attention or at ease help shore up the rep that gay men make wonderful consumers, like the patrons of the all-gay-white-male-run, community-based, mostly service-oriented institutions, some with multimillion-dollar operating budgets: often double-income in a single, fabulously decorated household, no kids, fashion-conscious, theater-going, bar-hopping, globe-trotting, time-sharing, alcohol-abusing, iron-pumping, steroid-shooting. It's no coincidence that Chelsea is where these superstores have all sprung up—Barnes & Noble, Bed, Bath & Beyond, Today's Man, Filene's Basement. This is the gay community that I am supposed to identify with. It's the upwardly mobile, queer-nationalist culture that turns me off the most.

B: In order to feel more at home, it's people of color-focused lesbian and gay networks which both of us have gravitated toward. We've had some involvement in establishing, supporting, or having active membership in several of the organizations in the "gay community" with which we identify: Other Countries: Black Gay Expression, APICHA (Asian & Pacific Islander Coalition on HIV/AIDS), GMAD (Gay Men of African Descent), Project Reach (a multiracial, youth- and adult-run youth advocacy, counseling, and organizing center), GAPIMNY (Gay Asian & Pacific Islander Men of New York), and the Lesbian & Gay People of Color Steering Committee (a coalition of almost thirty indigenous, grassroots groups). Most recently, we're working as members of the founding board of the Audre Lorde Project (a lesbian, gay, bisexual, two-spirit, transgender people of color community center based in Brooklyn, New York), a community space and spiritual home base whose vision includes multiracial, co-gender programming and organizing activities and an initiative that's not based on pathologizing our identities, experiences, or worldviews.

J: And it's through this community that we met. Though Bert may have a different recollection, I first met him at a meeting of the Lesbian & Gay People of Color Steering Committee to secure a spot in the People of Color contingent of the New York City Pride March for GAPIMNY, at the time a new affinity organization. I noticed Bert, one of the handsomest men I'd ever seen, who was really quiet and cautious—the opposite of me. He was a writer and refreshingly not a graduate of an Ivy League school, like my ex-lover. I was happy to learn that he didn't grow up with money and, like me, received financial aid to get through mostly all-white schools. I felt safe with him from the beginning, and not ashamed of unpacking whatever personal baggage I may have brought with me. I wondered about Bert being Black, having experienced too many Black people telling me that I wasn't oppressed enough.

B: I first noticed John at a general meeting of VOCAL (Voices of Color against AIDS and for Life), a fledgling group of lesbian and gay people of color who worked in AIDS. I was there to announce the marching order of the People of Color Contingent in the 1990 Lesbian & Gay Pride March. He reminded me of a high school friend I had, who was one-fourth Black and three-fourths Chinese. John didn't look anything like my friend, but they did share one feature: black hair. There was something about John that seemed familiar. We saw each other at a couple of other joint People of Color meetings—after one such meeting I asked him to dinner, and he accepted. After one or two other dates we got together and somehow developed a relationship. Physically, John is similar to almost all of the other men I've dated—slim. I was and am most attracted to John's mind, quick mouth, and energy, some of the very things that cause tension in our relationship. I was thirty-two when I met John, and feeling young but old. Old from so many consecutive deaths of friends from AIDS. When I found out John was seven years younger than me, I was a little reluctant to continue our relationship because he seemed politicized in a way I wasn't familiar with. There where some early signs that we have had very different life experiences.

First, the obvious: he's Filipino, I'm of African descent; I was raised in a housing project in East Harlem, he was raised in a house in Daly City, California; he worked as a counselor at a community agency in Chinatown, and I had just quit my job as an account marketing representative selling mainframe computers for IBM. Now the not so obvious—he had gone to private school since sixth grade and then to an Ivy League college; I went to public grammar and middle school, a specialized public high school, a small, east-coast private college, and had already graduated from a top-ranked public-interest private law school. My previous experience with men who attended Ivy League school also left me a little cold—they seem to never be satisfied with things. They always seem to have access to information and invitations to events and always acted as if they were entitled to everything they desired. I also felt I was considered desirable by these men because of my degrees and career track: they assumed I was their "class peer." John was very different—he is one of the few men I trust.

J: Even in a racially diverse city like New York, striving for visibility and recognition as an interracial couple of gay men of color is not very supported. Fact is, we've interacted with only two other Asian/Black male couples, one in New York and one in Boston.

Class determines a lot of the dynamics between Black and Asian communities in New York, where there isn't much widely documented history of peaceful coexistence, as with the relations between Korean grocery store owners and the inner-city Black neighborhoods they're often located in. In these same stores, check-out clerks never assume we're together, even as we talk animatedly and commingle items-to-buy on the counter.

B: When we began going places together, we'd sometimes take cabs, though I rarely took cabs myself, especially at night. In fact, I'd only flag down a cab when I was dressed in suit and tie. On some level I really resented being with someone who never had problems with gaining access to something like a taxicab. I'd been frustrated enough times by the indignity that passing taxicabs represent to factor in enough time for public transportation in my daily travel plans.

J: In fact, I didn't grow up in a place with cabs and didn't know until I met you that Black people were routinely passed by because of what the drivers assumed.

B: I think less of it is that I'm going to mug them; more of it is the assumption that I'd ask to be driven somewhere that might put *them* in a dangerous situation. The cab situation brings up how we negotiate on a day-to-day basis—you run up to cabs, stop them, or you run halfway up the block to flag one down. What allows you to do that, to think that it's safe, for you or the driver? Is there some intersection of race, class, and sexual orientation that gives you the freedom to run in the street? (Most Black men running in the street would seem suspect, and more than one woman would clutch their pocketbook.)

J: It's funny you perceive my running up to catch a cab as some kind of privilege or some manifestation of my level of safety. (A) I don't feel safe in New York generally, especially being on the thin side in a city where anti-Asian violence has topped the hate crimes stats, with queer-bashing a close second. And (B) when I see a cab, what I immediately think of are all the times cabs have passed me because, I assume, I'm not dressed like a businessman or whatever, or when they have refused to unlock the door until they know where I want to go (and agree to take me there). The cabs are supposed to be there for people, so I run up to the cab *and* open the door so as not to be passed over. It's an accountability thing and maybe there is some privilege I have to be able to do that. The dodging-traffic scenario is something I'll do only if I *have* to get somewhere. So it doesn't feel like a comfort or safety level I have; it feels like a risk I have to consciously take to get what I need. Also, in this city, I take public transportation more often than not. At times, when I'm on the subway, the racist vibe I get from people is that I might karate-chop them, so they'll keep their distance. However, at other times people generally perceive me as weaker and totally non-threatening because I'm Asian, like the time I was mugged be-tween the Delancey and Second Avenue stops on the F train.

B: Except when we were both treated similarly on our way back to New York from Montreal, when we were stopped by the U.S. border patrol, interrogated separately, our rental car strip-searched presumably for smuggled drugs, our gay guides ridiculed.

J: I also learned that we respond differently to authority. You became cool as a cucumber, not attitudinal, but terse, measuring your words per your lawyer training. I eagerly answered their questions and tried to send out easygoing energy, as if to say, "OK, officer, whatever-you-say, just-leave-us-alone."

B: Yeah, and you almost got us killed when you reached down under the seat for your shoes *after* they had already told us to get out of the car!

J: Well, we communicate differently according to the situation. We talk different, too. You easily flip between that teeth-flashing, IBM, "I'm going to sell you a computer now"-speak and Southern Black Baptist (which you fake).

B: We've known each other long enough to know which of each other's buttons to push. And how easily we fall into a competitive mode like the boys we were socialized to be, which is consistent with the survival strategies we developed as children.

J: For a long time one of the buttons was around HIV. When you tested HIV-positive and I tested HIV-negative, we needed some serious, relationship-oriented "technical assistance" to deal with being a "sero-discordant couple." You really surprised me 'cause I thought you'd be resistant to working with a couples therapist. But we did need some structured time to look at HIV-specific stuff *and* other, non-HIV-related issues.

B: I welcomed the chance to look at HIV/AIDS and its impact on my being able to be in a long-term relationship. In fact, the eighteen months we were together before I went for the test was the longest period of time I'd been with another man.

J: Therapy definitely helped us learn how to call out how we've been trained. You know, to question the norm to achieve, get more degrees, be active, make money and babies.

B: I'd say we're trying to center ourselves more, to carve out a life, develop more discipline and internal structures for us as individuals and as a couple, to create family and rituals, live with HIV and the gamut of health conditions: in short, less doing, more being.

J: I no longer live in fear of waiting for the other shoe to drop, for you to develop AIDS and die shortly thereafter. AIDS does not rule our lives. It has a place, it may even be a room in the house, but it is certainly not the roof, nor the paint on the walls. Structuring time together was our first step, and committing to planing was another, which I think helps us deal with our anxiety about the future.

B: Being in a "sero-discordant couple," I don't think of myself as opposites of things, but it's another box or demarcation. Given my level of education, I'm in a safe job in the sense that as a New York City school teacher, it's low-stress and it's something I enjoy. But the major reason that I'm there is the security that the benefits bring, mostly because the teachers' union is strong. I wasn't concerned when I was at IBM. Or when I was in law school, or before I was diagnosed as HIV-positive, I wasn't concerned with finding the security that a government job could offer. The bizarre thing is that when we became domestic partners in 1994, all the health and life insurance benefits started coming through my job, which recognizes same-sex couples, but people would say that *I'm* the most "fragile."

J: Because the HIV-negative person is the one who's supposed to bring home the benefits-bacon?

B: Right. So the roles would play themselves out in the relationship, and ultimately I would be rendered unable to work. That is, if you believe in the whole "hysteria" about how the progression of HIV disease eventually ends in a crisis-filled, downward spiral toward death.

J: What motivates me is not security at all. The full-time jobs I've had were not about security, but more to feel like I was doing something meaningful. What is interesting in retrospect is that, when I was old enough, I found myself landing mostly service-oriented jobs of the type I had known my parents and/or my older siblings to take. Like my first paid job was as a clerk/typist with a temp agency. When I was seven, my oldest sister had done temp work after high school; during one visit home, she and her co-worker at the time taught me to type. Other jobs were in and around restaurants—dishwasher, busser, salad-maker, bartender, host, waiter, valet—all of which my father, brother, and sisters had done. I volunteered as a buddy to a Person Living with AIDS with the knowledge that my mother frequently took care of older white women who were disabled, homebound, or abandoned by their families. Pursuing other "service-sector" jobs, I drove a college campus shuttle and registered with a couple of escort agencies. In fact, when I became a teacher, I felt a profound inadequacy, in part because there were no role models within my immediate family. But in any case, the motivation was not to save money to either buy a house or have for some "rainy day." I didn't grow up in a culture of saving. I now know my parents were committed to saving, but they never talked about it.

I remember poor and working-class Third World students I went to college with, who were clear about becoming doctors and other professionals because that was one way out of whatever situation they came from. But one of the things that made me *not* follow my classmates was coming out as a gay person. Coming out meant such a radical departure from so many expectations—so necessarily becoming a professional was one more that I threw into the trash. On some level, my mother doesn't understand why I'm not a doctor or a lawyer or otherwise capitalizing on what she perceives as "Brown University degree as ticket somewhere." And I think one struggle in our relationship is how much security should be a priority for me vis-à-vis *you*. I think up to now, I'm not preparing for your impending "downward spiral."

B: For me, not pursuing careers in law or with IBM has a lot to do with the expectation that somehow I would be connected to some sort of family unit. Security was less of an issue then, before I left IBM. I had saved, I had already built credit and was looking for the class/access/security issues of station and status, versus the kind of security I'm talking about now. I had a house already, but an investment-property house versus a house I wanted to live in. So I started to re-evaluate what kind of life I wanted to live.

The thing that's interesting to me is exactly *abandoning* the expectation of a nuclear family in the sense of "well, there's no

generation I have to look out for, so I can do stuff to feel self-fulfilled."
HIV stepped up my making personal fulfillment a priority. I am *not*
sick or dying; I remain asymptomatic at thirty-seven. What changes
do I need to make to get me to sixty, seventy, or eighty?

J: In fact, that's what I mean by "abandonment." Coming out as
gay (even if it was a certain narrow, white, middle-class definition
of "gay") let me off the hook to a certain degree so that I didn't
have to do what my classmates did. Whatever HIV has done in my
life and in the lives of people around me or through my job, it's
also stepped up my schooling in the importance of planning. In
particular for *us*. Growing up, planning was not an issue. I think
my parents relied on "God will provide" or "the Army will provide." They turned over a lot of needs that people would plan for
being taken care of. I think what's difficult as a couple is trying to
plan our future together, to make self-fulfillment a priority in our
personal and professional lives, and those are big choices (especially in a gay male culture that emphasizes being young and vilifies
getting older, and where premature death is so commonplace).
And I can think of people in our lives who are more concerned
about making money, in particular, gaining status, particularly gay
people/professionals. I see a lot of people overcompensating for
being gay by seeking status, even if it's not the status you get for
being heterosexual and family-raising.

B: There's also a lot of freedom and mobility in being gay. And
choosing not to raise children. Without the status of children,
we're not validated in society. My point is less wanting to get validation from someone else. It's more important to be self-fulfilled.
It's a point of empowerment. You're not trapping yourself by con-
vention, buying into status quo. I still think working toward self-
fulfillment will gain the same financial rewards or benefits that
"selling yourself to a corporation" would buy.

Having been in a different situation, it doesn't make a lot of
sense for me to use others' measuring sticks of how I should view
myself in the world. That automatically sets you up for failure.
Somebody always has a little bit more, someone else is a little bit
taller. Ranking is dangerous. Some kind of status that you fall short
of makes you self-hating, self-destroying. What's the value that soci-

ety places on you versus the value *you* put on yourself? What gives you status, or class, or station? Sometimes it's not education, or financial worth, or where you work, or how much you make, but rather it's about how you live your life.

J: Like our ceremony, the fact that it was such a public ritual. The ceremony was a series of decisions that we made according to measures that were important to us, according to our own standards. Exchanging beads instead of rings, planning logistics, inviting who we wanted to witness. People came from as far away as L.A. and the U.K. Five generations from your family and four generations from mine were in attendance. Like they say, it takes a village to raise a child *and* to sustain a relationship, no? That's the kind of validation that we're seeking.

B: So why do you choose to be in a relationship? Do you think that being in a relationship has anything to do with class or mobility?

J: Not to sound cynical, but I think that people are in relationships for themselves. You and I are both on our individual paths, doing what we need to do to feel self-fulfilled, and it's great that we can go down these paths while keeping each other company. Also, couples are far more validated than individuals. But it's healthy when we don't lose our identities. And we're each pretty independent, strong, survivor-types, but the challenge is, how do we create something new that goes beyond our individuality *and* integrates our values and who we are.

When we talk about our values, we reveal tons of information about how we feel about class. And values are things that matter, that we're passionate about, that we would die for—what's qualitatively important enough to keep us together. It's not just about co-existing; the plan is one thing we create together. Our joint plan is like a child and it's totally informed by our perspectives, our experiences, our values on class and other things, which come to the surface in the process. Our joint plan becomes the embodiment of our joint values; it's like we're developing common ground rules, values, culture. Not to say that we're becoming one person. At the point we're at in our relationship, it's a challenge to find what that "spiritual child" is.

B: The crucial question is: what does a child represent? What's our third thing? Sometimes it's community activism; our relation to our families of origin; how we make our loft a home. How does this stuff play itself out day to day? Exactly how does our home look? What kind of feeling do we want to have when we're inside?

J: My ideal is to be able to live in a space where I share the chores—the washing, the cooking, the cleaning. It feels more like everyone pulls their own weight. That roles are not so rigid. So many gay people I know hire maids to clean the house—and I'm not sure why that'd bother me if we did. Maybe because my mother cleaned and cared for other people, my father cooked for other people. I know we're busy people . . .

B: . . . this notion of always being busy—but busy doing what? How do you prioritize a commitment to what goes on outside with what goes on inside our home? If part of the motivation for hiring cleaning people is that "somebody's gotta do it so we can have time to be activists in the community," we need to talk about that. I mean, let's break it down: who did the cleaning in the house growing up and what is our relationship to chores, and what do we think about chores? What's interesting for me is that my mother cleaned the house, until my father left. And when my father left and we were all pretty much in our teenage years, we all got assigned specific chores. What's also interesting is that while I want a clean house, I don't want a clean house just to showcase to guests.

J: I sort of agree and disagree. I do want us and other people to feel warm, temperature-warm, and cozy. I don't want a space that's cluttered and prone to dust, but full of things, whether they're gifts or mementos of places we've been. Not to showcase, but to display things that have spiritual value to us. We should have a place where guests can sleep—you know, to the extent that hospitality is currency, because I certainly have relied on and been extremely grateful for people's floors and extra beds when I've needed them.

B: I also want to eat at home with you, my partner, and figure out how to make time for that. It's a very funny thing. My mother's a horrific cook, but some of the most fun and bonding I've had with my family has been in the kitchen. I remember that no matter what we were doing, we all had to be around the table at 6 p.m. No excuses.

J: Well for me, even though my father did all the cooking and my mother did all the cleaning (except in the kitchen), meals weren't a family thing. We rarely ate together. I think I learned the importance of meals from experiences that happened after I left home. Like when I lived in co-ops, and when I studied in Italy and saw how much value was placed on eating-as-ritual and sharing during meals, and I definitely want that with you.

B: We did pretty well with the McDougal Plan. For two months we planned, shopped, cooked, and cleaned up after three meals a day—low-fat, no-meat, no-dairy, high-carbo meals.

J: That was challenging, but fun. I know I was sleeping better, dreaming better, shitting better, and people at work said I seemed less stressed out! I appreciated the planning aspect the most and the fact that it structured time for us together.

B: Just like we're trying to do with financial planning, doing our wills and powers of attorney, naming beneficiaries, and every-thing that goes along with that negotiation. We're also doing the same sort of process with each of our mothers . . .

J: . . . which ultimately is about *our* own planning and our peace of mind as well as, hopefully, for theirs . . .

B: And having to commit things to paper, we're getting clearer on what's important and what *we* need to put in place in order to entertain all of the possibilities.

J: It makes a difference, too, to do this with you *in conversation.* Trying to get in touch with my views and feelings on class by myself was kicking up some of my negative history with school, like the pressure of having to write the perfect paper. Then there's the expectation of *our* collaboration of saying something super-significant together. But documenting our conflicts and differences of opinion definitely feels more real-world.

mir zayen do!/ we are here!

some notes on being a working-class jewish lesbian

TOVA

lesbians. working class.
jews.

bankers. slumlords. owners of all the businesses. owners of all the factories. run the banks. "jewish american princesses—j.a.p.s." middle class. upper class. owners of the media. rich jews. loud jews. cheap jews. all jews go to fancy colleges. all jews are doctors and lawyers—or married to one. jews are taking over the world with their money. jews and their money own the world.

lesbians. jews.
working class.

stupid. dirty. smelly. inarticulate. loud. garish. no manners. no etiquette. lazy. sap the "state" of money. trash. violent tempers. slow. dense. simple-minded. don't know how to manage money. spend all their money on junk and junk food. no taste.

working class. jews.
lesbians.

ugly. can't get men. look like men. want to be men. hate men. are afraid of men. angry. sick. crazy. sex fiends. don't know how to have sex. afraid of sex. social misfits.

i am a working-class jewish lesbian, self-conscious of the different orders in which those identities spill out of my mouth. i wonder how many would find those identities put together as a contradiction in terms. if i listen to what's around me, sometimes i begin to believe it's a contradiction.

what can i conclude if i look around the media, in "popular" books, tv, movies, newspapers, magazines, and advertisements? if i see jews at all, they are middle- or upper-class professionals, straight, maybe liberal, maybe religious. if i see working-class people at all, they are christian, dress loud, and can't seem to keep their homes clean. if i see lesbians at all, they are generally middle-class and "apolitical." i don't see working-class jewish lesbian feminists. but the invisibility of being a working-class jewish lesbian is not just in the world "out there," but in the communities in which i function—the lesbian and feminist communities, the "progressive" jewish communities, working-class circles, and the mix-over of all of these.

if i look around the lesbian community, i see many jews, and i feel support from them to be a jewish lesbian. i also witness much anti-semitism. the degree of anti-semitism in the lesbian community has waxed and waned over the years. when anti-semitism has been dealt with, it has been primarily because of the strong voices of jewish wimmin fighting anti-semitism and (re)claiming our culture and heritage. it is jewish wimmin who explain that not all jews are rich; that the term "j.a.p." is unacceptable; that some of us are loud and like it that way; that we have holidays we cherish such as passover, rosh hashanah (new year's), purim, and not just chanukah, which is *not* some "alternative" to christmas; that we have a deep history of activism in this country, in eastern and southern europe, in the middle east, and elsewhere; and that there is so much true richness about the diversity of our peoples across class, color, religious, and geographic lines.

while i have seen this (re)claiming grow again recently, i have also seen what seems to be a resurgence of anti-semitism. "suddenly," the only jews that exist are the ultra-conservative jews here and abroad (especially in israel) or the occasional sitcom jew with little or no jewish identity aside from some stereotypes (à la Jerry Seinfeld); jews are again taking over with money as lawyers, doctors, and those running hollywood; and jews are the ones and the only ones who started the patriarchy and totally destroyed any essence of wimmin's religion—the ultimate sexist culture that single-handedly destroyed goddess culture; and other assorted anti-semitic beliefs.

this revival of anti-semitism is multifaceted. some has to do with the increasingly more complex, more insidious situation(s) in the middle east in the last way-too-many years (i suppose one could say thousands of years, but i mean the recent past). while certainly the israeli *government* has the power and has used it in unconscionable ways in terms of the palestinians, the israeli government doesn't represent the ideas, feelings, politics, etc. of all jewish israelis, let alone all jews worldwide. the situation in the middle east has provoked a great deal of racist anti-arab sentiment in the u.s. and abroad, as well as a backlash of anti-semitism. during the gulf war, for instance, there were bomb threats in both mosques and synagogues in seattle.

contemporary anti-semitism also has to do with the depression in american economics and the accompanying rise of conservative and right-wing politics. service jobs have become the norm. factory work, such as in the garment district where my grandmother worked, has been "exported" to countries like hong kong and thailand with cheaper labor. farms have been taken over by multi-national corporations with high-tech equipment. jobs for the working class have decreased, not just affecting working-class people of color and jews (i.e., jews of color and white-skinned jews), but also white working-class christians. conservatives and the right wing have used economic oppression to try to rally white working-class christians who are angry at a changing economy that is kicking them out. these groups promote racism and anti-semitism, overtly and covertly, so white working-class christians have a place for their anger. if the jews own all the banks, hollywood, housing, etc., they are surely easy enough to blame for the economy. and where does all this leave working-class jews and people of color, who are affected at least as much, if not more, by these economic changes? where are the garment districts of today?

the pain of invisibility and separation as a jew in "my lesbian community" has overwhelmed me. if i look around the lesbian community i also see working-class wimmin, who give me support around being a working-class lesbian. again, i see issues of class and classism dealt with because working-class wimmin raise the issues and claim their culture. but classism persists, to say the least—assumptions about how to speak or write, what one can afford or not, one's worth in terms of one's so-called work, how one grew up, where one's been, what one knows or "should" know, and even seemingly absurd details like putting napkins on your lap, or even having napkins at all.

meanwhile, if i look around the jewish community, i find much classism as well as homophobia. surely, i find this in "conservative" jewish communities, but i find classism and homophobia even in places such as the progressive jewish community and feminist jewish community; and classism in the jewish lesbian community. i see classism and homophobia growing as the rise and influence of conservatism and right-wing politics grow and the u.s. and world economic situations grow more critical. attacking welfare recipients and the homeless; targeting gay bars, synagogues, mosques, and african-american cafes with bomb threats and drive-by shootings (in recent incidents in the seattle area); beating up and even murdering queers in mississippi, new york, oregon, and all over, is not only more common and sensationalized, but sometimes almost revered. and in u.s. culture, which pits oppressed group against oppressed group, one can see this homophobia and anti-semitism happening in working-class communities where jews as a group are seen as being rich "slumlords" and where queers are seen as taking over the neighborhood. classism, homophobia, and anti-semitism anywhere make me invisible and separate.

as one of the editors of *Bridges*, a jewish feminist journal, part of the work i do is focusing energy on making sure there are working-class voices in the journal and on the editorial collective. because of this i've had the *incredible* opportunity and pleasure of speaking with jewish working-class wimmin and many lesbians. because a lack of time (taken up surviving), lack of money (how many could pay to come to an expensive conference, for instance?), and oppression can make us so invisible and distant from each other, it has sometimes felt like a much-needed and long-awaited fix to be able to talk with these wimmin. when i put to-

gether a list of working-class jewish wimmin and sent out correspondence for an issue we did with a cluster of articles on class, i
was excited to realize there really are working-class jewish lesbians
out there. but i don't and can't live in *only* a jewish working-class
lesbian community. i function in a daily way, get my primary emotional, political, spiritual support from the at least somewhat larger
lesbian, jewish, and working-class communities. this makes the
pain of invisibility and separation as a working-class jewish lesbian
in all of these, "my communit*ies*," a pain and separation beyond
description.

recently, i've thought about the fear middle- and upper-class
jewish wimmin have about discussing class or talking about
money, and the connection of this to anti-semitism. people often
make anti-semitic assumptions about being jewish and having
money and class privilege. as is often the case, the values of various
jewish cultures (and there are many—ashkanazi, sephardic,
mizrahi, to name a few larger ones) don't always "translate" well
into the dominant culture. for instance, there are many anti-semitic
assumptions about jewish bankers and entertainers. yet the origins
of jews entering (*not* dominating or owning) these professions are
themselves a result of anti-semitism. anti-semitic policies of eastern
europe did not allow jews to enter many trades, schools, or "professions." two of the few things jews were *allowed* to do were to
loan money (hence their history of "banking") and become entertainers, traveling minstrels entertaining village celebrations (hence
a history of being in the "entertainment" industry). part of the origins of the very mixed influences of klezmer music come from
jews being traveling minstrels. ironically, the anti-semitism that
forced jews to be in these jobs has now been turned around to a
"newer" anti-semitism that accuses jews of "entering" these professions because they are "money-grubbing," "controlling," and
"loud." adding assimilation and capitalism to this mix, we can see
that when, despite anti-semitism, some jews are "allowed" at least
peripheral/financial entry into the middle class, they have many
mixed feelings. there is both pride—"i made it in amerika"—and
fear—"do i fit the stereotype of the money-grubbing jew? should i
hide my money to protect myself from anti-semitism?" in addition,
jews who have "made it" into the middle class are then criticized

for "making it." sexism strongly enters the mix here, as middle-class jewish wimmin are labeled "j.a.p.s" and are made fun of for wearing supposedly ostentatious clothing, jewelry, and fur coats.

i have seen middle- and upper-class jewish wimmin confuse and use anti-semitic (and sexist) assumptions as an excuse for being classist, for not being up-front about their class privilege, and for not confronting their own and other jews' classism because they are afraid they will be met with anti-semitic responses. they're right, but lying about their class privilege does not help erase classism *or* anti-semitism, and perhaps makes both worse. a person is not middle-class just because they are jewish, and feeding into that stereotype from any angle keeps the anti-semitism and classism growing. middle- and upper-class jewish wimmin need to be honest about their individual class privilege and how that differs from their jewish heritage; they must confront the anti-semitism around them as well as the classism within them. their *justified* fear of anti-semitism cannot erase their *unjustified* classism.

even as a working-class jew, i understand the fear of talking about money and being jewish. i know i have not said certain things or have masked certain things about money and class for fear that people will think i'm "really" a jew with money, not "really" a working-class womyn. for instance, i recently got some money from a bicycle accident i was in. i was able to pay back some debts, buy myself a new bike and a good stereo system, and keep some savings. despite the fact that i will likely have lifelong medical bills due to this accident, i worried when people came to my house that i needed to explain how i acquired these things. i worried about what could go on in wimmin's minds; would they think: "figures, some cheap, selfish jew who says she's working-class, doesn't have money, but puts it all away and buys a fancy stereo and bicycle." would middle- or upper-class jewish wimmin assume i was "another" jew with money, one of "them"? would they not see me as a working-class jew? would i need to or feel i had to explain because of my fears of how people in my own communities would act and make me invisible or not see the full picture of who i am? the fear and reality of anti-semitism toward *all* jews, of *all* classes, do not give anyone, including middle- and upper-class jews, an excuse to be classist in their lesbian or wimmin's or jewish or progressive or other communities. it does not give them the right to deny the full story of the existence of working-class jews—my existence.

i have seen and heard way too many wimmin, feminists, lesbians, assume that because you are jewish, you are middle-class, or at the very least assume working-class jews have a disproportionate degree of middle-class aspirations (we all go through wanting to pass to some degree). i have heard way too many people assume all jews, regardless of class, attend college, want to be professionals, have some sort of "in" with the jewelry business and can get discounts on diamonds... again, i have seen fear provoke my own actions. have i denied my jewishness to feel accepted as working-class? surely, i did that around the issue of lesbianism. when i first came out i went so far as to throw away all my jewish song sheets, wondering why i would need them anymore, now that i was part of the "lesbian nation" (and, thus, not the "jewish nation")? and while i can say this was a "sign of the times," something i would never do now, what is it about my jewishness that i deny in order to feel a part of a working-class or lesbian community?

there is an assumption that all jews want to be and are formally educated. while surely this is not so and does not address the diversity in the jewish community, it is true that certain segments of the jewish population historically and presently place a high premium on education. some groups of jews have called themselves the "people of the book." and there is an ashkanazi saying that words are so sacred, you are not even allowed to wrap a fish in newspaper. but what kind of education are we talking about? my grandfather, for instance, was revered for never having gone to school but being entirely self-taught, an avid reader, a political activist, and very knowledgeable about religious and secular jewish history and culture. these cultural values cannot be translated quite right into the language of the dominant culture, even after assimilation has skewed them.

some of the origins of a jewish stress on education involved certain jewish communities' stress on *religious* education. boys and men went to religious school to study torah, talmud, and other religious books and matters. so much so that often it was wimmin who were "left" with working inside and outside the home because men were "commanded" to study so much of the time. i should at least note the rather obvious sexism here. boys and men were forced to study, while generally wimmin were not allowed to study these religious works. however, these jewish wimmin, as is true in many cultures, created an intricate, complex, and influential "wimmin's" culture. for instance, wimmin had a strong influence over yiddish, which was the language of the "people" (as opposed to then ancient hebrew, which was for study), created their own set of prayers for wimmin in yiddish, and developed a large literary canon with such authors as miriam raskin, kadia molodowsky, malka lee, and esther singer kreitman. some of this "lost literature" is presently being revived and translated by such contemporary feminists as irena klepfisz, and in works such as *Found Treasures—Stories by Yiddish Women Writers*, edited by Freida Forman, Ethel Raicus, Sara Silberstein Schwartz, and Margie Wolf (Toronto: Second Story Press, 1994). in addition, religious education is now being embraced by many wimmin, as evidenced by the rise of wimmin rabbis and new feminist translations of religious texts by authors such as Marcia Falk. historically, for both jewish men and wimmin, education did not mean what it means in the u.s. today. indeed, in eastern europe, the more educated jews were the poorer jews, as they spent so much time studying, they had no time to earn a living. this is still true in a number of jewish communities today.

in my jewish home, education was stressed. even though i was a girl, because i did well in school, i was encouraged to go to some sort of college (as opposed to my sister). at the time, i was living in new york, and city college was still free. but for many complicated reasons, i was insistent upon going away to college. so i went to the only "reasonable" alternative that i even *thought* to consider, a state school, which at that time was still pretty cheap, but more than i could afford. i got scholarships, loans, and worked one to three jobs while going to school, and was rather traumatized by the "values" of the primarily middle-class community i found myself surrounded by—such as showering every day, keeping your voice soft, not wearing "loud" colors, etc. on more than one occasion, and even now, i watch myself trying to explain how i got to go to college. i feel compelled to explain all the jobs i had and scholarships and loans i got to stay there. to explain how having a degree doesn't erase my background, though it does afford me privilege. to explain how i'm not a "j.a.p." just because i went to college. sure, no one i know well would use that word (to my face, at least), but some part of those stereotypes are there, and i feel them and fear them. and i find myself explaining them because i fear somehow i will not be a "real" working-class womyn because of them. and ironically, this reaction sometimes makes me not pay attention to the privilege i have gotten from formal education.

what does it mean to be a jew and working-class? it has only been in the last few months, for instance, that i've figured out why i didn't fully relate to the term "white trash." no one has ever called me "white trash," despite my white skin and working-class background. yet i wanted to feel and use that term fully the way many white working-class wimmin i know proudly and boldly do. but something was not quite 100 percent there. and it's not quite there because, despite the fact that i'm a white-skinned jew, i'm not and wasn't ever really *white* trash. not all jews have white skin; not all jews can pass. many jews, especially ashkanazi jews (of eastern european descent), do have white skin or pass as white, and have skin-color privilege. but jews are not culturally what is considered "white" in this country, and are generally not considered white in other countries. so i guess i'm "jewish trash," which in this culture is certainly still garbage and still "stinks," but is from a different dumpster.

i've heard stereotypes about jews and class and money from wimmin of *all* classes, including working-class wimmin. i've been told that all working-class persons had wonder bread and jell-o molds, so i tried to figure out where my kosher jewish working-class childhood fit in, with rye bread and bread pudding. being working-class and knowing classist assumptions will persist doesn't give one a reason or an excuse to be anti-semitic. *justified* fear of classism cannot justify *unjustified* anti-semitism. wimmin from *any* class should not deny the complexities that have intermixed my class background with my jewish background to come out with something different from a working-class non-jew. working-class wimmin should not deny a part of their own working-class community and experience and diversity, because some working-class wimmin are jewish, and that makes a difference.

while i know there are many strong allies in my communities, and while many others would agree *in words* that anti-semitism and classism are "of course" not acceptable, i see anti-semitism and classism persist. daily, i'm afraid. in fact, the more i've thought about and talked about and raised these issues, the more shit i've heard about it, the more resistance i've gotten about dealing with it, the more painful experiences i've felt from it, and the more complexities around the issues i've had to sort out for myself, with varying degrees of success. in less than a year's time i stood up in tears (unusual for me) explaining to "my" lesbian community how i felt they were being anti-semitic, and then made the same "speech" substituting class for anti-semitism to a group of wimmin from "my" progressive jewish feminist community. i'm exhausted, and have to remember i'm part of these communities and that living isolated in a cave would be bad for my joints.

the "jews running the world because of their money" concept and the manifestations of that have been a major and primary source of contemporary and historical anti-semitism, and that issue must be examined. when dealing with jews and with class, we have to look at that—look at how this has affected our various communities, look at how this operates in and around us, look at how classism and anti-semitism are finely woven together. i believe more and more that one cannot talk about anti-semitism without including class. one cannot talk about class and not include the role of jews and other cultures and communities. and jews not dealing with class because of their fears of anti-semitism are, i believe, a major and primary source of classism in the jewish community. we have to look at that; look at how this has affected our various communities, look at how it denies the diversity found within the jewish, working-class, and lesbian communities, and how it is a part of our own internalized anti-semitism, classism, homophobia, etc.

somehow when i think of all these issues, i start remembering where i grew up in brooklyn. everyone in the neighborhood i grew up in was working-class or poor. the neighborhood was multiethnic and multiracial, and there were *lots* of jews. many people in my "immediate" family and rather large, multigenerational extended family were jewish and working-class or poor. as a young child, i didn't know many "realities" of middle-class or upper-class anyone or anything, and not many middle- or upper-class jews. and for all the "trouble" of that neighborhood and my family—and there was plenty of it—there were many positive values, including a strong commitment toward surviving as a community, that i try to carry with me today.

for too many and too complicated reasons to explain here, i had to leave that neighborhood, that family, and that community in order to exist; my lesbianism was certainly not the least of the reasons. in some ways i had to leave what feels like almost everything about my past life. the lesbian and jewish and working-class circles i live in today have allowed me to be myself and grow in essential ways my brooklyn life couldn't. but as my "neighborhood," my "family," my "community" expanded my worlds and myself in many ways, they closed me off in other ways. the classism, anti-semitism, and homophobia that exist in the communities i live in today also make me feel invisible, separate, or at least "split at the root" in all places. when i can only be part of myself in each community i am involved in, it makes me wonder if the whole of me exists at all. but it does, because there are working-class jewish lesbians. i'm one, and there are many others.

if we are going to survive with each other, have commitments to each other, be families, neighborhoods, communities, let's open our eyes to the truth of ourselves and each other. let us allow ourselves to exist in our varied and interwoven concentric circles of communities. and not only to exist and survive, but let us proclaim, as some of my ancestors did in "zog nit keynmol/never say," a song that has become known as the anthem of the jewish partisans of world war II, "mir zayen do!/we are here!"

The Glass Factory, 1980

HAROLD McNEIL ROBINSON

A week-long low-wage job on the swing shift
amounts to mindless manual labor
I smoothe brittle edges off
massive sheets of glass
Goggles, leather apron, and gloves
provide protective barriers
to the unthinkable
After all the education, applications, interviews
temporary assignments
attempts to find opportunity
through any imaginary window anywhere
I can no longer
shield myself from the truth
I must break the silence
It ain't happening here
No permanent job exists for me
in Sonoma County

Something adjacent to my heart
slowly begins to dissolve into sand

I think back to the warm morning sun
of the walk to a nearby shopping center
past rows of trimmed hedges
postwar cottages and bungalows
Passing motorists would do head turns
flip me the bird
jerk me out of fantasy
Black skin is still an oddity
this far north of San Francisco
My last sex partner
a business-minded blonde
said I seemed out-of-place
We functioned at best as machines
no longing remained for that touch

Ku Klux Klan stickers stood out
on see-through phone booth doors
Return to Oakland
might be wise
though thoughts resist
strive to assimilate
passively melt and bond
become like the massive transparent sheet
in my outstretched hands
that hits the metal sander
at the wrong angle
and shatters into a hundred bits

To Market, To Market

Considering Class in the Context
of Lesbian Legal Theories and Reforms

RUTHANN ROBSON

Considering "class" in any context requires an interrogation of both status and relations. In the first instance, economic status is a social marker that engenders bias or privilege in ways similar to other identity categories. In other words, "class" operates to mark certain persons as "classed," the usual inference being that such persons are "lower-classed" in the same manner that marking someone as "racialized" means such persons are "non-white."[1] In the second and equally important instance, economic relations are the structures of participation in the market economy, including not only monetary exchanges for goods but also the "market for symbolic goods,"[2] which would include artistic and legal production. In the context of lesbian legal theories and reforms, both class status and market relations must be addressed in a specific and explicit manner.

Nevertheless, I continue to struggle with the degree of specificity and explicitness required because I (too often) conflate a lesbian politic with an anti-classist one. For example, in *Lesbian (Out)Law*,[3] I made certain choices regarding language, publisher, price, and content that implicated both class status and market relations. I conceptualized the book as an accessible one in terms of the symbolic (language that could be understood by non-university-educated lesbians) and the material (priced relatively affordably), as well as including content that addressed issues such as prison and crime that disproportionately impact lesbians with less privileged class status. Yet I articulated these choices—to myself and to others—as lesbian choices grounded in lesbian theories. Thus, despite an educational background in classical theorizing derived from Karl Marx, I conflated lesbianism and class consciousness.

This conflation began to unravel as many lesbians—those embodiments of lesbian theories—began to advise me against the "lesbian" choices I was making. This advice consisted of recommendations to pursue a hardcover university press book that would concentrate on issues relevant to the "majority" of lesbians. Such advice was based in part on class biases, but also on an assessment of the market economy, the relevant commodity being the book itself, especially in terms of the symbolic prestige, as well as the commodity of my academic "career."

While I do not believe that such advice is malicious or unrealistic, I have long been interested in the ways in which we police each other with the best of intentions. Often these intentions reinforce certain class norms and standards. Yet we rarely, if ever, articulate these norms and standards in terms of class identity or with any reference to economics.

This policing also occurs in my teaching. For example, in the context of discussing discrimination in a feminist legal theory class, I pose a hypothetical that places the students in the role of attorneys on a hiring committee at a legal services office. This role will become a reality for many of these students in less than a year, assuming that legal services continue to exist. The hypothetical provides that the committee members conducted initial interviews in pairs and now the entire committee is meeting to decide which applicants to call back for a second interview. On the interview notes for one applicant, the interviewer noted, "dressed inappropriately." The issue to be discussed is, of course, whether an assessment of the appropriateness of dress constitutes "discrimination" in either a legal or ethical sense.[4]

As in most law school classroom discussions, we freely revise the facts to uncover differences between analytic structures and results. If under a particular set of facts the applicant's dress can be interpreted as cultural, ethnic, or religious in some manner—a kente cloth, a yarmulke, a veil, a sari—the students have absolutely no problem concluding that the "dressed inappropriately" notation is discrimination. If the applicant's dress can be construed within a gendered context—a man wearing a dress, a woman in a man's suit, hair too short or too long—the students discuss the situation for a longer time but ultimately conclude that discrimination is occurring, although opinions differ as to whether the discrimination is based on sex/gender or sexual orientation. However, if the applicant's dress is attributable to a lower-class status—my favorite example is a woman wearing a dress made by her mother; it is pink and satiny and has rick-rack stitched on its borders—the students are not troubled by the specter of discrimination. No matter how much I try to make my hypothetical applicant in the pink satiny dress sympathetic (describing how she had to save to buy her mother the material for the dress, describing how she picked out the pattern in a McCall's book), the students raise all the arguments that could have been raised in the ethnic and gender contexts but were not: arguments about the potential of her attire to be perceived negatively by judges and opposing counsel and clients. The word "professional" dominates the discussion.

It may be important that while the racial, religious, and gender identities of the students are diverse, their economic status is less variable. These students are themselves predominantly from working-class or impoverished backgrounds. Yet they roundly condemn this hypothetical applicant: "She should know better than to dress like that." They irrevocably link the *display* of class status to knowledge, yet another commodity. While they do not advocate legal redress, they do offer solutions: She should borrow a suit from a classmate, she should go to a thrift store, she should get *Dress for Success* from the library and pick another pattern and different material.

When asked about the distinctions between a woman applicant wearing a veil or a man's suit or a rick-rack bordered dress, one student explains the differences not only in terms of knowledge, but also in terms of choice. The veil is a viable cultural choice; the man's suit is a viable gendered or sexualized choice; but no one would *choose* to wear the attire of the lower classes, at least until such attire had been appropriated and stylized by the higher classes. Further, many students consider appearing as a member of the lower classes as inconsistent with their avocation as public interest attorneys, specifically attorneys for impoverished populations. As cultural critic John Guillory expresses it:

> For while it is easy enough to conceive of a self-affirmative racial or sexual identity, it makes very little sense to posit an affirmative lower-class identity, as such an identity would have to be grounded in the experience of deprivation per se. Acknowledging the existence of admirable and even heroic elements of working class culture, the *affirmation* of lower-class identity is hardly compatible with a program for the abolition of want.[5]

Thus, it is not simply that "lower class," or "poor," is a rhetorical category or identity that allows prosperity to be normalized and other economic conditions to be pathologized, creating a group of "others" who are deviant.[6] The same process of categorization occurs in racial, ethnic, religious, and sexualized identities, and may serve liberatory as well as repressive interests.[7] However, although many identities that have been politicized may provoke debate over the relative merits of separatism and assimilation, such debates have little currency with regard to class. One explanation may be the inability to recognize class as an identity at all: "Classlessness is congruent with the basic tenet of the American creed, namely civic equality, and with the defining values of American society, notably equality of opportunity and individual success."[8] Related to this are our individual inabilities to definitely denominate our own class identities.[9] Yet John Guillory's insight is perhaps most basic to the failure of lower-classed persons to entertain separatism as a viable option. While the condemnation of materialism, affluence, and consumerism is often part of progressive and humanist agendas, the maintenance of an insular and impoverished underclass is incompatible with the goal of economic justice. In other words, almost all of us—whether postmodern or liberal or even conservative—at least theoretically advocate the abolition of poverty, the condition by which poor people are defined.[10]

After the discussion about "inappropriate dress" and the limits of discrimination, my office hours are especially busy. Students come to discuss the readings and request recommendations, and, if they are female, almost always manage to broach the subject of the interview outfit. They describe their outfits in detail. The unasked question hangs in the air: is this outfit the equivalent of the pink satiny dress with the rick-rack border from McCall's Pattern #24457, although I am borrowing it from my roommate/bought it at a thrift shop/borrowed *Dress for Success* from the library? Even a blue suit is not automatically safe, because there is fabric and skirt length and blouse and shoes and "legs" to consider.

For lesbian students, sexual orientation issues complicate the discussion but do not change its fundamental nature. Because we are in New York and the students are applying to progressive legal employers, students do not consider sexual orientation itself to be a problem. The problem is not that one is a lesbian, as long as one is "the right kind" of lesbian. This "rightness" is expressed through appearance and style. As Danae Clark, in her excellent essay "Commodity Lesbianism,"[11] might phrase it, the students are not so much concerned with being "out" as with seeming "in." Seeming "in" requires both knowledge and money.

My role in this exchange is to impart knowledge (although I have also on occasion loaned out clothes). In doing so, whether or not I believe I am being less than rigid, or even liberatory ("the most important thing is to be comfortable"), or even subversive, I am ultimately agreeing to police them. I am agreeing that it is important to appear as if one belongs to the class of persons that one wishes to join. I am telling them what I did: how I learned to pass as a hippie student, as a member of the progressive bar, as a lesbian law professor, rather than as a poor kid in a homemade dress, perhaps not pink, but definitely with rick-rack. I am saying: you can do it, too. I am telling them they should.

Yet I am plagued by two political concerns. First, my advice to the students is an accommodation that I believe should be unnecessary. The applicant in the shiny pink homemade dress *should* have a cause of action for discrimination, just as surely as the applicant in the yarmulke and the female applicant in the man's suit should have causes of action. This does not mean that racial, religious, gendered, or sexual identities are commensurate with class identities or with each other: each is unique and has its own histories and manifestations. It also does not mean that the category of "class" should trump all other categories or become the exclusive category of analysis or the exclusive identity entitled to legal redress for discrimination.[12] Further, the inclusion of class as a protectable identity does not "dilute" other established, protectable identities such as racial and religious identities, or other seeking-to-become-established identities such as sexual minority status. Rather, I believe it is vitally important for the ultimate protection of all "minoritized" identities—be they racial, ethnic, religious, gendered, or sexual—that economic status be equally protectable. Otherwise, economics becomes the acceptable explanation for discrimination and other forms of legalized violence.[13]

Second, I am increasingly troubled by the rift between class and sexuality. At one point, I could comfortably express both class and sexuality concerns within the rubric of lesbianism, specifically articulating a lesbian legal theory that could address both class and sexual minority concerns. Theoretically, this should not have been possible, given the disparate sociological groundings of economic class and sexual status. Nevertheless, a coincidence of interests seemed plausible. Such a coincidence of interests gradually dissipated, but the fracture is most revealed by the discovery/invention of lesbians as a "market" segment, an innovation in which lesbians and gay men have colluded. Obviously, lesbians have always been economic actors; not only do we routinely participate in the market economy, we have a long (and complicated) history as consumers and purveyors of specifically lesbian cultural items, from magazines to bars, from recordings to crafts. Yet the present situation is marked by a scale far surpassing women buying or selling handmade ceramic labyris at a lesbian festival, or frequenting the bars that operate at the edge of legality.[14] Measured by capital's own rod—the dollar—the present lesbian and gay marketing phenomenon is a multimillion-dollar enterprise involving multinational corporations, advertising campaigns, and orchestrated consumption.[15] While we gain a somewhat positive presence in the straight media as well as advertising dollars for our own media through such an invention, our place in the dominant market economy effectively commodifies lesbianism as a style (which can be purchased) rather than as a politic (which must be lived). As Clark expresses it, lesbians are invited "in as consumers" to be "part of the fashionable in crowd" while negating "an identity politics based on the act of coming out."[16] Thus, capitalism's notorious search for additional markets creates a rift between class and sexual identities by commodifying lesbian and gay identities for the lesbian and gay consumers who can afford to purchase them. While the creation of the lesbian "market" may have lagged behind that of the gay male market, recent sources proclaim its viability.[17]

The commodification of lesbian and gay identities is certainly not unique. For example, bell hooks writes of the problems caused by the "commodification of blackness": it "strips away" the potential of black identity to "subvert and undermine the status quo."[18] The commodification of blackness makes it possible for "white supremacist culture to be perpetuated and maintained even as it appears to become inclusive."[19] Similarly, the commodification of lesbianism makes it possible that heterosexist and sexist culture is perpetuated and maintained even as it appears inclusive.

Importantly, hooks' theorizing in this area includes a discussion of complicity, which she theorizes as rooted in the equation of "capitalism" with "self-determination."[20] Lesbian complicity is derived from these same roots. Or as lesbian theorist Robyn Weigman expresses it, "products" are equated with "political progress."[21] In fact, commodification may not just be the process by which products are merged with politics, but may also include a specific rejection of politics. For example, as Sue O'Sullivan brilliantly argues, the present media images of how "cool it is to be a dyke" depend on the retreat of the "boring old lesbians" who represent not only "unattractiveness" but also "politics."[22] To collude in the denunciation of the stereotyped image of the outdated political lesbian is to reject the "radical political agenda of feminism, including its analyses of the social, cultural and economic."[23]

Nevertheless, it is difficult to resist the temptations and treats of being trendy, especially after one has been ignored or despised for so long. And it is even more difficult to believe one *should* resist. The participation (even if it is more negatively termed "complicity" or "collusion") by other lesbians makes difficult any resistance to an enterprise on the basis that the enterprise is not truly "lesbian." Such a resistance would rest upon the positing of an authentic lesbian existence, a ground no longer available in a postmodern

world. Yet the alternative—whatever a lesbian does must be good
for lesbian survival—is at least as problematic. Indeed, it is the alternative that may be even more essentialist than the positing of
authenticity, because the alternative fails to interrogate the differences—including economic ones—among lesbians. The alternative
denies the reality that the ability to derive benefits from commodification presupposes a degree of class privilege.[24] Although it may
be that none of us can escape participation in this commodification,[25] such participation nevertheless has disparate rewards and
disadvantages depending on one's class status.

Not only does the dissipation of class analysis in lesbian and
"queer" legal theorizing result in a lack of resistance to commodification and the maintenance of heterosexist structures, it has also
resulted in our failure to adequately respond to those who advocate our demise. Relying on statistics derived from "marketing sur-
veys" designed to convince advertisers that lesbians and gay men
could be a profitable market, the New Right utilizes rhetoric with
shocking similarities to pre-World War II anti-Semitism to portray
us as economically privileged. The portrayal of lesbians and gay
men as economically privileged serves New Right rhetoric in at
least two ways. First, the depiction taps into already existing class
resentments and anxieties. Second, the myth of economic advantage counters any claim that lesbians and gay men are discriminated against.[26] Yet our own rhetoric has often not effectively
countered these falsehoods;[27] instead, we have employed class-
biased stereotypes to deride adherents to the New Right, ranging
from polite implications concerning a lack of education to more
explicit insults like "trailer trash" and "shitkicker."

The dissipation of class analysis means not only that we cannot
respond, but that our own positive legal reform movement is problematic because it fails to take into account both the economic dis-
parities among lesbians and the market economy's operations
upon lesbianism. The present emphasis on marriage is but one example.[28] Marriage is widely touted as being an advantage that will
provide economic benefits for lesbians and gay men, but this obscures the fact that it will not be an advantage for lesbians in all
classes. The very availability of marriage could work to the economic
disadvantage of lesbians receiving public entitlements because the

state will impute the income of one "partner" to the other, who might otherwise be eligible for "welfare" benefits. Notwithstanding concrete harm to economically disadvantaged lesbians, marriage as an economic arrangement that supports the market economy is delegitimized, as if the feminist-marxist critiques of marriage are inapplicable to lesbians and gay men. Even more fundamentally, the very notion of the marital relation as a propertised one–including the theoretical basis of monogamy in private property–is considered irrelevant.[29] What is considered relevant–although often expressed in a joking manner–is that lesbian and gay attorneys will profit economically if marriage and its corollary, divorce, are legalized. Our communities are converted into client bases; the professional status of some of us is secured.

I am suggesting that a serious consideration of economic structures might yield a very different emphasis in the lesbian and gay legal reform movement. But I am also suggesting that lesbian survival–both in the sense of the survival of many individual lesbians and the survival of lesbian as an identity–depends on an agenda of economic empowerment and redistribution of wealth. Economic deprivation constricts choices, including the opportunity to create a life in which one's lesbianism can flourish. The historical work of gay and lesbian community historians and theorists demonstrates the link between economic conditions and the abilities of lesbians (and gay men) to survive, as individuals and as communities.[30] The theorizing and historicizing of the economic realities for lesbians and gay men–the homo/economy–has only just begun.[31] We need to apply historical and economic insights to our own time and work toward realizing the conditions that promote lesbian existence.

It is not enough to have a policy–or even a statute–prohibiting discrimination on the basis of sexual orientation in a world in which so many lesbians cannot find any work at all, and so many more cannot find work that is meaningful or rewarding, and so many must work so hard and so long for so little. It is not enough to have justice for only those lesbians who can afford to purchase it.

Notes

1. The comparison between race and class is a comparison in the manner in which such categories operate within a world of privilege; it is not an absolute confluence.

2. Pierre Bourdieu, "The Market for Symbolic Goods," *Poetics* 14 (1985), 13.

3. Ruthann Robson, *Lesbian (Out)Law: Survival under the Rule of Law* (Ithaca, NY: Firebrand, 1992).

4. We are not only considering extant doctrine, but also the ways in which a person who believes in nondiscrimination would act even if not required to by law. I have labeled this latter situation "ethical."

5. John Guillory, *Cultural Capital: The Problem of Literary Canon Formation* (Chicago, University of Chicago Press, 1993), 13.

6. See, e.g., Thomas Ross, "The Rhetoric of Poverty: Their Immorality, Our Helplessness," *Georgetown Law Journal* 79 (1991), 1499 (noting that the creation of the abstract category of the "poor" is a rhetorical device employed by the courts to abnormalize the poor).

7. The category of homosexuality is paradigmatic in this regard. As Foucault argues:

> There is no question that the appearance in nineteenth-century psychiatry, jurisprudence, and literature of a whole series of discourses on the species and subspecies of homosexuality, inversion, pederasty, and "psychic hermaphrodism" made possible a strong advance of social controls into this area of "perversity"; but it also made possible the formation of a "reverse" discourse: homosexuality began to speak in its own behalf, to demand that its legitimacy or "naturality" be acknowledged, often in the same vocabulary, using the same categories by which it was medically disqualified.

Michel Foucault, *The History of Sexuality: An Introduction*, trans. Robert Hurley (New York: Pantheon, 1978 (1976)), 101.

8. Stephen Edgell, *Class* (London: Routledge, 1993), 121. As Edgell notes, however, the notions of classlessness and equal opportunity have long been recognized as inherently contradictory, "since if everybody is equal, there can be no superior or inferior positions to move into."

9. Although as Julia Penelope notes, in the introduction to her excellent anthology on lesbians and class,

> We may have an unclear sense of our "class identity," but each of us surely learns our "place" and that of others. These lessons are taught to us by our parents, guardians, whoever takes on the job of raising us. And they tell us explicitly, almost every day of our lives, "who we are" with

respect to the family next door, the family upstairs, the family down the street. We are taught to compare, contrast, and gauge our differences. Oh yes—we have some ideas about where we stand socially and economically with respect to other people we come in contact with.

Julia Penelope, "Class and Consciousness," in *Out of the Class Closet: Lesbians Speak,* ed. Julia Penelope (Freedom, CA: The Crossing Press, 1994), 13, 22.

For an excellent interrogation of the meaning of class boundaries, see Victoria A. Brownworth, "Life in the Passing Lane," in this volume.

10. The commitment to the eradication of poverty, however, is obviously a different matter. As Professor Thomas Ross points out, Americans commonly hold that poverty is inherent, irremedial, eternal ("there have always been poor people"), the result of abstract forces (the "politics of distribution"), or a demonstration of moral weakness on the part of those people who are poor, yet "all that has ever been required to eliminate poverty is a redistribution of wealth." Ross, 1509-10.

11. Danae Clark, "Commodity Lesbianism," *Camera Obscura* 25/6 (1991), 181.

12. For example, one suggestion has been to eliminate affirmative action based on minority racial status and replace it with affirmative action based on economic disadvantage. Richard Kahlenberg, "Class, Not Race," *The New Republic* (April 3, 1995), 21. Such suggestions impose a divisive either/or model of access as well as promoting false notions of scarcity.

13. As I have written elsewhere, the dichotomy of the good lesbian/bad lesbian is a dangerous one; it ensures protection for some of us at the expense of others of us:

> The discourse of discrimination measures us not only against a heterosexual norm, but against each other. If a company employs four lesbians, a new manager can fearlessly fire the one who has her nose pierced or who is most outspoken or who walks the dykiest. The remaining three lesbians insulate the company from charges of discrimination on the basis of lesbianism. Antidiscrimination is thus partial, allowing the selection of only the whitest and brightest of us, the ones with the best clothes and accents, the smoothest legs and apolitical pasts.

Robson, 87.

14. For a discussion of the ways in which the law operated on "gay bars" in the 1950s, see Joan Howarth, "First and Last Chance: Looking at Lesbians," *Southern California Journal of Law & Women's Studies* 5 (Fall 1995), 153.

15. See generally, Grant Luckenbill, *Untold Millions: Gay and Lesbian Markets in America* (New York: HarperCollins, 1996).

16. Clark, 193.

17. See, e.g., Jeff Barge, "Moving Out and Upward: Lesbians Attract Marketers," *Crains Small Business* (February 1995), 9.

18. bell hooks, "Spending Culture: Marketing the Black Underclass," in *Outlaw Culture: Resisting Representations* (New York: Routledge, 1994) 145, 149.

19. Ibid., 150.

20. As hooks argues,

> the contemporary commodification of blackness has become a dynamic part of that system of cultural repression. Opportunistic longings for fame, wealth, and power now lead many black critical thinkers, writers, academics and intellectuals to participate in the production and marketing of black culture in ways that are complicit with the existing oppressive structure. That complicity begins with the equation of black capitalism with black self-determination.

Ibid., 148.

21. Robyn Wiegman, "Introduction: Mapping the Lesbian Postmodern," in *The Lesbian Postmodern,* ed. Laura Doan (New York: Columbia University Press, 1994), 1, 3. Weigman's insight is especially important because she describes lesbian complicity in this equation:

> Music, clothing, vacation cruises, festivals, artwork, publishing—in all these areas, lesbian identity functions as the means for defining the specificities of both production and consumption. While this relation—of lesbian-made, -sold, and -owned materials—approximates in the 1990's a tamed separatism, it is more than disturbing that the commodification of the lesbian as a category of identity is often what passes, inside and outside the lesbian community, for evidence of political progress. At a recent women's music festival, for instance, the growth of the merchant area—in terms of both the number of products available and their diversity—was lauded by one performer as a sign of growing lesbian political power. . . . Can we unproblematically herald the consolidation of the lesbian as a category of being when this being is increasingly signified by our saturation in commodity production, both countercultural and, to a limited but growing extent, "mainstream" as well? Must we, in other words, embrace a liberation contingent on production, marketing, and then vampiristically consuming "us"?

Ibid., 3-4 (footnote omitted).

22. Sue O'Sullivan, "Girls Who Kiss Girls and Who Cares?" in *The Good, The Bad and the Gorgeous: Popular Culture's Romance with*

Lesbianism, eds. Diane Hamer & Belinda Budge (London: Pandora, 1994), 78, 90.

23. Ibid., 91. Sullivan notes, however, that just as the strident lesbian politico is a stereotype, so too is the lesbian who is young and "provocatively attractive and fashionable." "Both images are fantastical; neither image corresponds anymore to the multilayered realities of lesbians' lives than any other media caricatures of women do." Ibid., 92.

24. As bell hooks writes, "when the chips are down it is usually the black folks who already have some degree of class privilege who are most able to exploit for individual gain the market in blackness as a commodity." hooks, 147.

25. According to Robyn Wiegman, "We have little alternative action but to participate." The "commodification of the lesbian" is "not a check we deposit by choosing to sign our name on the back. *That* signature will always precede us." Wiegman, 45 (emphasis in original).

26. As Suzanne Goldberg notes,

> Take Back Cincinnati, a group organized to promote a voter initiative to amend Cincinnati's charter to exclude lesbians, gay men, and bisexuals from protection against discrimination, explained in its literature that a "group wanting true minority rights must show that it is discriminated against to the point that its members cannot earn average income, get an adequate education or enjoy a fulfilling cultural life."

Suzanne Goldberg, *Lessons from the Cultural Wars: Lesbians and the Religious Right* (forthcoming).

27. M. V. Lee Badgett's work demonstrates that gay or lesbian status (defined by sexual behavior) results in a negative economic impact at a rate of 11 to 27 percent for men and 11 to 14 percent for women. M. V. Lee Badgett, "Economic Evidence of Sexual Orientation Discrimination," in *Homo/Economics: Capitalism, Community and Lesbian and Gay Life in the United States,* eds. Amy Gluckman and Betsy Reed (New York: Routledge, forthcoming).

The Lesbian/Gay/Bisexual Policy Network (c/o Professor Badgett, School of Public Affairs, University of Maryland, College Park, MD 20742) is one of the few groups attempting to research and disseminate accurate economic information about sexual minorities in the United States.

28. For a discussion of specific cases in which a failure to adequately consider class requires a rethinking of the litigation's positive outcome, see Darren Rosenblum's excellent article "Queer Intersectionality and the Failure of Recent Lesbian and Gay 'Victories,'" *Law & Sexuality* 4 (1994), 83.

29. For further discussion, see Ruthann Robson, "Resisting the Family: Repositioning Lesbians in Legal Theory," *Signs* 19:4 (1994), 975.

30. As John D'Emilio argues, by the beginning of the twentieth century,

gay men and lesbians began to invent ways of meeting
each other and sustaining a group life....Lesbians formed
literary societies and private social clubs. Some working-
class women "passed" as men to obtain better-paying jobs
and lived with other women—forming lesbian couples who
appeared to the world as husband and wife. Among the
faculties of women's colleges, in the settlement houses,
and in the professional associations and clubs that women
formed, one could find lifelong intimate relationships supported by a web of lesbian friends. By the 1920's and
1930's, large cities such as New York and Chicago contained lesbian bars. *These patterns of living could evolve
because capitalism allowed individuals to live beyond
the confines of the family.* [Emphasis added.]

John D'Emilio, "Capitalism and Gay Identity," in *Making Trouble: Essays
on Gay History, Politics, and the University* (New York: Routledge,
1992), 8.

Other important works that discuss the relationship between economics and the formation of lesbian or gay identities and communities include Allan Bérubé, *Coming Out Under Fire: The History of Gay Men
and Women in World War II* (New York: Free Press, 1990); Lillian Fader-
man, *Odd Girls and Twilight Lovers: A History of Lesbian Life in Twenti-
eth-Century America* (New York: Columbia University Press, 1991);
Elizabeth Lapovsky Kennedy and Madeline Davis, *Boots of Leather, Slippers of Gold: The History of a Lesbian Community* (New York: Routledge, 1993); Esther Newton, *Cherry Grove, Fire Island: Sixty Years in
America's First Gay and Lesbian Town* (Boston: Beacon, 1993).

31. As Jeffrey Escoffier notes, we "have only the barest sense of the
economic history of the lesbian and gay communities." Jeffrey Escoffier,
"The Political Economy of the Closet: Notes Toward an Economic History
of Gay and Lesbian Life Before Stonewall," in *Homo/Economics: Capitalism, Community and Lesbian and Gay Life in the United States,* eds.
Amy Gluckman and Betsy Reed (New York: Routledge, forthcoming).

I owe much of my own thinking about the relationships between economics and lesbian/gay community to discussions with Jeffrey Escoffier
and other members of the Thompson Square Queer Theory Discussion
Group, 1993-94, and the conference Homo/Economics, sponsored by
CLAGS (Center for Lesbian and Gay Studies) in November 1993.

Currency

JUSTIN CHIN

"It's always about money," my grandmother said. Every family fight and feud that I grew up witnessing was about money. How much was left, how much could be used, how much was taken advantage of, who was left out of a share.

I grew up quite suitably upper-middle-class. In five years, from scratch, saving and borrowing, my family managed to move from a dingy shop house overrun with rats and centipedes at the back of my dad's clinic and buy into a new development, frightfully expensive at that time.

My father was the first person in his family to graduate from university—medical school, no less. There is a picture of him in his graduation robes and mortarboard, rolled-up diploma in hand; standing proudly and grinning beside him are my grandmother and grandfather and my mom in her beehive. I was always told that he was terribly clever and had wanted to go on to a further degree, but by then my brother was already born, and my father had to support his younger sisters and brothers through school.

The years we lived behind the clinic are a haze to me. I was still a little tot contentedly playing with Rupert the Bear. My folks, my brother, and I slept in one room; my three aunts slept in the other. But the place always seemed more crowded with uncles, cousins, and my grandmother visiting often. The "New House," as it was referred to, did not hold much gravity in my mind; in retrospect, I probably didn't even know what the hell was going on. One day, my folks took me for a drive and we drove the familiar road to the beach, but then we took a detour and ended up at this huge frame of a house. It was two stories, with a massive garden, a slight spiral of a staircase, wooden paneling, air-conditioning, and the promise of many, many rooms. I learned the term "dining room." But more importantly, there would be a Study Room. Education was an important factor in "being comfortable in life," we were always told. "We make sacrifices so that you don't have to." The Study Room was for my aunts who were still going through school, but ultimately it would be for my brother and I.

Money and status were always uncomfortable subjects growing up, and they continue to be. Dad is a general practitioner. An ex-boyfriend used to leer at me, making some snide and cutting remarks about how I was nothing but a rich kid who had everything I wanted, Dad's occupation informing his ideas. But in Malaysia, and in Kuantan where my dad works, a regular G.P. is so unlike the doctors in America, who charge exorbitant consultation fees. When my dad started his clinic in Kuantan, he was one of maybe two or three private practitioners. In twenty years, he and my mom (and the very same receptionist all those years) built up a practice with a loyal patient following. In some cases, he's been the family doctor for three generations of a family: the children that used to be brought by their parents now bring their children. There is very rarely a consultation fee, and the money is made in the dispensary run by my mom. Maybe $10 to $12 Ringgit (US$4 to $5) a patient. Nothing made Mom and Dad happier than when a flu virus befell a family of six.

The funny thing is that I never felt like I grew up with money. More than money, we grew up with a strange sense of privilege and expectation. We were always reminded that we were "doctor's children." We were expected to get excellent grades, be super-smart, and become doctors (preferably), lawyers, architects, or engineers. Classmates in school whose parents weren't doctors, lawyers, architects, or engineers looked at us with a certain awe. Sure, we were more well-off than some other folks, but not as well-off as others, but then again, doesn't everybody fall into this pattern? We were always urged to save, to be thrifty, to spend money wisely.

My parents, like practically all Chinese parents, believed in a good education for me and my brother. They believed that we should not have to go through what they went through, and they lived in fear that we might go hungry. So they spared no expense, working day and night to provide for us. But, as comfortable as I was, there were always so many other kids in class who had pools in their backyards, took yearly trips to America and Europe, and had the latest electronic gadgets and games; they also had their own rooms. I was always envious.

At the same time, my family could still afford to hire even poorer folk who attended the same church we did to help with the cleaning. I remember a friend's amazement that we sat to dinner with "the servant." His eyes widened in horror and amusement; in his house, he explained, the servant ate in the kitchen. Somehow, I think we never figured out the whole idea of hired help. For the ones who worked out, we always looked at them as a sort of family friend. When my maternal grandmother got older and more arthritic, my mom hired an older woman who worked as a road sweeper (which we were often told was one of the lowest occupations one could descend to: "If you don't study hard, you'll become a road sweeper/taxi driver–then you'll know!") to help out with a bit of cleaning and doing the marketing. There were days when Mama-Chou and Ah-Sim would be lying on the floor eating peanuts and gossiping and watching daytime soap operas (with my grandmother translating inaccurately).

A few years ago, there was a news report on the front page of the *San Francisco Chronicle*. It proclaimed that gay and lesbian households were significantly richer than heterosexual households, since most often, both partners were working and there was no family to support. That report–a national study, we're told–was reprinted and hailed as a milestone in gay and lesbian rights. We got an IKEA ad out of it, as well as a host of entrepreneurial products: rainbow-motifed wotzits all the way up the wazoo.

Similarly, we're told that Asian households in the United States make oodles more money than those of other races, that Asians don't go on welfare like the other colored folks, that they are sig-nificantly wealthy, amassing riches starting from nothing.

What we're not told is that many gay and lesbian households simply eke by and that many Asian-American households make more money simply by the fact that there are two or three families living, working, and sharing a household—and asking for help and going on welfare is a horribly shameful thing.

When the L.A. riots broke out, there was a lot of talk about Korean shopowners who have shops in Black neighborhoods. The newspapers reported that there was a certain sense of resentment that "these people" had a store. What was not reported was that often, in an extended family, each member puts up money for a store, and when that store makes good, each member again puts up another kitty for the next family member to start a business. Even if that were hardly the case, the anger directed at the shopowners may have been misdirected when one considers who really owns the property the shop stands on. It is easier to hate a very real working-class Korean family than it is to hate the real fat-cats behind the vague sign of Tri-City Realty.

What we get, then, is bitterness toward the Asians who "come over and make more money" and a resentment toward Asian-owned businesses, when such businesses are bought through the graces of three families pooling their money together. What we get is the idea of special rights over civil rights. And what we get most is a seething loathing from our enemies—or those we think are our friends.

Of course, when I speak of Korean shopowners in L.A., I'm speaking of a community I'm not privy to, and perhaps I'm over-generalizing and over-romanticizing it all; whatever information I have is second- and third-hand, from articles and interviews I've read. "Asian" is certainly not a uniform race; it is a convenient socio-political grouping of many different Asian ethnicities. I must shamefully admit that some Asians can be as xenophobic and racist as anyone can be in this country.

Still, this I know: My dad and his older brothers put their younger brothers and sisters through school and college. An ex-tended family of uncles and aunties helped my parents put my brother and I through college. When my dad's younger brother visited San Francisco, we met up for drinks, and before I left he pressed a few hundred-dollar notes into my hand. I protested; he said, "When I was in school, your daddy gave me money to help, so it's okay that you take this, too." When I left for the United States, uncles, aunties, and cousins took me aside quietly and gave me red packets with money "to help out." When my cousin left to go to England to get a further degree, I sent her what money I could, too; it wasn't like I had that much money to fling around, and she certainly wasn't expecting it, but it was something that I deeply felt I should do.

My mother tells me a story: Her dad had been bilked out of the family timber business by his brother. To show his care and family responsibility, he decided that he would give my grandfather a weekly allowance. My mom, being the youngest, was dispatched every week to her uncle's house to collect the allowance. She would arrive and be made to sit in the corner of their lavish living room and would be ignored for hours until her uncle came and tossed her the envelope.

"It was so humiliating," she tells me. "That's why I want you to get a good education and a good job, so that these things won't ever happen to you."

Once, on her way back from school, my granduncle's Mercedes passed her, and she spat at it. My granduncle saw this and immediately called my granddad, who caned my mom severely. "Even though he treats us like shit, you still have to respect him," he said.

My mother tells me this story one night, and she admonishes, "When you don't have money, people treat you like shit. That's why we always tell you to study hard."

We're supposed to let bygones be bygones, but I can't forget being dragged to visit relatives during Chinese New Year, as is customary. We arrive at my granduncle's mansion, ring the doorbell, and wait at the gate. After a few minutes, his servant comes out and says that the family is not in; they're out visiting. In the car, my grandmother remarks, "But both his cars are in the driveway."

Recently, in the *San Francisco Bay Area Reporter*, one of the area's gay weeklies, the writer of an angry letter to the editor complained of an Asian-owned diner in the Castro that was rude to him: "Perhaps they will feel more comfortable in Chinatown," the letter writer hissed. *They* want to take *our* money but don't want to be respectful to us, he ranted.

We see each other and we don't see each other at the same time, and for those of us who live in more than one world, we perhaps see too much. The samples and the methodology lie, and we don't read between the lines enough before waving that new proof, new evidence that we can fit in the class that we feel we deserve to be in. The misreading of numbers and newsprint and the belief in them starts a frightening chain reaction. Sometimes I have this strange feeling in my gut: that the Left is very willing to forgo the Asian-American community in favor of the African-American or Latino/a communities, that Asians have to prove themselves as "People of Color," that gays and lesbians are growing increasingly hostile to People of Color.

In San Francisco, the head of the Log Cabin Club, a gay Republican organization, is a Chinese-American who actively speaks on behalf of the group. In one election, the only Republican candidate running for San Francisco mayor was a Chinese-American. A local city supervisor who is Chinese-American, though a Democrat, is often cited as the "conservative one." There are many Asian-Americans in the Republican Party, locally and nationally. There are many Asian fundamentalist churches in the Bay Area. During the drive to oust the Boy Scouts from the San Francisco school districts for their exclusionary policies, and during the fight to implement Project 10, a counseling project for gay and lesbian teens, there were many Asian-Americans in the meeting halls opposing "gay rights." Sometimes I would like to think that the queer community has the ability to differentiate among individuals, organized groups of a particular ethnicity, and an entire ethnicity. But I can't be sure. I'm not even sure of myself: When I see or read about Asians so wholly expressing a rabid conservative ideology, I do cringe inside of myself. Just as some more old-fashioned Chinese folks think I'm making the race look bad, I think the same of them. It's easy to want your communities to share your understanding of class values, Asian values, and family values, but different people understand differently; we don't all think alike, nor should we.

I wonder how the man in that diner in the Castro who wrote the letter would have reacted if he got the same rude service but the restaurant was run by Whites, or African-Americans, or Mexicans, or Cubans, etc. Would *they* still be taking *our* money? Perhaps I'm doing the same: unable to differentiate between an individual and a group, condemning the queer community on the actions of one silly faggot. But in the afterglow of the mass hostility toward immigrants in the state of California, I'm not sure if that man doesn't represent a large part of the queer communities' attitudes, and whether the server's rudeness represents a large portion of antagonism toward the more privileged populace. The divide is great, and all we have to negotiate the chasm is a rickety wooden bridge of words, op-eds, media darlings and celebutants, and impotent politicos who make the lowest common sales pitch.

My great fear is that the Left, and the liberal/radical queer community at large, is fast equating Asian values with conservative values without as much as a blink of an eye.

I know these aren't terribly great examples. And I can't really put any real solid proof on the table, but I know it goes beyond general paranoia and a sense of victimization. It's a wry observation, the way one may observe that a car crash victim has on the same shoes one is wearing the same day.

I grew up and came out in the '80s, what is now known as the "me-greed generation," the filthy stinking rich '80s. We had *Dynasty, Dallas,* and other soap operas that glamorized wealth and demonized the poor. The poor characters in these soaps were always evil bitches and scheming bastards trying to get a piece of someone else's pie. My friend tells me that she used to watch *Dynasty* in a bar in West Hollywood; she enjoyed watching the queens want to be Alexis and Krystle. Back home in Singapore, being one of the women on *Dynasty* was also a fascination among the queens. They would assume names and characters and act out these people, remembering the bitchy lines and exchanging gossip about the stars. The allure of glamour and the idea that one could have so much money to simply fling away was terribly great.

The fascination with *Dynasty* among a lot of gays is interesting. First, many of us wished Alexis were our mother. She was powerful, had tacky outfits, and was accepting of her gay son. But deeper than that, through that soap and its camp sensibilities (*Dallas* was way too down-to-earth), many gays lived vicariously in this fantasy of power and wealth and uppercrust living. In Jennie Livingston's film *Paris Is Burning*, a young black drag queen looks at the camera, purses her lips, and says, "I want to be rich, I want to have a rich husband who will take me places and buy me expensive things....I want to be a rich, spoiled white girl." There are drag queens in Asia who enter contest after contest in search of glamour, a sense of belonging—who search for a metaphoric "Whiteness."

It is also interesting to note how rich-white equates to power and a preferred class status. Once, I said, to a friend's annoyance, that gay white men must be the most bitter people in the world: Here they are told that white men own the world, but simply because of their sexual orientation they are ostensibly denied easy access to this realm of "power," whatever that means these days. So we're told that gay rights are important, and we're asked to fight, fight, and fight for them. But when there are gay rights, people of color will still be people of color, and women will still be women, and they'll still be fucked while the happy white fags run off to the disco. My friend said I was being divisive.

Gay rights are important, but that's not all. I remember Molly Ivins once saying that women's issues are violence and poverty; everything else was just "fluff," she said. We need to rethink the packaging our struggles come in, check the fat content, the preservatives, and the sell-by date.

Drag has always been a strange thing for me. I have some unresolved feelings about it. Not because of the effeminacy of it. I do admit that sometimes it can tumble into the terrain of misogyny, which I do not care for. There are nice drag queens, and then there are really mean-spirited drag queens, who will use race, class, and gender for a cheap gag, a silly tittle. But what is most unspoken is that drag ridicules and disparages what is seen as "trash." And just who exactly is "trash"? Then there is "rich trash." Even in the make-believe fantasy world of drag, wealth can't buy you out of your trashdom.

Drag is firmly rooted in the long history and tradition of camp. In drag, the audience is asked to marvel at the kitsch, the send-up, and the ludicrousness of it all. But at the same time, we laugh, and unquestioningly we are laughing at some very real and valid appearances in a certain realm and a certain culture. A polyester suit may seem silly, but for someone it may be the only good suit he has; a velvet painting or an airbrushed scene of Waikiki on denim may seem so utterly crass, but for some folks, they mean a lot and are real decorating items, not campy artifacts. Laugh if you may, but know when to stop, too.

Here, we have class status and difference as defined by decor and accessories. It goes beyond good taste and bad taste. And besides, these style and taste judgments are rooted in the profoundly abrasive stratosphere of class.

Returning to the idea of the metaphoric whiteness-as-class-status thing. Yup, I, too, was trapped in the '80s; I wanted the glam life. I was dating this aerospace engineer from France when I was 17. He was stinking rich: he drove a Porsche, lived in a luxury penthouse apartment, and had all kinds of really expensive things. I was so taken by all those trappings. I loved walking in his house and simply taking it all in. But up to this day, what I remember most about our time together was his thinking I had stolen his Cartier lighter and his laugh when he saw that I had misset the table settings.

Thinking back, as only one can do in times like these, I wonder about what was going on in that whole situation. I simply wanted to be a rich, spoiled white girl, too.

The thing called class is a weird thing; it seems that you're trapped in it and you can't buy your way out. And even if you do, possessions and wealth do not equal class status; *that* is attained in ways I still cannot possibly comprehend.

Something that never occurred to me before: I was enrolled in a pretty prestigious school. (Pulled strings: uncle was vice-principal, hence we skirted the grueling application processes.) Each standard (or grade, if you Yanks so please) was divided into ten or more classes. Every year, based on our final examinations, we were either promoted or made to stay in the same standard. The final grades were tabulated, and the first forty highest scores went to the A class, the next forty to the B class. It was a matter of prestige to get to the A class, of course. The J, K, L, or M classes were for the kids everybody knew would not amount to much. Most of the time, those classes and the kids in them were synonymous with the term "Chinese-educated," which was synonymous with lower-class, uncouth. The kids in the upper classes were synonymous with "English-educated," which was everything Chinese-educated was not. There were Chinese-educated kids peppered through the top classes, but they were few, and they stuck together, disdained by the English-educated kids.

I never realized how the structures that I grew up in, even as a young pup, segregated us. Class is all around, and sometimes we don't see it until it is too late. Then again, even had I known these structures and been aware of them, I really don't know how I would have lived differently.

My parents did not let me want for anything. They made sure I had all my basic necessities: food, clothes, shelter, education, books. They also believed in saving money, in being thrifty, in a good savings, a good sale, a good discount, in not being frivolous.

Being the first person in generations to break out of one class and into a more privileged one is a very strange thing. It is very much like immigration and exile: unless you're there for a long, long time, you remember too much of where you came from. You start to get nostalgic, you start to describe so you won't forget, you visit a lot and think that maybe one day you will return, but most of all, you realize that too much of your body is invested in too many places, too many memories and warnings flow in your blood. You never really fit in, you're always a stranger in a familiar land. You can try to pretend, you can be comfortable in your disguise, but you know you still can't buy your way out.

You know that the next generation and the next will be the ones who will really fit in, who will clearly define that break. Negotiating the spaces between classes is a terribly tricky thing.

Much of it depends on one's personality and moral sensibilities, perhaps. A lot probably depends on where one has come from and what one has learned in that span of life. Looking back on what I have just written, I realize, too, that perhaps I have romanticized it all a little too much, taken way too many liberties, and I probably will continue to do so through my life. Romanticizing, of course, occurs when one is moving from one class status to another, is in transition, and is forced to look back. The move, this transition, may take years, generations, more than one's lifetime to accomplish. You can't just load the U-Haul and get there. It is crucial to know that class is hereditary, too, in a way, and that it changes so much from one generation to another, that it is ever evolving even in one's own life. For many of us, this state of transition *is* our class status; it is not as simple as checking a box on a tax form, and it certainly goes beyond earning potential.

In speaking about class, we are forced to look more deeply at our identities. Class is inexplicably contained within our understandings of sexual orientation, ethnicity, and gender. It also influences how we see the world and how we want to change it or not, and how much we feel we can. And with identity politics, this realization can either free or cage a person.

It is important that we impart our sense of class values onto the next generation or to the people who may be at similar crossroads. We need to leave better records that these conversations, these discussions, and these arguments about class in our communities happened, so that the discourse on identities, on class and race and queerness, can evolve and move on to another, hopefully more positive, place. Understanding one's identity is a process, and I look back on the Civil Rights movement, the ethnic studies strikes, Stonewall, all those marches on Washington, ACT UP and Queer Nation; those bits of memory, records, and history, blended with literature and art, have given me much raw material. With this, I can better articulate who and what I am to the people who would rather I did not exist.

Putting Down Roots

KENNETTE CROCKETT

I t was a sunny Sunday afternoon in July. My lover, Monica, and I were enjoying a barbecue at a couple's home in Naperville, a suburb thirty-five miles west of Chicago. Conversations centered on suburban issues—garage-opening mechanisms, yard upkeep, and the best places to go for things that would make their homes look more like a Norman Rockwell painting. Finally someone turned to Monica and me. "Where do you live?"

"The city," we both responded. Everyone shook their heads as if to offer sympathy as the conversation turned to tales of city horrors and advice about how we, too, could make our great escape.

Despite the appearances and sounds of heterosexuality, most of the people were gay. The couple, Hope* and Andrea*, friends of a friend, had just recently moved to the burbs from the city, and the Fourth of July get-together was supposed to serve as a dual celebration. "Yeah," joined in Hope. "Moving out here is the best thing that we could've done. It's clean, safe, and quiet." All of the other suburbanites agreed.

I could not argue with her. Where they had moved was cleaner and safer, and the homes were more affordable. Yet I could not say

*Some names have been changed.

that I was persuaded then or now to move to the suburbs. Not because I rejected a cleaner, safer existence but because the suburbs have always represented a great divide. Growing up, I knew this division was racial. Back home, the suburbs were places where whites moved to get away from Blacks in the inner city. Today we know it as "white flight." East St. Louis, Illinois, my hometown, is a small, predominantly Black city surrounded by small white towns. It borders the Mississippi River and serves as a bridge crossing from St. Louis, Missouri. Hence the name; we are east of St. Louis.

Living in a homogeneous Black subculture was just a matter of course for my parents. My mother and father were born into a segregated world, and, though Illinois and Missouri are not Mississippi, both had their color lines. My mother would tell me about how Blacks couldn't go downtown unless they worked in the kitchen of a restaurant (around the same time, Blacks were confined to the back of the bus). Dad was one of the first Black babies born in St. Mary's Hospital in East St. Louis. This achievement was overshadowed by the fact that the hospital kept him in a room separate from the white babies.

I heard these stories repeatedly, told in endless variations by countless relatives, friends, and acquaintances who had each experienced such injustices and indignities. So I was always aware that there were "lines" between Blacks and whites. My personal interaction with whites was largely as an observer gaining many of my insights from episodes of *The Brady Bunch, As the World Turns,* and whatever other TV shows I could catch. Then there were the real life experiences. I have vivid memories of shopping in Fairview Heights, a nearby shopping mall in a white community. Though we stood out as Black faces in a sea of white, the white salesclerks rendered us invisible. "We were next" became my mother's mantra, as we were always being overlooked or bypassed by the white salespeople trying to serve the white customers.

So I never wondered why we didn't live around whites. It was hard enough to shop around them. And when I did hear of a Black family moving to a white town, the follow-up story would usually involve a cross-burning.

Segregation was everywhere for me. My schools were all-Black, and the only time I saw white students was when my school com-

peted against theirs in sports, band, and debate. College would become my first real one-on-one experience with white people my
age. I selected Mundelein College because it was a small women's
liberal-arts institution. "Why an all-girls college?" teachers and
friends back home would ask. This was my standard reply: "I like
the fact that it's in Chicago, a city of urban diversity." Why an all-
girls college? Where else to meet a girlfriend, I told myself.

Now, recalling the exchange at the barbecue, I wonder why
Hope and her girlfriend have given up the diversity and gay camarade-
rie of city living for this more isolated, heterosexual-like existence.

"We just wanted a nice home in a clean neighborhood," offered Hope. Hope is white and in her thirties. I am not quite sure
what she does for a living except that it involves a lot of travel to
Alaska. Andrea is Black, about the same age, and a school teacher.
"Yeah, it's nice out here," she agreed.

I don't think that they were moving to get away from minorities
per se, since many of the couples at the gathering were interracial.
Maybe it was just to distance themselves from poor people. After
all, most major cities have close dividing lines between "good"
areas and "bad" ones. Case in point: Chicago's Gold Coast neighborhood, the richest part of the city, borders Cabrini Green, one of
the most notorious housing projects in the United States.

But listening to Andrea, I couldn't help but wonder. Living in a
predominantly rural white area when you are Black has never
seemed like the ideal way of life. Andrea was from St. Louis, not
too far from my hometown. Although St. Louis is not predominantly Black like East Boogie, it is still a far cry from farmland.
Hope, I was told, is from a small, rural white area, so I guess her
move to the burbs from the city was like a homecoming.

That was last year. Now Hope and Andrea have parted ways.
Hope kept the house. Friends said that it was in her name all along.
Andrea—well, I'm not sure where she is. I don't know if she remained in the burbs or moved back to the city. I have my hunches
that it's the latter.

Hope and Andrea's reasons for moving to the suburbs sound a
lot like those of straight people. They are not alone in this migration to suburbia. Rich, a forty-two-year-old gay white male whom I
met on America Online, expressed similar motives. "I moved out

here [Woodstock, Illinois] for a relationship, but it fell apart. I stayed, though, because I like the calmness, the quietness, and the safety."

~~~~~✕~~~~~

The big city once held an allure for young people looking for excitement, a dream, and abandonment, especially those hoping to escape the often constricting convictions of small-town mentalities. Take Camille, Pascale Bussieres's character in the film *When Night Is Falling* (directed by Patricia Rozema), who realizes she can no longer live in her small Christian college community after she falls in love with another woman, Petra. This present-day love story deals with issues of self-acceptance and homophobia. Love is the overriding motivator for the relationship between two women who come from different racial and cultural backgrounds. In the beginning, Camille is involved with a man and sees herself as part of the religious college community that she later must leave. Camille jumps the biggest hurdle of them all when she accepts her own desire for another woman. Together, Camille and Petra go in search of their own community. Naturally, the film ends with the couple heading west to the "Gay Mecca," San Francisco.

That pull toward America's metropolises always seems more pronounced in young gay people from rural areas who seek freedom from the small-town minds and the chance to be out in the streets with other gay people. Look at the films *The Adventures of Priscilla, Queen of the Desert* and *To Wong Foo, Thanks for Everything! Julie Newmar,* which deal with gays venturing outside of their city environments and into small towns. And what happens? A strange version of *The Wizard of Oz,* where Dorothy and her friends are trying to escape from Kansas rather than return to it. The gay characters in *Priscilla* and *To Wong Foo,* for all of their outrageous dress, blend into the Sydney and New York scenery. In *Priscilla,* when Mitzi, Felicia, and Bernadette begin their road trip, there is a bon voyage party for them. And in *To Wong Foo,* when Noxeema, Chichi, and Vida depart from New York, hundreds of queens and other well-wishers see them off. Felicia, the young drag queen with a mouth as exorbitant as his wardrobe, sums it up best when he says that he can't wait to get back to Sydney. Felicia's and the others' return to the city is, after all, a homecoming. That is largely because in the city meetings are spontaneous, bars are easier to find, and the dream of living in a place with other "people like us" can really happen.

At least that's what I thought when I moved to Chicago to attend Mundelein College. I wanted to come out. I wanted to have a full-blown lesbian relationship. Chicago gave me quick and easy access to a gay community that my hometown did not. And despite my own middle-class background, I didn't care whether the woman was Black or white; rich, poor, or middle class; working or studying full-time. What mattered, even more than race and class, was sexual orientation. If a woman was gay and interested in the community in general and me in particular, that could be the start of a beautiful relationship. I thought that our struggle for equality would bind us together and that love among the exiled would and could conquer all.

Oppression is an interesting two-way mirror that influences the oppressed's perception of themselves and the oppressor's perception of the outcast group. So members of a minority group are often lumped together. When a group is persecuted, that oppression strips away other factors, like class, that also contribute to hierarchies in the eyes of the oppressor. Take, for instance, Black Americans. At one time in their history, Blacks could not live wherever they chose. Confined by segregation to certain homes, jobs, and occupations, Blacks had no choice but to live and work and play together. There were still internal hierarchies. But because Blacks were in one place, to an outsider they had one look, one identity. So my great-grandfather, who was a minister, was the same as any Black man to white society, regardless of his class.

But the great emancipator, integration, was supposed to give Blacks the opportunity to earn more and to live wherever they could afford. Yet no matter how often and how far Blacks moved, the neighborhoods were all too soon predominantly Black again. In theory, integration gave Blacks the chance to exist as individuals and to challenge the stereotypes of a monolithic identity. Reality was white flight carrying thousands of white families outside of the inner-city limits and into any areas where white faces were the only ones to be found. Today, thirty-odd years after integration, I find myself living outside the predominantly Black neighborhoods but still living within the confines of the stereotyped, monolithic view of Blacks created by white society.

Like the Black community, the gay and lesbian communities were drawn together by oppression. The oppression that many gays and lesbians faced became a catalyst in creating what many refer to as "the gay ghettos." Clustered in large cities, these areas were a friendly harbor for gays seeking refuge from the hostile straight world. The differences between the gay ghettos and the Black ghettos are based in economics. Apartments, bars, and businesses all grew out of these gay sections of the city. And again, because they were in one place, gays and lesbians were stereotyped into one identity, one existence.

When I first moved to Chicago, I was pleasantly shocked by the area that gays had christened "Boys Town." This trendy part of Chicago located between Belmont and Halsted was full of guys cruising, laughing, eating, and doing things that their straight counterparts did on Rush Street, only with more flair. It was not until a few years later that Chicago lesbians would party in "Boys Town." Eventually women would stake their own claim to Andersonville, a northside neighborhood. Now, women-owned businesses catering to lesbian and bisexual women offer us our own space. The freedom that I felt just being able to see others like me walking the streets has only been surpassed by the overwhelming feelings I get from gay pride parades and just recently at Stonewall 25 in New York City.

Today it seems that some gays and lesbians no longer need to live around each other to experience that sense of community. Some of us don't even need to socialize in gay circles. Hope and her friends rarely get into the city. And even when gay suburbanites gather together, their groups suffer from what I call the mirror complex, where everyone present looks the same. To be reminded of this, I only had to visit a suburban bar. Walking into Temptations, all I could see were blonds, everywhere. The crowd did not have that ethnic mix that you find in most city bars. There wasn't even the white pierced set. Gays who live in the city have more of an opportunity to mix. I know many urban interracial couples and couples with different salaries and educational backgrounds.

So just being gay is not a large enough factor to keep some gays in the city. For them, the need for "people like us" has been replaced by different needs: for safety, security, and ownership of property. The need to be a part of a group still exists, but what has changed is the kind of group and the perception of the seeker. Blue- and white-collar queers move regularly to suburbia, not so much to live around people of their same race but to live around people, gay or straight, of their same class.

But is race completely removed from the gay equation? Is gay flight a by-product of white flight? A person is aware of their race and gender. So white gays who move to the suburbs are reacting out of their race and class. Some might say merely that the chickens are coming home to roost. I believe that a person's upbringing stays with them their entire life. My parents' middle-class lifestyle plays a big part in my outlook. So a white person raised in a lower-class home brings those experiences to their present economic state. At the same time, gay flight could arise out of a greater need to assert individuality, to challenge the stereotypes of a monolithic urban identity. For Blacks this need is compounded.

When I first came to Chicago, I sought out gay friends. My earlier friendships were mainly with other Blacks, and I selected my friends by mutual interests. By the time I accepted that my dreams of kissing women were not going away, I decided to take steps to meet lesbians. As a Black lesbian, I have always challenged the monolithic identity. There are times when I straddle the fences of both the gay and Black worlds. My Black identity has always been nonsexual. My early memories of homosexual feelings were linked to white women. Maybe it was because all the Black women I knew seemed so straight (not to say that I didn't have crushes on Black women). But I always thought that white women more than Black women were experiencing the same sexual longings as me. So I ventured from a Black world into a gay/white world. My voyage did not leave me fulfilled or with a sense that I had come home. My encounters with white women were not complete, nor can I say they were satisfying. There just seemed to be a bridge to cross that I wasn't aware of until I had been in the gay/white world for a few years. Connecting because of our physical attractions was easy. But our perceptions on important issues were different. When we went out to eat and waited while white couples were being seated, white women thought that race couldn't possibly be the reason for the delay. They didn't understand about my hair and the extra care that it needed. They couldn't nod their heads in affirmation when I reminisced about eating greens, looking with admiration at my older siblings' Afros, and grooving to the sounds of Parliament. Explaining my culture and experiences to white girlfriends got old. So once my sexual identity was solidified, I began to search for people who shared my class and racial/cultural upbringing.

It wasn't until I met my life partner, Monica, a Black bisexual woman, that I realized that my identity was not so much middleclass, Black, or gay, but rather a strange fusion of race, class, and sexual orientation. A lifetime committed relationship turned my focus again to my class and culture, and how I wanted us to live our lives. It was then that I realized that I had to be aware of my race, class, and gayness. I had to learn how to survive and thrive in a larger society that stigmatizes my race and sexual orientation, and harbors doubts about my middle-class status.

The associations of poverty and illiteracy with Blacks still linger in the minds of some whites. So when I drive my Jeep Cherokee Country, am I the girlfriend of a drug dealer in the minds of the white couple on my left? Why is the ownership of my Jeep constantly being questioned along with my knowledge of wines, good food, travel, and strong coffee? Race, culture, and sex drive us, and, depending on the person and the events, one may override the other. Most people want to be with, as Archie Bunker would say, "their own kind." People believe that they know what to expect from their own, whereas someone of a different group is capable of anything. Yet somehow, beyond the masks of race, class, and sexual orientation, people manage to connect. Why? Maybe it is the strong bond of mutual interests and simply having a fondness for someone.

The people Monica and I meet and form friendships with today are gay, straight, Black, and white, but they are usually from the same economic backgrounds. So does class transcend other differences? Yes and no. I have met white people from middle-class backgrounds, yet we don't connect. I have even met Black people who share my past experiences of growing up in a home where both parents were present with good careers, and had very little to say after the small talk ended. The friendships in my life must strike a chord in me. Sometimes the chord combines my race, sexual orientation, and class; the combination depends on the individual.

⁓

Who gets to go to the suburbs and have a good life? It's not easy for a person struggling in the city to pick up and move, especially to a place where money and its trappings go hand in hand. Not to say that the burbs are filled with rich people, gay or straight. But many of the people there have some sort of job security, whether blue- or white-collar. The gays and lesbians I know who live in suburbia tend to have a formal education or work steadily in well-paying blue-collar jobs. Put the very same homes, which are so reasonably priced, in the city, and they would be unaffordable. Money can go further out in the hamlets. Of course, there are still lesbians like myself who could afford to live "better" in the burbs but prefer the city. You can say that I like the feel of concrete under my feet.

People move for different reasons. Gays and lesbians who move to the burbs do so because something changes. The things that once held them to the city are no longer as much of a factor in their lives. Their need for community goes beyond gender and sexuality to the more familiar bindings of race and economics. I believe that a person can live in the suburbs and remain active in the community, but their location might affect how active they are. Does a person become more invested in their neighborhood? And can a person truly have a gay experience and live somewhere so far removed from most members of the community? To me, it's like going to college but living at home, or going to the Michigan Women's Music Festival and staying in a hotel room miles away from the campgrounds. When the women are sharing, how much can you hear in your room?

Like their straight counterparts, gays and lesbians who move to the suburbs usually move to burbs that reflect their race and class. They see themselves moving outside the gay and lesbian tribe to a tribe that represents them racially and economically. Marilyn*, a Black, middle-aged friend of mine, lives in Calumet City, a southern suburb with a large Black population. She moved there because she wanted to buy a home. Her search started in the city. But she could afford to buy one in questionable areas. And a home in the trendy areas of Chicago was over her price range. As a native Chicago southsider, she naturally leaned toward the southern burbs.

Now, out among the trees and houses that cover the land as suburbia's chain restaurants cover the main strips of road, she and her lover enjoy suburban living. "I like my home," reveals Marilyn over dinner one night. "But sometimes I hate being so far away from the city and my friends." I don't get the chance to see Marilyn that often—only when there is a party that brings her into the city or when Monica and I can muster up enough motivation for the drive out there.

Marilyn and most of the gay people I know who live outside of the city tend to lead lives very similar to their heterosexual counterparts. Home, property, and in some cases children tend to be the order of the day. They now occupy bastions of traditionalism: get a well-paying job, buy a house in the burbs, settle down, and have a family. I sometimes wonder how they look to their straight neighbors. Maybe no different than Monica and I look in our predominantly hetero-inhabited apartment complex. But in a big city, people are used to seeing uncommon sights. Rich in Woodstock told me that in suburbia, "one doesn't come on to someone right away. It's more closeted." I would like to think that as long as the grass is mowed and the house looks good, maybe, just maybe, straight suburbanites are not concerned with their gay neighbors.

If there is a great price to pay for integration, maybe it's the scattering of minority groups when we have more choices of places to live. A breakdown occurs in the community when people bound together by a cause no longer live around each other. Not to say that every gay person should live in the gay parts of the city or that every Black person should live in the Black areas. We just have to work harder to stay in touch with each other. There is power in numbers.

Often, people socialize and live around people of the same means. Money inclines people to accept you on an economic level but not on a social one. So the great drama continues, and gays will move to the suburbs along with their heterosexual equivalents. Maybe they will have children. And maybe those children will feel the need for excitement, freedom, and escape from small-town mentalities. And maybe the gay 10 percent will want to live in the city and put down roots among people like us.

Inconspicuous Assumptions

DONNA ALLEGRA

Notions about class thread their way through literature and fabricate beliefs we put on without a moment's thought. Horatio Alger rags-to-riches stories are an all-American favorite. In our national mythology, second to the tale of poor-boy-makes-it-big is the fable of the boy from the wrong side of the tracks winning the love of a rich girl. A variation on the gender-pointed theme is the old saw about the man who marries the boss's daughter.

Even with the obvious gender bias, these aren't necessarily noxious fairy tales. Such dreams can come true more readily in the U.S. than in most other countries. But this is not the most telling parable about class in America. The downside to having a high class to aspire to and a low class to shun is the resulting snob culture. The snob position assumes that some forms of written expression are more valid as pure artistic conceptions than others.

The English course party line would likely welcome a sing-song lyric about the moon in June, while an innovative saga told would be soundly trounced. Perhaps you've experienced that people take you for a serious reader if you leave the library with a hardcover, but those same people feel free to interrupt your involvement in a paperback science fiction, mystery, or romance novel.

Defenders of the status quo always harken back to some time in the distant past as the pinnacle of achievement and regard all else as mere shadow. The assumptions in back of this posture do not acknowledge that under particular situations and times, the thrust of writing is aimed at specific purposes that stem from cultural circumstance. Over the past thirty years, feminist scholars and people of color have revealed in countless ways that what is passed off as high art issues from the people who inhabit the class of power and privilege.

Individual writers who happen to be white and male may well have starved in garrets, been rejected, and gone unrecognized in their lifetimes. Still, it always works out that the men who run this world eventually declare that the only true art is that which reflects life as they experienced it.

During those blank moments when people of color and women remain unacknowledged, we can clue in on where class plays out beyond its conjunction with race and gender position. It used to bewilder me how some people could readily embrace William Faulkner's convoluted sentences but wrinkle their brows over Toni Morrison's complexities. I'd stare in open-mouthed disbelief as E. L. Doctorow was hailed as an innovator and literary pioneer, while Ntozake Shange was pooh-poohed as an impostor for her invention of the choreopoem in *for colored girls who have considered suicide/when the rainbow is enuf.* This shows that class attitudes infiltrate our value systems so thoroughly that we can't detect them without conscious effort. As with environmental pollution, we're so used to inhaling this noxious element that it seems natural.

One way class snobbery pervades the atmosphere of literary discussion is when we disdain what people say on account of how they say it. Most people have a hard time recognizing value when a writer comes from a cultural base that does not fashion itself according to their own cultural style. That style is called the standard without acknowledging the fact that "standard" replicates the culture and vocabulary of those in dominant positions.

No matter that Shakespeare's English and Chaucer's diction must be studied and translated for contemporary readers even to get a clue to their meaning. Such translation is deemed a worthy intellectual venture. The fluidity of language that marks the change from Old English to our modern language is regarded as a natural evolution, yet African American dialects are connoted as "slang."

In another instance, if a writer takes on subject matter not easily understood by arbiters of good taste, that writer's labors are discounted for not being universal. A man's ejaculation on the page is revered a holy rite of passage as compared to a woman's infinite variety of orgasm, which is greeted as a subject for derisive laughter.

How can we talk about quality and not assume the ruling class's values, which serve to keep us all "in our place" and uncertain as to our inherent worth in the scheme of things? We're so used to this class assumption that it seems to be the norm the entire world is subject to, or certainly ought to be. We must consciously look past the ruling-class viewpoint we're acclimated to, having grown up reading through its voice.

As a book slut who could gladly spend time bedded with a different author every night, I'm still unable to make claims that only a few authors are the greatest. Different writers have particular offerings to succor and ply me with their delights. I'm too promiscuous a reader to settle down or even limit myself to a single school of literature. It seems unreasonable for anyone to crown as queen a particular way of literary expression, barring all other genres from the heart, never to lust outside the fold.

Those of us in the lesbian-feminist and queer social activist movements have learned to be more sensitive to context so that we can view literary and other arts more fairly, but attitudes of competitive snobbery still abound. I've seen power brokers in literature wield authors' names the way some males talk sports—as extensions of their egos, metaphoric weapons to exclude and put down others. "Well, you've read ＿＿＿＿'s latest, haven't you?" "Oh, ＿＿＿＿, he keeps writing the same book over and over again."

It seems to me that queer people need to keep their social and political awareness keen despite the temptation to put on airs that would make some individuals appear superior to a group more despised on the social scale. If we reproduce conventional society's modes of oppression, it's only to our detriment.

Currently, the "mainstream" is huffing out the lie that comes in the guise of sneering over "political correctness"—as if such social consciousness is a force of oppression. In taking on that line of conversation, we've fallen for the bait. The radical right has great copywriters. They come up with terms like "Feminazis" and "P.C." to sway public opinion and manipulate perceptions about people who protest social injustice.

I believe that as lesbians and gay men, we have the added challenge to avoid the traps laid out for us. When we fall for our enemies' tricks, we waste precious energies that we need to protect our very lives. There's a real war going on in the culture. We need to be ready with counter-offensives to the radical right's often brilliant and effective propaganda. To survive, we must identify and promote our lesbian-feminist queer cultural values, or we, too, will die in polluted water as we try to navigate the so-called mainstream's double-talk.

I've been talking of "we," and I just said "our" values. Shaky ground here, but let me try to map some out. I see lesbian-feminism practiced when I read calls for submissions to lesbian-feminist anthologies and journals that read "people of color encouraged to submit" or "nonsexist, nonracist material only." No mainstream house has ever voiced such a concern.

Indeed, how many lesbians and gay men want to live in the white-house-and-picket-fence monogamy that is presented as the all-American way? Isn't the nuclear family dependent on the fact that the woman bears the burden of being the man's emotional support and ass-wipe? Do we want to procreate domestic violence, incest, and collusive silence around these all-American norms? As far as a countercultural dream of building a cabin in the country goes, no thank you. I'd be scared to death if I had to live in an isolated area without a large and immediate population of people of color.

＊＊＊

A telling marker of the ruling-class viewpoint has to do with whose lives make it to the page and just whose story is told. The upper classes had their dramas enacted as the experience we were supposed to take as "universal." Shakespeare's leading characters were court royalty. Well, I'm not exactly the queen of England, but I first recognized myself as a lesbian by name in the story of a British noblewoman. Before I finished Radclyffe Hall's *The Well of*

Loneliness, I knew my common bond with Stephen Gordon made us sisters. I had all the symptoms of her situation. As a tomboy long past the age when I should have outgrown the "phase," I waxed romantic over pretty girls; boys were fit companions, but of no interest beyond that. Clearly, I was destined to ride horses across the British countryside and become a champion fencer!

My emotional identification with Stephen Gordon was so all-encompassing that it didn't occur to me that my prospects as a nine-year-old Black kid from Brooklyn were not the same as a character like Stephen Gordon, who inherited wealth and class position. I didn't see my race and class then. How could I, having grown up on American myths in a Black neighborhood—not the slum that immediately comes to most people's minds when I say "a Black neighborhood"? Coming from a racially mixed neighborhood meant I didn't have white children taunting me with their privileged place in society by pointing out that I was the "nigger." That was to come later.

The next lesbians I could find in hardcover came via Jeanette Forster's *Sex Variant Women in Literature.* I unearthed that gold mine from the Brooklyn Public Library's card catalog under the heading "lesbians." The literary lesbians the book directed me to, such as Natalie Barney, Sappho, Gertrude Stein, and Djuna Barnes, wrote about the concerns of upper-class women. They who lived on unearned income would likely take one look at me and imagine a cleaning woman or, at best, a housekeeper. Not much probability that they'd recognize a sister spirit, because class identification is so much more rigid in the upper registers of the social scale.

Nor did I understand much of what I read by Stein and those others. I was in my teens looking for evidence of my lesbian self at the library. The literature that spoke clearly of my possibilities was the soft-core lesbian porn of the 1960s—writers like Ann Bannon, March Hastings, Joan Ellis, Dallas Mayo, and Sloane Brittain, whom I happened upon in the adult books section of drugstores. Later I searched for these books with an eye peeled for paperbacks that wore suggestive covers and had blurbs that spoke the titillating promise of unnatural lives. I kept these "trashy" books even more furtively hidden than *True Romance* and *Real Love* magazines. These softcovers were my bridge to lesbian likelihood not offered by the literary novels whose minor lesbian characters *Sex Variant Women in Literature* recommended to me.

That was thirty years ago. Since then, feminist presses have widened the spectrum of whose lives can be revealed on the page. Publishing for the mainstream American audience has also broadened to include more of the world than British royalty and the American upper classes.

I am a writer. I work a full-time job and write after work hours, or during times of unemployment that I extend as long as I dare. That's the reality for most of the writers that I know. We are of a class that must pay for our right to write. Virtually everyone has a day job to support her writing ventures. We pay more in postage and xeroxing fees than we are remunerated for in our efforts to publish in feminist, lesbian, and gay literary journals and anthologies.

The work of the literary artist may merit admiration in some circles, but in dollars and sense, this work is considered an extracurricular activity. Very few writers are paid the superstar salaries that we hear bestseller-list authors command. My peers skeptically mock these authors as sell-outs who couldn't write their way out of a paper bag. We frown on those who we perceive to write for a commercial market, and hold ourselves superior because we write to the calling of art. But until recently, I did not know that the people who originally could speak of "art for art's sake" came from the class of inherited wealth. Many people take on that notion without awareness of its class implications.

The deeper meaning of writers' refusal to aim for the commercial market is that we refuse to reproduce mainstream values that decry queers as "cowardly perverts" and render heterosexuals the only heroes. This is a brave and revolutionary stance. The facts of our lives as lesbians and gay men speak a greater truth than the common morality's prejudiced misinformation. The courageous work of telling our particular truth as lesbians and gay men does not result in the kind of profit-making product that heterosexual Gothic romances or police procedural mysteries—genres that have delighted me when written in dyke—are for their makers. Even on the left banks of the mainstream, heterosexist ethics hold as firmly as they do in *Cosmopolitan* and *Penthouse* magazines.

Frankly, I envy people who don't have to work for survival. I want to hear of their lives and not sneer as if my working-classness were superior to their owning-classness. Most people I know express scorn about people who don't need to hold tight to a job for an income—"His daddy pays the bills"—even as we all want that hallowed situation—"Wish I had me a trust fund to live off of." Yet I think these sentiments carry an honest recognition that the class system is so grossly unfair.

We live within an economic system that allows some people to have such astronomical wealth that luxury cars like the Mercedes Benz and the Lexus are selling better than ever. This economic environment accounts for people who *have to* work three jobs in order to pay the rent and be able to call themselves "middle-class."

Too many people simply do not question the belief that somebody has to be the low class by which we measure human worth. One aspect to some African American men's homophobia, as it is expressed in hip-hop culture, is that these young Black men—who are slated for America's rock bottom—finally have a people they can look down on—queers.[1]

The current intensification of diva bitchiness and dissing that is so popular these days seems to me a variation on Lady Uppercrust looking down on the commoners. It serves the ruling class when people who are in the same boat put down and attack one another. The "divide and conquer" strategy is set in motion when we fight for the crumbs of an imagined social status rather than taking on the difficult, fearful work of standing up to our true oppressors.

The desire to be "better than" and rule over others derives from identifying with the ruling class, never unmasking the assumptions that go with "ruler." In *The Wizard of Oz,* Dorothy didn't strongly challenge the "little man behind the curtain," but exposing his machinations forced him to release some of his illusory power.

***

Given survival needs, what do we write? Is it poetry that we perform in poetry slams? Do we compose short stories and write "flash fictions" more often than taking up a novel with its enormous demands for time? For a long time I couldn't even consider a novel. Some of the reasons had to do with earning a living and dealing with the world that makes unfair, extra demands on me to dance around white racism, sexism, and homophobia.

A Black woman with little money doesn't have the same social leeway as a white man who is also a literary artist. People who consider him romantic in his financial straits scorn me if I show monetary caution. They show flickers of suspicion as they readily call to mind headlines about welfare fraud and transfer my face to the photo above the caption "welfare cheat." But such is not the case for a white man who puts out that he is "short on cash flow."

His poverty has a certain romance and classiness to it. Most people applaud his noble efforts to earn a living. They somehow believe that his ship will come in, he'll get on his feet to stand firm financially and get his due artistic acclaim. And in a sense, they're right: he is more likely to make it, given the cultural bias in his favor. This seems the literary equivalent of cabs that screech to a halt at the feet of those who need only to push back their blond tresses to hail a taxi, but others have to wave dollar bills in the air and show seriously bad attitude for twenty minutes just to get a cab ride across town.

I witness how often my spoken claim that I'm a writer is met with surprise. "What do you mean you're a writer?" said with cynical assurance that I'm covering up some kind of hustle, probably drug-dealing. If I speak of limited monetary resources, the world at large has no tolerance, much less understanding, that a societal structure is at work beyond my individual choices. Poor people, particularly those of color, receive no compassion for the fact that the class structure makes it a lot harder for us to gain social status and financial security as rewards for hard labor.

The average American's training to accept class hierarchy fogs our vision of its existence, but we can discern its reflection of the world at large in the work arena. The writing realm is an editor's market—more wordsmiths exist than places to publish our wares. We supply the labor and raw materials, work for no pay beyond the eager hope of acceptance, will rewrite on the possibility of further consideration. Would that I could buy my fruit and vegetables at the market or drive a car from the lot on such a basis: let me try it out, and if I like it, I'll pay you.

But as someone who wants her work published, I keep my ears tuned to what songs publications play. I will aim work for specific anthology topics because the opportunity to be published is a distinct factor in the give-and-take of being influenced and influencing. I also know full well that editors need their publications to profit. Alternative presses have other concerns, but the financial bottom line is just as clearly written on their list of things to do.

I think that because I grew up believing my family was middle-class rather than working-class poor, I didn't feel that writing was only a distant star to wish on. I could set my sights on that desire and think it just as possible for me to achieve renown as it was for anyone else. I am grateful for my naive ignorance of the social realities surrounding who I am. It served to keep my impulse to write alive in the face of the expectations that I would grow up to be a domestic worker, crack prostitute, or welfare mother.

What did galvanize my desire to be a writer was reading Paule Marshall's *Brown Girl, Brownstones*. The picture of Marshall on the book's back cover gave concrete evidence for my own possibility. A further incident that seemed to have no great merit at the time, but that gave a solid form to support my dream, was happening on TV programs that featured Lucille Clifton and June Jordan broadcast into my family living room. Here I witnessed two more African American women paid homage for their work as writers.

Certainly I'd heard of Gwendolyn Brooks and the canon of Black male writers from the Harlem Renaissance, but those literary figures somehow didn't make an impression on my sense of possibility. I've only recently understood the importance of such "role models," particularly for young people who do not see anyone who looks like themselves giving life to their dreams.

I grew up on the American mythology that success was guaranteed to anyone who worked hard enough for it. Children in my neighborhood were schooled that merit and quality would outstrip any social ills—in my adolescent years, racism held prominence as the injustice we'd have to overcome. My parents, both people from Caribbean immigrant families, also absolutely believed that truth and justice as the American way would prevail in all realms. Not until my early twenties did I acquire a body of knowledge steeped in life experience that proved otherwise. Political movements for social justice led me to notice and factor in my African descent, my female caste, my queerness.

Eventually I came to see that my best bet for publication would be within the lesbian-feminist community. Having a greater sense of racism and homophobia, I couldn't imagine that "mainstream" houses would want to hear my take on the world. American culture is sodden with racism, sexism, and homophobia.

I did find a home for my work in lesbian and feminist publications. I might have enjoyed reading *Black World* and *Black Scholar* when I went to college, but I knew they wouldn't welcome my feminist insights, lesbo characterizations, or any queer motifs in my writing. I am still continually surprised when African American, queer, and real-life women writers are published and praised on their merits rather than from tokenism, fetishization, or crass exploitation.

I came of age during an era when the stuff of a writer's life was encouraged to be her subject matter. This marked a shift in class perspective. Previously never-to-be-considered "crude" and "low-class" notions, like the point of view of African Americans on themselves, my rites of passage as a lesbian, or a person of color's perspective on the world, have come to be sought after by one branch of the power structure: mass media. Such was not the case as little as forty years ago.

I could recognize tokenism and racism behind some of my opportunities to get into print. And I sought to reap what advantage I could. I'd felt encouraged by white feminists' early, awkward grapplings to get beyond their racism. Sometimes this resulted in efforts to put women of color in the forefront. Fortunately, for the ego of my younger self, I didn't fully grasp the off-note when some women didn't seem truly to be coming from the heart. I later realized this dissonance was liberal guilt, not a heartfelt sense of sisterhood.

My grasp of the situation led me to submit work to publications that have been criticized for their overwhelmingly white mastheads. I suspected that editors would be looking to be sure their next issue was more strongly populated by people of color.

A level of good intention and the struggle to not be oppressive are at work when publishers want to hear from "minority" and oppressed people. Though these motivations are praiseworthy,

I've yet to see such efforts go so far that the people in power relinquish all their privileges to the ones to whom they feel so generous during any particular era of heightened political awareness around race issues.

In fact, many whites think they're doing the coloreds a favor. They actively deny the fact that their systematic power and privilege come with prices paid by depriving colored people of dignity and respect. What these white people don't acknowledge is that American society's class structure is premised on the kind of affirmative action that gives white male people the first pick of everything.

In situations where racist beliefs have not been deeply rooted out, politically conscious good intentions degenerate into a one-upmanship among whites. An example I've witnessed is when white women have used the lack of colored women's representation as a weapon to score points against one another. Believe me, the fruits of racism taste no less bitter when delivered by lesbian or gay practitioners.

One of the functions of class has to do with limiting what people believe they're entitled to reach for. The correspondence in literature is that people in the lower class have traditionally supplied stories for middle- and upper-class writers. We latter-day peasants were not expected to write our versions, nor were we encouraged to spin our class visions on the tales we told.[2] We could be mined and exploited for raw material, but we didn't yet have the natural right to narrate with our own language and be respected for our analysis.

Only through the efforts of African American and feminist movements for social justice have some of the veneers of psychological colonization been unmasked. We know that history, a literary form, has been written by the victor and the oppressor, and that the majority of peoples have been left out of the text. The keepers of the castle were shown to have lied about the underclasses when poor folks made it even to the margins of the pages that highlight privilege and power. The missing gaps are like a difference of opinion between a Mack truck and a pedestrian. As a direct result of

African American struggles, other oppressed groups have also sought to unearth the bigger picture and write their own histories.

In true American fashion, this alternative truth-telling has become a product that is marketed and sold to those it has relevance for. The net effect is that the publishing corporations run by ruling-class white boys, some of whom are female and colored, are once again enriched off our backs.

Yes, we get to write during the time we can spare after taking care of survival needs. The catch is, given the class set-up of the publishing industry, the usual suspects still profit from work that was, at its first inception, derided for being "on the fringe," "off-beat," "stridently feminist," or by "crazy niggers."

Lesbian-feminist and gay presses that first took the risk to pub-lish this new and exciting material were lucky if they broke even financially. Mainstream publishers and popular media take note of a new market and step in to reap a handsome profit. It seems the more things change, the more they remain the same.

Still, I write. It's not as if knowing the air is polluted can restrain anyone from breathing. Putting my vision out there works like emission controls on vehicles—unclassified truth helps prevent the pollution from getting worse and allows us all to breathe easier.

Notes

1. This thought was passed on to me by Maua, Yvonne Flowers, elder in the lesbian African American community.

2. Essays by Elliot and Joanna Kadi in *Out of the Class Closet: Lesbians Speak,* ed. Julia Penelope (Freedom, CA: The Crossing Press, 1994).

mother poem

MIRANDA MELLIS

pouring juice from a blue jar
braiding my hair
throwing a paint bomb at a billboard
sweeping up anguish
broken glass from a fist through a window
with her wing-tipped broom
she's been told she leaks a poison from her heart.
i inherit the feeling, and her barricade, like a fence
that only spirits get past
she was framed and so i, unnamed
redress. because i can't live that silenced way
—daughter of the shamed—
so i honor her.

sequence of events:
burrowing into her bare back
p o l i t i c s filet of sole j u s t i c e
blueberry pancakes p o r k c h o p s solidarity d y k e .

all those churches housing banner-makers at night
we wore gauchos and tried to feather my curly hair
cut off our barbies' heads
while she postered/smoked/wept for sunrise tanks
she
consulted oracles on her children's behalf
availed herself of the opiates of the masses
went on strike/wore combat boots/taught at high schools
    called
Sunshine, and Opportunity.
she had a girlfriend
named diana that
disappeared
i was eleven
(something to do with retributive armed robbery
by which i was inspired to dream
of redistribution
of wealth)
diana was a goddess, right
underground like persephone (and in case you're a cop
    maybe
diana's not
Her Real Name)

guerrilla
third generation axis/con/artist
there is room for
all that scavenging pain, knowledge, and depression
mind a stinging hive and longing for human liberation
the mural in the hall, and the welfare check for toast today

and your voice downstairs i heard
(when politics was just a word)

she threaded my young mind incrementally
with simple values, like
always fight back
only steal from the biggest stores
work the landscape as outlaw
view it as mutable
imagination is the weapon of choice
your will is not the measure of all things
we are masked by contingencies
and revealed in action.
i perched on her bed
to drink desperation's wisdom
precious like untold history
a circuitry
of mated worlds–tenderness, war, abuse, and resistance
vanity and insurrection, poverty and extravagance
joy and beauty in a terrible state
and despite governments
this is one who knows her mother from the frame they
    give her

"it has not paid to cherish symbols
when the substance is so close at hand"[1]
earth, beneath concrete skirt;
fill my mouth and eyes with your daughters
    i am taking a very old way

Note

1. Audre Lorde, "Walking Our Boundaries," in *The Black Unicorn: Poems* (New York: Norton, 1978).

A Boy's Own Class

WILLIAM J. MANN

Our deck this summer has afternoon sun, something to which we've all resigned ourselves. "Our *last* deck," I tell visitors, "faced the east. Not only could we see the bay, but having coffee first thing in the morning with the sun full on your faces..."

I don't need to finish. They understand.

Here in Provincetown, decks matter. The strategic placement of the deck—whether it takes morning or afternoon sun, whether it looks out over the placid bay or the cacophony of Commercial Street—directly affects a house's summer rental price. "But where's the *deck*?" we always ask, first thing.

Sitting here now, moving my chair to follow the arc of the sun despite the sunblock plastered all over my face, I'm thinking about decks, and views of the bay, and summers in Provincetown. We've been coming here for five years now, my boyfriend and I and our closest friend. Always a different house, each one better than the last as we become more precise, more particular about what makes for good summer space. Except, of course, for the concession this year regarding the deck: but still, the place has two and *a half* bathrooms this year as opposed to two, and somehow we've managed to snare *three* precious parking spaces—among the rarest of rare commodities in this burgeoning queer resort town. Such things make up for the lack of morning sun: we shall, as my boyfriend says, survive.

And sitting here, baking in the midday rays, my cellular phone on a table near my elbow, I laugh. "How the hell did you ever wind up here, kid?" I ask myself. "Who the fuck do you think you are?"

"I don't know, Ma," I answer, still laughing. "Some days it's sure hard to figure."

My mother, of course, never used words like "hell" or "fuck." My mother has much more class than that, but it's *her* voice that I hear, nonetheless.

"I try to be a little classy every now and then," she's telling my boyfriend, showing him around her house, pointing out the baskets she's hung on the walls, their little "Made in Taiwan" stickers still clinging to the centers. "This is the style now," she says, pointing with her thumb over her shoulder. "Baskets on walls."

A few days later, when I tell her that we will take a house on the Cape for the summer yet again, she echoes: "What's that, the style now? Going back to the same place every year for your vacation?"

"It's not really a vacation, Ma," I explain. "It's a place we go to get away."

"Get away from what?" she asks.

You see, my mother and father have always had a much different view of time off. They worked hard: my father as a shoe salesman, my mother as a secretary. Vacations meant a break, but not necessarily a rest. Vacations were an opportunity to do the things they didn't have a chance to do the rest of the year—like cleaning out the attic or painting the garage. My parents always made sure to take their two-week vacations while we kids were on summer break. That way, between coats on the garage, we could all pile into the Chevy and head down for a day at Rocky Neck State Beach, with dinner at the Big Boy ending the day. "Go ahead," my mother would consent, "have the brownie sundae with the peanut butter ice cream. Can't get that at home."

Once back home, there'd be another coat of paint applied to the garage. My father would have us mowing the grass or trimming the hedges. I used to cut the grass in geometric patterns—stars, spirals, curlicues—lording over the lawn on my father's ride-on mower. These were days free from school, from homework, from early-to-bed rules. These were vacations.

If vacation means a respite from work, then it has a different connotation for the working class. "What do you *do* when you go up there?" my mother asks about our time on the Cape. "There's only so many times you can go on a whale watch."

Ah, Provincetown. That sublime spit of sand at the very tip of Cape Cod, farther away from the rest of the world than anyplace else on the planet. At least for me: here, on my deck—in morning *or* afternoon sun—I lie and dream lazily about stories I am writing, characters I am creating, scenarios I am manipulating. It is a place grounded in creativity, culture, tradition. Here lies buried the very first Pilgrim ever to set foot on American soil. The Mayflower docked here, in the winter, before moving on to settle at Plymouth. Later, in the mid-nineteenth century, Portuguese fishermen settled here, bringing with them their ships and their nets and their wives, forging a hardy community that weathered not only the blistering summers but also the deep and bitterly isolating winters. Devoutly Catholic, the Portuguese prized hard work and family: they would have found common ground with the Pilgrims buried off Shank Painter Road.

But by the turn of the century, immigrants of another sort had arrived: artists, who found in this place at the end of the world the sanctuary they needed to create. That, in turn, opened the door for the queers: wherever the arts thrive, we aren't far behind. From art colony to gay resort—complete with drag queens barking at tourists to come see Liza and Cher and Marilyn, and buffed bar boys parading down Commercial Street in nothing but lycra shorts—Provincetown has long accommodated two very different populations, and not always with as much tolerance as the publicists would like to suggest.

"Shall we just turn our heads and ignore what they do?" asked one outraged fisherman a few years back, when controversy swirled about the late-night activities of the gay tourists, who were congregating in the street after the bars closed. There were reports of sex on the tops of cars, drunken carousing in backyards of year-round homes. "Shall we just let them take our town away from us?" the man with the deeply creased face and pipe between his teeth had asked.

Of course, there were the usual homophobic slurs and the resultant accusations of bigotry. "These *fishermen*!" sniffed one gay summer resident, as if to say: *Don't they know I should be able to do whatever I please because I've paid good money for a condo here and that keeps this miserable little fishing village alive?*

That summer resident might actually have passed by one of those fishermen at 3 a.m., trudging down Bradford Street toward the wharf, heading out for another day at sea. The summer resident, of course, would be *ending* his day, just back from the dick dock, tired and sated, looking forward to that comfortable bed in that comfortable condo on the bay.

"*That's* unfortunate," said a friend, as we cut through the Portuguese section of town on our way to the Love Shack.

He was gesturing to a small house with a neatly trimmed yard. The house was quiet and dark, the family asleep, as most families are at midnight on a Monday. In the short driveway a child's tricycle was trimmed with long green and red tassels. Along the edge of the house were planted pink and blue plastic roses, presided over by the Virgin Mary in a clamshell.

"*Plastic*," my friend said. "They're plastic. Can they not afford *seeds*?"

My mother's voice, again: "Oh, thanks, they *are* pretty, aren't they? But they're not real."

The geraniums in the window boxes on the side of my mother's house were plastic. "I wanted something really bright over there," she explained to the neighbor who commented on them. "Something that'd stand out."

Once, I thought there was nothing wrong with plastic geraniums. There was an entire aisle of plastic flowers in Woolworth's that I would parade down as a boy—Princess Anne on her wedding day, strolling under a trellis in the gardens at Buckingham Palace. Artificial flowers entice a young gay boy's imagination—but I came to learn they offend an adult gay man's sensibilities.

The first summer I ever spent in Provincetown, I tricked with a beautiful dark-eyed boy who said he was in town only for the weekend. The next morning, he confessed.

"I was born here," he said. "My parents still live here. I'm home visiting."

"Really?" I asked. "That must have been interesting, growing up gay in a gay town."

"It was hell," he said plainly.

His name was Peter. His last name told me he hailed from one of the large Portuguese families in town. It was hell, he said, not because his parents were necessarily homophobic—although they'd been known to make fag comments every now and then—but because the gays were viewed as the rich out-of-towners, coming in to take away their village.

"It's not so much that you all are gay," Peter said to me, "but because *they* think *you* think you're better than them."

The twist on the conventional gay-straight dichotomy was not lost on me, nor was the significance of Peter's reference to me as "you all"—as if I were part of something he was not. This was a man with whom I had just made wild, intense love for nearly four hours, and yet he saw us as different, as part of two worlds, separated by a chasm as large as the one he no doubt felt between himself and his parents.

How to explain I, too, felt that way? That sometimes I had this unnerving notion that my life here, on this deck, in this sun, was a charade? "*How the hell did you ever wind up here, kid?*" I've asked myself, time and again. From the little factory town where I was born and those vacations at Rocky Neck, how did I end up sharing a house in the tony west end of Provincetown, every summer for the entire summer, year after year?

It's simple: I'm gay.

Had I not been gay—had I been my brother, for example—I would never have discovered the access that led me to a different place. My brother and I attended the same college, a state university not far from where I grew up. But only *I* ventured into a world my parents had never known. Had I not been a gay kid, I would never have been invited into that world. A visiting gay lecturer took me to dinner and later introduced me to well-known activists and writers when I visited him in Boston. I became involved in the effort to pass a gay rights bill; I made friends with the state's liberal politicos. Every June, I'd head down to New York (my mother a nervous wreck) to attend the gay pride celebrations. I met people, I read books, I listened to speeches.

For me, my awareness of class arose along with my queer consciousness. They are inextricable. Had I not been gay, I wonder, would I be like my brother, secure in his class, happy to be a

Knight of Columbus chugging beer on a Friday night, playing bas-
ketball with the guys, taking his kids to spaghetti suppers at the
local Italian eatery and his wife to the annual Spring Fling thrown
by the Junior Women's Club? There's a beauty in that, of course, a
simple but nonetheless profound beauty. Had I not been gay, that
could well have been me, and I might not have been unhappy.

But that's *not* me. I make less money than my brother, but I
have stepped out of my class origins while he has not. Money matters little in any discussion of class, except for the access it offers. If one does not aspire to use such access, however, all the
money in the world will not transform one's class. My brother
takes his kids for a day at Rocky Neck still; I summer on the Cape.
My weekends are often spent in New York seeing a Broadway
show or the opening of a Manet exhibit. Yet dinner at a Big Boy
still suffices as much as at the new Thai eatery our gay friends all
rave about. I enjoy shopping at the mall nearly as much as I do the
boutiques of SoHo. (*"Really,"* I can hear my mother saying, "the
parking's *so* much easier at the mall"—and I find myself agreeing
with her more and more.)

What does it mean to be gay and working-class? The first gay
people I knew were not working-class: in fact, I've known precious few, even now. Perhaps that's because to be working-class—
or at least, to show the *signs* of it—is anathema to a particularly
dominant part of gay male culture. We eroticize the image of the
oil-blackened mechanic or the stable boy who creeps into our bed-
rooms in the middle of the night: Who can ever forget that scene
in *Maurice*, where the unspoiled nature of the working-class lover
transforms the jaded, unhappy aristocrat? Yet to admit one's
mother displayed plastic geraniums would be "unfortunate." Our
sexual desires may be rooted in our humble pasts, but not our cultural tastes, which determine how we are or are *not* accepted by a
society that devalues our lives. They are rooted in our own homophobia. Being gay is bad enough, we reason: we must prove that
we at *least* have taste. And so: the stereotypes of the opera queen
and the beer-guzzling straight man.

The very first out gay men I ever met, back in the early 1980s
when I was still in college, were two wealthy white men who
lived in a great apartment, held great jobs (architect and graphic

designer), and had great taste. They taught me the importance of being out, but also the importance of being—well, *classy*. But not in the way my mother used the word. I learned that to be "classy" really meant something else: "Oh, he has no *class*," the men would sigh over a local salesclerk with a mustache and a 1979 Pontiac Firebird—two accessories I would have found, in my closeted high school days, very attractive. I quickly observed that to be gay meant one had to "have class"—in other words, to assimilate into the rarefied world as quickly as possible, to reject anything in one's background that was less than fabulous, and to learn all the requirements of a gay culture that seeks to give the impression we're all upper-middle-class: an appreciation of opera, classical music, literature, film, art, design, fine dining. And to act as if—even when it wasn't the case—we all have plenty of disposable income to throw around.

I observed something else as well, something that undercut the refined image but was nonetheless just as essential in becoming gay. And that was an appreciation for other, less genteel things: tea rooms and rest stops, bars and dance floors, Jeff Stryker videos and *Honcho* magazine.

Those latter categories I had no trouble with. In those places, in those activities, the class divide was less apparent. The dick dock in Provincetown is a great equalizer: I've watched my share of condo owners suck off their share of houseboys.

But I struggled with the other categories, the ones of culture and rarefied achievement. My parents' taste in music had not ranged very far from Perry Como and Dean Martin. They never sidetripped to the Museum of Modern Art on our way to Rocky Neck. And it didn't matter how many forks one used at the Big Boy.

The divide in Provincetown is a class divide. It is not about sexuality. It is about working folk who have accepted homes in the less attractive part of town because the wealthy summer people have claimed the best real estate. It is about a way of life that threatens to be disrupted not by sex on the tops of cars in the middle of the night but by a blatant disregard for people's place, the humble but nonetheless well-guarded niche they have managed to carve for themselves.

"I understand," I said to Peter. "I really do."

He doubted it. Still, he took me to meet his parents, although he debated the wisdom of doing so. Not because of their reaction to me: their acceptance of his queerness had been lukewarm but real. It was *my* reaction he worried about, something I understood fully. My first lover had been upper-middle-class. I never brought him to my parents' home. He never saw their faux oakwood paneling and the fact that we had no dining room, that we ate every meal in the kitchen.

Peter's parents asked me to stay for dinner. "It's just frozen fried chicken," his mother apologized, but I *loved* frozen fried chicken. Always have, ever since my mother would serve those Swanson's TV dinners. Peter's parents warmed to me then. We talked about student loans and car payments and the problems with health insurance and cash advances on our credit cards. We had both used such advances to pay bills in the past: paying off debt by accumulating more. I'd used cash advances a couple of times as my share of the deposit on our summer places. "*That's* how you afford it?" his father asked me.

"That and friends," I said.

They were fascinated by our rather socialist arrangement: each of us put in as much as we could, and somehow we always managed to end up with enough to rent a place every summer. That some ended up paying more was not an issue, a fact that troubled Peter's father. "Seems everybody should pay equal," he insisted.

That was a point of divergence for us. We could relate about many things, but this was not one of them. Neither was the sex at the dick dock. "But it's on private property and the owner doesn't care," I argued, "and there are no houses anywhere around." But there was no persuading Peter's father. "It's just *wrong*," he said. He wasn't wild about the drag queens walking down Commercial Street in their sequins and pumps, either. But when *Roseanne* came on we all laughed together, and the homemade chocolate cake with the sugar frosting and M&Ms on top, served for Peter's birthday—exactly the kind my mother always made for me—was better than anything I'd ever tasted from the trendy French bakery all the queens patronized on Commercial Street.

"It's all in how you beat the eggs," his mother confided to me.

A couple of years later, I am at another gathering, in another part of Provincetown: a condo with a fabulous deck on the bay, with skylights that reveal the stars. The party is peopled with gay white men, whose first names are interchangeable with their last: Chandler. Forsythe. Carter. Somehow the topic has become classical music, one area in which I have not yet given myself a crash course.

In my quest to acclimatize myself to the cultural requirements of the gay set, I had sought out all the appropriate texts and cultural artifacts I hadn't been exposed to growing up. Film I had already mastered as a college kid; literature came about the same time; politics a little later. But I was still in the catch-up phase for classical music. And so, at this party, I sit singularly silent.

"Was Chopin gay?" they ask each other.

"*Please*—you actually *like* Brahms?"

"Don't you think gay men tend to prefer rococo sonatas?"

Before the topic of sonatas had overrun the conversation, we had been talking about the dick dock. I had delighted in exchanging tips on cruising and public sex with these men. They were new to me, friends of friends, and I knew little about their backgrounds except for what I assumed. Of course, assumption is always a dangerous thing—not to mention unfair. "I trust no one who has never had to struggle," a friend once said to me, and I wondered, sitting there, about the adversities these men had faced. Not to deny them their own particular struggles, but I wondered nonetheless. What family network had eased their way into a prestigious school? What connections landed them their first jobs? Which Ivy League professor had found them the internship that launched their careers? What college chum of their father's had sublet them their first apartment in the Village? Class is, after all, about connections: that invisible chain of helping hands that keeps the rich white boys in power, a de facto reverse form of affirmative action. And the twist is: many are not even aware of their good fortune. The surest sign of privilege is the assumption that one has a right to it, and so one often remains blithely unaware of another's struggle.

Sitting there, I felt once again the divide between two separate parts of myself. I was *expected* to know the difference between a rococo sonata and any other kind, just as I was *expected*, at Peter's parents' house, to reject the notion of sex on the beach if I were to truly be accepted by them. To which world did I belong, if either?

Yet I choke back my own resentment and try to give the bene-

fit of the doubt. Perhaps many in that room overlooking the bay
had grown up in factory towns similar to mine. Perhaps many had
had to hold down jobs while going to college. Perhaps many were
still struggling with student loans and car payments. Perhaps many
secretly delighted in a meal at the Big Boy or a shopping spree at
Wal-Mart. But once the conversation moved onto sonatas, one
might reasonably suspect all of these men had come from the
same exact place, so complete was their presentation.

The schism between the classes is very real, and it is likely even
more apparent among the gentrified world of the gay elite. It is, perhaps, a uniquely gay *male* phenomenon: the lesbians in Provincetown, at least, do not move in the same set as the men, and my
lesbian friends both there and elsewhere say the class demands I
describe are not the same for them. But other gay male friends,
when pushed, admit to a certain pressure to hide their particular
classed culture, that to be out as a working-class gay man means to
restrict their gay community in many ways.

I know the fear. In that room overlooking the bay, we all were
male, we all were queer, we all were white, we all were (roughly)
of the same generation. Yet my world only barely intersected with
theirs, and even at those points, only through my own determined
manipulation. As I sat there, mute and uncomfortable, I felt as if I
were about to be discovered, my secret revealed. "You're from
where?" they'd ask. "*Where* did you go to school?" And I'd
promptly be kicked out of their exclusive club.

Now, sitting here on my deck, as the afternoon sun begins to
set, I muse about that term: *out working-class gay man.* How
many do I know? How many do I see in the gay media, in positions
of leadership in the queer movement? Can I even claim the term
myself anymore, sitting here on my Provincetown deck? How
many of us can—despite how much we owe, or where we went to
school, or how much we know about sonatas. How many of us
have so deeply hidden our origins that even a sincere attempt at
beauty like planting plastic flowers becomes "unfortunate"?

But fortune lies not so much in the trappings of an exacting
class, but rather in the simple integrity of my mother's definition of
the word. "I try to be a little *classy* every now and then," she says—
and my mother has a lot of class.

Growing Up
in Two Closets

Class and Privilege in
the Lesbian and Gay Community

DAVID P. BECKER

I n a 1978 article for *Gay Community News*, I wrote about growing up in two closets, about being both gay and very rich. I
talked then about the contradictions of being a member of such
different minorities—one oppressed, one the oppressor—and the
ability to pass in both "normal," heterosexist culture and the
marginalized lesbian and gay community. At that time, I wrote
under a pseudonym, more afraid about revealing my class privilege
than my sexuality. In so many ways, the money has been much
more difficult to speak about. There are justified negative feelings
about great wealth in a politically oppressed and aware community, and it has been personally risky to come out of my "privilege
closet." However, it is vitally important to establish such a dialogue in order to build a strong foundation for social change at all
levels, and my political work over the past twenty years has been
directed toward that goal.

Today, I write under my real name, and again I name my multiple
privileges: white, male, rich, graduate school-educated, upper-class-
connected, health-insured, etc., etc. My father's father founded a
sizable bank; my mother's grandfather founded one of the largest

corporations in the country. Above all, growing up in a rich family is an incredibly *protected* experience. We had a very large home, 200 acres of land, lots of possessions, private schools, servants. There were virtually no interactions with people not of my background, except for the servants, with whom I was often closer than I was with my parents, and who were the only working-class people I knew for years. I grew up alone and was not encouraged to meet people in the nearby town. The spoken and unspoken lessons I received to uphold the status quo of the class structure and our family's place in it were very thorough and effective.

My various closets were very inefficient. For years I separated my life into different compartments: I couldn't tell my family I was gay, I couldn't tell my gay friends I was rich, and I certainly couldn't tell the rest of the world I was either. This effort took a *lot* of energy, and I felt very isolated. I spent a lot of time trying to disguise my true identities in all aspects of my life. In the sixties, for instance, I often lied about my trademark middle name—Pillsbury. It wasn't particularly cool then to be an heir to a corporate fortune, even if it was in cake mixes. It can be difficult to work through all this baggage toward an analysis of its origins and effects, particularly when awareness of its obvious inequity produces strong guilt feelings and a desire to hide or avoid the contradictions.

Silence is my family's preferred method of dealing with doubts or resistance around both sexuality and social change. Any questions in such a family about poverty or violence are met with smooth, reassuring explanations. Non-assertiveness is a prized attribute; after all, if one controls the means of production and policing, one doesn't need to be outwardly assertive (although there are complexities here in comparing male/female, straight/queer conditioning). More and more, I realize what a narrow escape I made from following the path laid out for me (i.e., toward the executive suite and the country club). One of the biggest potholes, of course, was my sexuality; treated with total silence, it told me early on that in one important respect, at least, I did not belong. I think that in rich families, however, silence around money is even stronger than that around sex. There are many secrets in rich families around both subjects, and any breach of the silence is regarded as a betrayal. My coming out publicly in the media about my sexuality and privilege did not go over too well. I was asked just why I felt I had to *talk* about it, *if* I was asked about it at all. I actually think my family has been much more freaked out by my philanthropy, both its extent and its non-traditional direction. They seem to think I'm actually throwing the family money away. This goes for families of origin and such family hangers-on as bankers and lawyers.

I still haven't figured out what combination of circumstance and character has enabled a few upper-class (I sometimes use the term "ruling-class") women and men to overcome and analyze the disparity between their lives and those of the majority of the world. (Thanks to the feminist movement and other factors, I must add that more women have succeeded in this transformation.) College was my first opportunity for some clarity. Even in Maine during the 1960s, the combination of Vietnam, the Civil Rights movement, revolutionary folk songs, and personal relationships with working-class friends managed to wake me up. In addition, inheriting a million dollars as a college student quickly introduced me to many contradictions in my life: privately giving away thousands of dollars, privately still enjoying some of the perks of being rich, and publicly trying to maintain a fairly cheap lifestyle. In my case, the realization that I experienced discrimination as a gay man came quite early on, but the acknowledgment of my own privilege and its implications came much later, and I am still learning.

Finally, I did what many of us did, even before we realized why we did it. In 1975, I moved from small-town Maine to a big city—in my case, Boston. There, I soon fell into two communities that were to change my life considerably. The first, of course, was that of the many lesbians and gay men who were leading open (even happy) lives and helping others to do the same, working for our liberation; I was led to a valuable volunteer stint at *Gay Community News*, which also inspired me to help fund it for years. The second community was a fairly new group of people with similar backgrounds to mine who were meeting together and building new models of philanthropy, trying to build bridges between our resources and the different communities that needed them. In Boston, these efforts were centered around the Haymarket People's Fund, with which I have worked ever since. What I learned from my involvement within these two communities in particular was the vital connection between my own privilege at one end of the social scale and my distinctly underprivileged status as a gay man, among those toward the other end of the scale. *GCN* and Haymarket formed the foundation of my politics, illuminating an analysis of the class structure and the necessity of working in coalition to achieve social change.

Money and economic status play as powerful a role within the lesbian/gay community as they do in the larger society, even with racial and gender complexities and the often underground nature of our oppressive social systems. Within white gay male culture in particular, youth and looks of course are major considerations, often at least superficially overriding class. However, much as in the rest of culture as a whole, economic status retains in most instances the ultimate power. Inevitably, my own economic status has appeared sooner or later in all my interactions, serving to remind me of its force. It has reinforced a strong sense of isolation, for in reality I am a member of a minority within a minority, mirroring the fact that so much wealth is controlled by such a minuscule proportion of society.

In my early *GCN* article, I described my sexual coming-out process and my beginning attempts to own up to my privilege and to use it for social change. I argued then and still maintain that, though it is certainly not without risk, it is easier for lesbians and gay men with wealth to come out sexually. We can literally afford to come out, and we never lose our class privilege. Rarely will we lose anything, materially. Our privilege almost always affords us safety from physical and financial harm—if not from emotional pain, which of course does cross all classes. (I also don't advise progressive future heirs to jeopardize their financial inheritances without a good deal of thought!) As a result of our connections, too, we can often bring our concerns to very high levels. Money talks in our society, and many of us already have a great deal of political access because of that. It is very important to be visible in establishment settings, despite the discomfort, homophobia, and marginalization we experience at times. As much as I believe in individuals coming out sexually whenever they can, I believe it is *especially* important for those of us with money and privilege and access to come out, both for the individual and the society.

Coming out sexually, of course, is an essential step toward political awareness of heterosexual privilege and thus—ideally—a first step toward awareness of other forms of social and economic privilege. I have consistently urged other wealthy lesbians and gay men to make the connections between their privilege and their oppression, and to work toward social change. Over the years, I have met many rich lesbians who have done their analytical homework; the response from gay boys, however, has been underwhelming. Making these connections between privilege and underprivilege has inspired my work in the lesbian and gay and social change communities ever since.

Being visible is risky, and being visible around money carries its own particular problems. I mentioned earlier the feelings of isolation and fragmentation I had growing up rich and gay. Those feelings occasionally resurface even today. I am part of a minority, and our particular position of privilege and power within the lesbian/gay community isolates us at times. We need to accept that our money gives us power within our own and the larger communities, and acknowledge that that separates us from most of our allies in important ways. At the level of personal relationships, money can have a very touchy effect, of course, requiring a great deal of effort to deal with it. Within our larger community, those of us with money are the subjects of admiration, envy, attraction, stereotyping, flattery, on down the line. We also need to deal with the larger stereotype prevalent in the popular media, and especially the far right, that all lesbians and gay men are a monolithic wealthy elite. Most of us in the community (especially those without money!) know what a damn lie that is. That characterization is a perfect right-wing wedge issue, effectively isolating us from each other and other disenfranchised groups, in addition to echoing anti-Semitic slurs of the past. Such efforts require those of us with money to come out about our privilege in order to expose these lies, as difficult as that can be sometimes.

In my own case, this did not come about easily. Remnants of the old class-training were still present, and my own activism has been at times tempered by a certain inbred reticence. Confrontation is a very big no-no; I have not often been active in the streets. Instead, I have done a great deal more work understanding my own background, working with others from similar circumstances to understand theirs, and developing my own processes for giving money to social change efforts. My family's rule for philanthropy was to be "charitable," but not extravagantly so. The cardinal money rule is "don't touch the capital," much less give it away.

How do we encourage other gay men and lesbians to come out of the "privilege closet"? There has been some progress over the last decade, at least in the realm of fundraising for gay and lesbian organizations. The most notable example, of course, is the tremendous amount of money that has come from the community in response to AIDS (for too long, no money came from anywhere else). In addition, considerable funds have been raised to support electoral politics, exemplified by the success of the Human Rights Campaign, now one of the largest PACs in the nation. And slowly but surely, funds have increased for other types of community organizations, such as legal advocacy groups, community centers, and health clinics. We have come a long way: In a study commissioned in the late 1980s by the Working Group on Lesbian and Gay Funding of the National Network of Grantmakers, it was discovered that between 1982 and 1984, 100 of the largest foundations in the country gave only $42,000 to lesbian and gay organizations—representing 0.004 percent of their total resources. (Those foundations, of course, were founded by the richest families and corporations.) Now, at least some gay donors are giving gifts in the millions.

However, so much of this money has been given to reformist, assimilationist groups rather than more progressive, radical efforts, particularly those in communities of color or those working to build coalitions between groups. While legal reforms are undeniably crucial (especially for those without class privilege), other needs for change in the underlying system should not be passed by. There will be no true liberation if we fail to make such connections. These have included the efforts of gay liberationists in the anti-apartheid movement, and of lesbian and gay activists in the labor movement, such as queer supporters of striking mine workers in Great Britain, who organized a 1984 benefit with the fabulous name "Pits and Perverts."

It seems so simple to realize that the gay community cuts across all class lines, and that those with considerable class privilege could realize that AIDS strikes everyone, rich and poor (and access to health care is so often restricted to those who can afford it); that we are all subject to hate violence; that we are still criminals in many states if we "commit" sodomy. And, therefore, that we *all* are in this struggle together; that indeed we are in *all* struggles together. However, so many gay men and lesbians with money (both unearned and earned) have opted for self-protection from a hostile society through cultural consumerism and self-righteous complacency, while perhaps working for "civil rights"—for themselves. Such escapism was more understandable, perhaps, in the McCarthyite 1950s, but not in the Helmsite 1990s. I know many, many more ridiculously underpaid activists who tithe, who give away 10 percent of their income, than I do people with a *lot* more disposable income. Discouragingly, those with privilege, especially rich white guys, often just don't get it, and it's important for those of us who *do* get it to challenge that status-quo mindset.

From the moment I realized the implications of my inheritance, I knew that I wanted to somehow return money to the communities from which it came. I also learned it was important to give the community the choice of where that money could best be used, thereby giving up the inherent power that donors (especially large donors) have over organizations and agendas. This principle has been established by such groups as Haymarket, which turns over the funds it raises for grassroots political organizing in New England to funding boards made up of community activists. I have been giving money away for more than twenty-five years, and funding within the lesbian and gay community for twenty. In 1990, I set up OUT—A Fund for Lesbian and Gay Liberation, an activist-controlled national foundation based at the Funding Exchange in New York. I drew on the community foundation model represented by Haymarket and the Astraea National Lesbian Action Foundation, among others.

It is also important for progressive lesbian and gay donors to continue this work and call our own organizations to account and be witnesses to the larger social change movement. We don't generally have too many safe places to discuss the problematic aspects of class and money. In such a short space, I have been able only to sketch my own perspective, barely scratching the surface of the tremendously complex workings of class in the queer community. It is a difficult but important dialogue, and one that has been subject to its own painful silence. My own journey has been a long, continuing process of study, trust, and some fear (will I be seen only as a checkbook?), but what I have realized is that privilege is a tool, and must be used in working for liberation. Audre Lorde has spoken to this question eloquently: "To use privilege requires admitting to privilege, requires moving beyond guilt and accusation into creative action. Unused privilege becomes a weapon in the hand of our enemies."[1]

Note

1. Letter to *Gay Community News*, vol. 17 (January 21-27, 1990), 5.

Lucky

a conversation in many parts

SCOT NAKAGAWA & CATHERINE SAALFIELD

CATHERINE: The continuation of our spoken dialogue about dykes and fags and class—money and (as?) social structure—from Portland to Manhattan will now take place on the ever-expanding Internet as we e-mail each other bits and pieces of our related thoughts, pushing toward overdrive in the middle of this hot day, trying to avoid a personal system breakdown but working for the capitalist system breakdown. First, we need to lay out the process of this "dialogue." At my desk, I work out this explanation. You'll read it in Portland. Think a bit. We only get to sit across from each other at the kitchen table once a month or so when your work brings you here or when we're crashing together on someone's floor in a town neither of us calls home. We never get any writing done then. But this writing is some of the total of our dialogues—our spoken conversations—that do occur when we're in the same physical space or on the phone.

By interrogating the nature of dialogue that serves the purpose of social change, I think we've discovered the necessity of endurance, the role of long-term individual participation. In reference to a draft of this article, Susan Raffo called our kind of reflection and regurgitation "the slow drip-drip that leads to changes in thinking."

We cannot afford to forsake the thinking component of this process, the part where you and I don't talk for a couple of days, where we type up memories or personal analysis and then shoot our words over the fiberoptics into the other person's house and await a carefully constructed, thoughtful, cohesive, and challenging response. But enough about all this. Let's start talk-writing and see where it takes us....

SCOT: I believe we are living in a time of tremendous and unprecedented peril. All around us we are witnessing the rapid assembly and consolidation of a powerful, right-wing, reactionary movement that intends to destroy us—to turn us toward fascism. Though hardly a mass movement (37 percent of eligible voters determine electoral outcomes, and just more than half of them elected the last Congress), the right wing is exercising often definitive influence at all levels of government. The right represents a plurality of the vote rather than a majority of eligible voters, yet they are transforming our culture and changing the terms under which those who fall outside of their conception of the "traditional family" will live.

The right is winning in part because, while the major political parties cynically construct policy on the basis of opinion polls rather than on real human needs, the left provides no alternatives. Instead we are fractured, under siege, and in disarray. Our lack of unity is killing us. We can speak volumes about all the ways in which we are different from one another, but we struggle when called upon to describe why we should be working together. We share no analysis of the things we have in common.

So here we stand, blighted, benighted, and divided, as the right wing lays the groundwork for social and economic changes unimaginable to those of us raised in the wake of the striking of the New Deal between labor and capital. It's time for us to come together and, to repeat an often used phrase, establish some common ground. We need to add to our analysis of how we are different, which we have forged in the fires of prejudice, and, in response to the very real rejection of our issues by the left, move toward an overarching analysis of what we have in common. To me, that means talking about the economy, because I believe that it is in this facet of life, more fundamental to our survival than any other, that our destinies are most intimately and inextricably intertwined.

Their side has already begun the discussion. They are talking about the economy and providing false but nonetheless radical and resonant "alternatives" to business as usual. The leaders of the right have made no bones about appealing to the economic insecurities of middle-class white voters who are reacting with anger to falling wages and job loss resulting from "structural adjustment." Morality, individual worth, even citizenship have always been based in class in our country; now, in response to the anger being ignited over conditions created by global industrialization, the right wing is creating a new meritocracy.

In this new social class system, resentment toward the rich is being replaced by resentment toward government regulation of capital. This shift of focus is being achieved by spinning conspiracy theories that blame those traditionally hated in our society for government takeover—according to them, we've ruined it for everyone by demanding "special rights" and social programs that breed "dependency and immorality." The right-wing response to this mythical takeover? Take the government back by any means necessary. They want to form a new nation based on morality, productivity, and "culture." California's anti-immigrant Proposition 187 and Colorado's anti-gay Amendment 2 are examples of the arsenal of scapegoating strategies they have and will continue to employ.

Poverty, crime, greed, and hopelessness may well reach proportions unprecedented in American history if the right wing gets its way. We need to provide some alternatives of our own or we will ultimately appear as selfish as they say we are. Even queers are answering the right wing's call for an end to social programs and for "taxpayer" (read white, middle-class) revolt. I wonder, will queers who choose right-wing economic solutions eventually be forced to accept repression more profoundly devastating to our humanity than sodomy laws or lack of civil rights protection to secure the class privileges the right is offering to a society of hungry people?

As queer organizers we need to respond, and respond strongly, by talking about and organizing around the economic interests we share with straight people. However, doing so requires us to create a new analysis of queer identity that focuses on class—not an easy thing for a community that, as an organized and identifiable group, is so based in capitalism, industrialization, and the emergence of bourgeois society.

C: My mother thinks my friends and I talk about sex too much. At the dinner table, on the phone, to the television set. We get chatty about dildo sizes and we'll be happy to elaborate on whatever made someone giggle right before she came. Talking about sex can be sexy, intimate, and inspiring. Talking about sex is a lot more fun than talking about money. Of course, having sex can be that precious, satiating, remaking of a day, so the conversation already has that advantage. Nevertheless, discussions about money have a lot in common with banter about what we do in bed. Talking about money also can be intimate, inspiring, and funny.

So maybe it's not that sexy, but then again, talking about sex isn't always sexy either. I have done a lot of explicit safer sex training in my work as a videomaker and HIV workshop facilitator. Communication in detail about sex is necessary if we are to protect ourselves and our lovers from unwanted pregnancy, disease, and infection. For both the speakers and the listeners, these conversations can be and have been scary, maddening, invasive, alienating, and embarrassing. All of those things can also be true for money talk. But people, especially queer people, still talk about sex a whole lot more than they talk about money.

Although I'd much rather talk about sex with you, Scot, we've set before ourselves the task of deciphering some meaning from the messy, confusing, powerful, and challenging web of growing up in the profoundly class-stratified United States in the latter part of the twentieth century. For me, being rich in and of itself doesn't carry much objective significance, but to load the symbolic imagery down a bit, I'll add that I'm white and female and began rolling around with girls in my sophomore year at college. The convergence of such accidents of birth have gotten warped and solidified, nurtured, and discredited over and over in my life through all sorts of demanding experiences, mundane habits, emotional observations, and familial, professional, and social interactions.

A friend and mentor of mine, Stephanie Clohesy, sums up our challenge well: "In terms of class, both you and Scot ended up believing in and doing things that wouldn't necessarily be the expected fulfillment of either of your lives. The working poor often end up as very consumer-oriented and striving middle-class folks with little time for politics and social change. Rich people often end up in pursuit of pleasure or recognition, wanting to do good but not necessarily wanting to change the world in a way that would kill the goose laying the golden egg." She has asked me, "Where did you each hear the message?"

S: Some of the primary obstacles facing us in this essentially political process appear to me to be personal. In order to succeed in meeting this challenge, those of us convinced of the need for this project must focus on the experiences that brought us to a place in our lives where dealing with issues of class have become so central to our queer identities.

I'd like to talk about that with you as one way of starting that dialogue. However, I understand that in many ways the risk to me is minimal. I mean, the one thing that all the Catholic saints I grew up with have in common is that they suffer—and they are often poor. When I share my experiences of growing up poor, I become a sainted character—I solicit unmerited respect and awe, and become one who cannot be challenged or contradicted, as if the experience of poverty in and of itself constituted some kind of special education. As patronizing and tiresome as I find this kind of special treatment among those left of center, I realize it has its privileges. Even leftists appreciate a good rags-to-riches story.

You face a different kind of exposure. Are you willing to take the risk of talking about being rich and engaging in a public conversation about class from that perspective with this poor brown man who loves you? I think it would be a service to a lot of people who are grappling with issues of class and trying to find a way of thinking about class and the economy that allows us to deal with these issues without guilt, or individualism, and without establishing moralistic hierarchies—a canon of saints if you will—that ultimately make it harder, rather than easier, for us to organize wage earners around economic issues.

C: As far as recognizing similarities and differences along the way, I was keenly aware of class from the jump. My friends didn't have swimming pools and a choice of which car to drive to the supermarket. After having played hide-and-go-seek at their houses for weeks, we wouldn't discover still more closets—or even rooms—to hide in. My family moved several times in my childhood, and we usually had a three-story house with a basement. Most of my buddies didn't have private lessons in anything. For me there were a few on the piano (which didn't last—in fact, I recall *you* suggesting I'm tone deaf). Several winter ski vacations started off with the four of us kids practicing behind some rustic, blond ski instructor.

The overwhelming majority of people of color that I knew were working-class or poor. The African American woman who watched us when I was very young had to take the bus in from another part of town. I sensed that place was far away and that everyone who lived there was also black, was her family, was her people. Of course, I never assumed all the white people living on my block were "my family" or "my people." Isn't that how white folks end up believing that the only people with race are people of color? The more I acknowledge my race, the more I need to fight racism because people of my race are the ones demonstrating and nurturing racism and destroying people with it, ourselves included.

The only reason I didn't conflate race and class completely was due to the working-class and poor white people I came across in my public school experiences. I find it interesting to talk to people from all classes with all different kinds of backgrounds about when they became aware that there were other races, when they became aware that some people had bigger houses and some people had smaller houses, and some people traveled to different countries and some people didn't. I think that's fascinating, and it's not just a story about rich people. Because the dominant society paints such a prosperous picture of people living in this country and maintains the hegemonic notion of class mobility, it can perpetuate that wholly inaccurate image of this as a classless society. We have bought in, so to speak: most everyone, it seems, will define herself as middle-class. That is, until she starts talking specifically about the parameters and experiences of her life. Then everyone has a story. These are the voices, the stories, the dialogues that could create change.

When I came out as a lesbian, I suddenly understood part of what made me so different from other people, and the naming of this difference made me feel comfortable. Identity (and by extension, community) became very important to me. I was no longer a person who felt she didn't have one (or the other). A dramatic insecurity lies at the root of this society's obsession with "classless" identifications coming from all sides. That, and the fact that people just don't want to be different. At my best, I feel different and secure. Even though I feel like being a lesbian takes me outside of most things coddled, most things reassured, most things acceptable, I find myself in communities (straight and gay) of support, of celebration, of struggle, and of love.

We can be ever grateful that these communities aren't homogeneous, and finally, our differences are what (will) challenge us most. No matter how dykey I am, no matter how whatever, I'm still rich (which definitely provides freedom, power, opportunity, and stability). Many only see that. Many only feel that. I can't separate it from myself; I can't separate myself from it. Are people always going to hate me for having money, for having more than they do, for having so much? Are people (some overlapping with the last set!) always going to "love" me because of my money, because of what I can do for them, because they want some of what I've got? The lesson for me has to do with getting to be a rich person who can be loved, truly. Even by people who have felt the hate or the false love (and from some who have felt both).

You're right that examining our differences up close won't get me sainted (especially if I explore a lot of the true experiences, real observations, core feelings, or unless I kneel down to deny my happiness, luck, and love). So, Scot, we continue on down the road. What are your flickerings of learning the class ropes? When did you first identify the reality of different classes? From childhood until now, how have your daily rituals been informed by your (lack of) access to money and that kind of power? How have you negotiated intimate relationships across class (our friendship and this article being no exception)? Why did you decide to dedicate yourself, your time, your money, and your passion to, among other things, challenging the class system as you know it? How do you personally go about doing that?

S: My mother, like so many working-class women of color in Hawaii, thinks I *have* sex too much. Talking about sex is not the issue so much as the way in which it signals the doing of it. She would rather pretend that babies come from cabbage patches and queers are discriminated against for nothing more than holding hands in public.

Class, on the other hand, is an issue with which she is very comfortable. Talking money and talking class were the staples for a great many family discussions, and factored into every decision we made. In this way, class is to the poor what race is to people of color—we deal with it because we have no choice. Not dealing with it is the luxury of those for whom class does not present material barriers to mobility, to enjoyment, to eating, and to paying the rent.

My parents spent most of their growing-up years as agricultural workers. I also worked in the fields in my young life. As a kid I took great pride in being the best pineapple picker on the line; I could pick flowers faster than anyone I knew, and my skill with a machete and a pickax would take your breath away. In elections the union endorsement automatically got our vote, and in life my status as a worker was explained, demonstrated, and forced on me in my family and outside of it.

C: When Susan Raffo and I first talked about this anthology, I wondered out loud if any other rich queers would be contributing. She said no. (This has since changed, and David Becker's excellent exploration of his donor activism is also included in this anthology.) Internally I rolled my eyes, more out of frustration with wealthy people's inability to participate in the dismantling of a painful and unjust system than at the fact that I would be "speaking for," literally, a whole class of people. The burdens of representing others by default and not design are much lighter than the ultimate burdens we all bear under a system that keeps us so divided. For certain, we are kept divided by design, by capitalism's design.

Among queers (or lefties), this twisted translation allows ruling-class people to co-opt the notion of "coming out of the closet" about class. It's like straight people hiding their sexuality among sexual deviants, taking over the language of the oppressed without working to truly transform the system that forced them all into such narrow positions in the first place. It's an arrogant notion that anyone can just be quiet about their position of privilege, that two sides of the same coin are equal, that individual experiences dominate over hegemonic structures. It won't work.

I'm not going to speak for anyone else. Actually it's not a choice, I just don't. Readers shouldn't assume that anybody else who grew up in a big family that had a big house (or more than one), who had choices between public and private schools, regular exposure to the "fine arts," the opportunity to travel to different countries and cultures, and various other luxuries thinks the same way I do. The more I define my space within class-specific commonality, the less likely it is that anybody will share it with me. I can identify parental lessons in social justice philanthropy, in education as a means to empower each member of society, in the power of creativity and innovation to transform individuals and society as a whole, in supporting democracy by voting, and in supporting people by voting for liberal politicians. I recall the backlash my parents experienced campaigning for McGovern while living in Greenwich, Connecticut, a town everyone in my family despised for its elitism, ignorance, and serious dearth of culture.

I come from an athletic family made up mostly of girls—tomboys, to be precise. We talk loud at dinner, hug each other when we're feeling good, and flash ugly sneers when you piss us off. With my parents, brother, and sisters, participation was of primary importance. My siblings and I competed for the most endearing wit, charm, and intelligence. Creativity and independence of thought and action were where it was at. No worries about the safety of "a good government job." We inherited security and safety from our skin, and our class. Being a political activist, an artist, and an out lesbian were all things that wouldn't (and didn't) topple my world or my parents' world, wouldn't compromise my safety or my ability to succeed. That's how it was in my rich family.

My dad was the headmaster of the school I went to after we moved from Ohio. By the time I was seven or eight, each of the four kids in my family had a single room. We went skiing in the West every winter. I never went for dolls, preferring to organize things, read books, and play kickball in the yard. I hated TV, drew pictures, and wrote page-long stories in my illegible penmanship.

Drawing and painting were definitely the best things going except for my two stuffed rabbits, who to this day look like truck drivers in their patchwork dresses with soft ruffled collars. Now, the two of them sit on the bookshelf in our bedroom waiting to spark memories of a lucky child, a happy woman, and dreams of a better world, one more satisfying in its opportunity and freedom for everyone.

S: The biggest way the issue of class got confusing for me was when issues of class and race seemed to merge. After all, I lived in Hawaii, most assuredly a colony of the U.S., and identified with the brown people—nearly all of whom are of working-class origins— among whom I grew up. In Hawaii, rich people were white, and poor people were brown. Poverty and lack of power often seemed to me more a function of race than class. There were, of course, exceptions. Japanese and Chinese Americans in Hawaii have moved up the class ladder into the lower echelons of the middle class. However, the truly rich, those who traveled often to the mainland and owned beachfront homes on estates behind tall walls, were uniformly white. Asians seemed to occupy a place in the middle.

This confusion was expressed in many ways. Early on, when I was in my teens, on my way to dropping out of school to find work and make a living, I became deeply and passionately involved in the early Hawaiian sovereignty movement. In life I existed mostly on its edges, but in my imagination the movement and its ideas consumed me. I was deeply and profoundly moved by the notion of a cultural nation that would break free from the colonial power of a United States government that had terrified me ever since I saw TV coverage of the Vietnam War and watched brown people who looked like me being killed by U.S. soldiers.

This movement, I thought, would one day set me free. But then, at 17, I became a social worker, and dealing with the painful injuries of class for poor and working people, experiences that reach across race and culture, became my life's work. I quickly learned that poor people come in all colors and all deserve our compassion. I found new theories to help me name and explain my world, that brought class as an issue into the forefront of my thinking.

The new theories I learned gave me hope and helped me believe that winning justice—real justice—and change was more than

a quixotic pursuit for college students and the white folks in socialist parties. Organizing around class had the potential of reaching
enough people to build real power. I became intoxicated with the
notion of collective power and what we could do with it, and was
determined to get some or die trying. At the same time, finding a
queer community made me more compassionate.

I fell in love with white men who have died of AIDS and white
women who live with the fear of breast cancer and loss and discrimination. I have befriended rich white men and women who
share my experiences of discrimination on the basis of sexual orientation, and who understand the fear of violence and the humili-
ation and shame of the closet that I have lived with and continue
to live with as I struggle every day to overcome the internalized
effects of oppression. Queer people are my people. There are
those who call me Uncle Tom for calling white gay people my
people, but I can't help myself. We have too much in common,
and the burden of the struggle to end race and class oppression is
too big for this brown man to carry on his own. I love my white
and middle-class or rich brothers and sisters out of hope for something better for those who suffer, whether they be brown or
white.

In the course of all of this change, I made a career as an organizer and entered into the ranks of white-collar labor. I left Hawaii
because I wanted more experiences, more sex, more challenge,
and because I felt that I, light-skinned, Asian in appearance, had
privilege on these bases and should exercise them, here, in the
belly of the colonial beast.

And here is where I met you, Catherine. And in answer to your
question about why I struggle still and dedicate my time, money,
and passion to challenging the class system, I say, I think we both
struggle for much the same reasons. My reasons may look a little
different from yours. When I draw the images of the people whose
lives I want to make better in my mind, their names, faces, tender
hands, and warm hearts that have loved and supported me may
look different from those who inspire you. The specific points of
reference that anchor me to the work *are* different from yours, but
the primary motivations all boil down to the same thing. I work to
challenge the class system as an expression of, as Ivy Young once

put it, "love for those who deserve better than they are getting now"...and so do you.

C: Each family, of any class, is different from the next. Myths and generalizations fail us in this case as ever. Some rich folks say, "Having been taken care of all my life, I'm happy to learn now that I can do some things for myself." From the start, my parents instilled in me independence of the most garden variety—tough, true, and resilient. I know exactly what I can do for myself, feel quite capable, and find great meaning and peace in maintaining a home and the plants, taking care of the dog, cat, and fish, fixing things when they break down, fall down, or come apart in some way. I relish the preparations for gatherings and the consequent wet, refreshing, clean-up process.

I have a lot of privileges. Money is only one of them. I have an incredibly close relationship with my family, and with my mother in particular, and that's something that I value as a much higher privilege in my life than money. And it's also something that I could feel guilty about. I could feel guilty that a friend's parents kicked her out of the house when she told them she's a dyke. But guilt is not going to do me or her any good.

Some rich folks I've spoken with over the years talk of isolation, alienation, being warned off of "those people," discouraged from playing with anyone unlike themselves. We, on the other hand, were taught to make friends with whoever crossed our path, a noble pursuit to be sure. In others I still value an outgoing character, a friendly approach, an openness of spirit. This too, however, has its privileged perspective. The lesson implied a reciprocity that couldn't and shouldn't be counted on. In certain ways, I was taught that anyone might want to become my friend, when, in fact, other children or adults may have plenty of reason not to play with me because of how my race and class background may manifest itself in style, ignorance, and (political) beliefs. I guess rich folks can be isolated either by choice or by circumstance. I have learned some hurts of racism and classism in this firsthand way as well as through empathetic projection or "enlightened self-interest."

E. B. White once said, "If the world were merely seductive, that would be easy. If it were merely challenging, that would be no problem. But I rise in the morning torn between a desire to improve the world, and a desire to enjoy the world. This makes it hard to plan the day." As you and I continue to plan such long, long days, I'm grateful that we have the gift of being both pleased and challenged.

S: Because people and my love for them drive me in my work, I am forced to be humble enough to deal with folks as individuals, at least most of the time. Because I am of the working class I have no romantic notions of who and what the working class is—we are people, all kinds of people, both kind and cruel, generous and selfish, good and bad. The same is true of every race and class of people. Within their particular locations within the system of capitalism under which we live, people are good and bad, they struggle with hardship and with privilege, differently perhaps, but in ways that are still all too human. I am not better than human. I am not better than these people.

Freed from the class structures that separate us, we are capable of love across classes. I know that there are limits. I understand that we are products of the culture and economy that made us and that people act in their own self-interest as defined by the dominant culture. I am not blinded by love, only humbled in the face of it, so that the answers are not so easy for me.

I believe in class struggle, and I believe that until poor people have power, rich people as a class will never respond to our calls for justice, and the world will continue as it is, largely unchanged. In the world as it is, poor people suffer, toxics are sprayed on farmworkers, old people too often die lonely and impoverished, racism runs rampant, women are raped, beaten, and murdered just for being women, Mexican laborers living in the waste produced by U.S. factories just over the border have babies that are born without brains. Fifty million children will go hungry tonight. A gay person will be beaten today, a gay child will commit suicide, and my brothers are dying of AIDS. This world must change, and that will require us to organize, mobilize, and agitate, and that process will make some people very uncomfortable.

However, I think I understand that the theory that guides me speaks in generalities, while people live in specific locations and are the products of diverse experiences, all different within their separate but connected categories. That's why I can love you in spite of your privileges. With all that you have, you are willing to struggle with me, laugh with me, talk about sex with me, and love me. You are my sister. If only change required something as simple as getting the rest of the human race into the family, we could change the world.

C: It would be so awesome if the hegemonic notion of family values meant getting everyone into *our* family of values! I feel like we are tirelessly working on it, though. I feel tireless sometimes. Like no matter how much I do there will have to be more done and more done specifically by me. That definitely keeps me going. And makes me want to massage your shoulders and the back of everyone I love who works so hard to make changes in this world. I'm reminded of a story related by Alice Walker at Marlon Riggs' memorial service in San Francisco. She described visiting him sick in the hospital with HIV-related illnesses. She spoke of massaging his aching feet. She finished with the admonition that "We must rub the feet of the people who stand for us."

S: So, tell me, Catherine, how did someone like you, rich as you are and with all the privileges, and isolation, that come with that status, find her way into class struggle? How does that play itself out in your life and your work? How do you negotiate privilege and power in a world in which you have more than most? What part of what leads you to struggle across class is about being queer? Would we be writing this together if we weren't?

C: Without knowing those answers right off, I must say it's the questioning that moves me along. I recall attending the "Choosing Children" conference in the '80s in Boston with my middle-class white activist girlfriend of the time. At a workshop about class, the speaker addressed participants by our class identification, specifically poor, working-class, and middle-class. As an afterthought she waved her hand across the air and said, "If there are any upper-class women here, you *know* you don't represent your class."

My girlfriend of the moment turned to me and in a whisper asked, "How does it make you feel when people say things like that?" Although superficial, it felt good, since people I respected identified me as doing good work, venturing beyond an elitist approach to living. It also made me feel different because this middle-class woman—who appeared to have the same values and similar experiences as me, who spent energy fighting the same powers-that-be as I did—was saying she didn't know my experience.

She joined a chorus of voices that hasn't stopped engaging with me in dialogue. Like you, Scot. Like this. Like now. Thank you. May our kind of love and this type of really queer relationship become more and more desirable, encouraged, and common. That would certainly scare the fascists a little. As Suzanne Pharr once said, more or less, "Bigotry on the Right unites them. Bigotry on the Left divides us." If we could work to eradicate the divisive character of our communities, we might actually see the dawning of a powerful lefty, queer, people of color-led movement that would change this system once and for all.

S: In my childhood community, women worked outside of the home. There was no such thing as staying home or being a home-maker unless you were rich, and we knew no one rich. Betty Friedan went right over our heads—the basic ideas resonated, but the experiences of women in my life were so different from those she described.

Class played a role in how my mother saw herself and saw us. My mother was a "lady," and she referred to all of her friends that way as well. At parties, the "ladies" would sip wine coolers while the men chugged beers or slugged down hard liquor. The "ladies" wore makeup; they painted their faces pink and wore their hair up. Their favorite activity was going to the beach. Capri pants or baggy stretch shorts and hairnets in shades of green or blue were beachwear. They never swam, never exposed their bodies in public, and never talked about sex. Homosex was never even considered, much less talked about.

Feminists like Gloria Steinem only annoyed the "ladies," and the very idea of leaving legs or armpits unshaven, as they imagined all white feminists did, solicited leers and smirks and expressions of utter disgust. Those white *women* probably didn't even bathe! To the "ladies," the term *woman* was an insult, a word that in their world was a bitter reminder of how they were treated by the white "ladies" on the plantation.

C: A good transition for me was when I moved to a place of understanding philanthropy and funding as activism, understanding my place as an activist with class privilege and the multitude of possibilities and responsibilities that entailed. Many have done it before me. (But, sadly enough, not *that* many.) I could name most of them, whether they're dead or alive. The Funding Exchange offers a good model of how some rich progressives paved a way to collectively disseminate mounds of moolah that they inherited by way of birth.

The book *We Gave Away a Fortune: Stories of People Who Have Devoted Themselves and Their Wealth to Peace, Justice and a Healthy Environment* begins, "Never before have so many people stood to inherit so much.... Over $8 trillion–the personal net worth of Americans over 50–will soon pass to a younger generation." Only a few baby-boomers stand to inherit those trillions. Scary seeing how much smaller and smaller the pot of privileged people becomes as the pot of gold increases. And that so few of them are actually moved to do anything with their "good fortune."

S: In the often queer and sex industry-driven life of downtown Honolulu where I discovered my gayness, class also defined us as different from the bar life and the tourist-infested gay community in much the way gender identification separated the "ladies" from the women. Women of our sexual orientation were not lesbians– god forbid anyone would call them something so queer. They were *gay*. "Butchies" is the still popular term for gay women of color in the islands. And being a stone butch was more the rule than the exception for the butch gay woman. The nearer one gets to the earth on the class ladder, the more gender roles seem to play themselves out in extreme and, I think, stylish fashion.

Boys were *mahū*. We were either the world's biggest queens or we were butcher than any gay boy on the Castro could ever hope to be. Those who fell somewhere in between seemed out of place. Either way, if you messed with us, you would be lucky to go home to the mainland with your teeth still in your head. Lately, I've discovered the fem side of me. I wonder how much of that has to do with being richer than my parents ever hoped to be. Or perhaps I'm just turning into a "lady" in my old age. I do sometimes feel old, even at thirty-three.

C: Being a rich white lesbian is different from being a rich white straight woman. Being a lesbian has taught me a lot about the world in general and particularly the world I live in from day to day. And it has also given me lessons on not being everything that is being spoken to in the world and not being the accepted thing. I'm not the accepted thing. But although I don't feel like an insider, I enjoy a lot of the privileges. Yet I don't feel like I'm stepping out of something. I feel like I'm on the outside of something.

People talk about marrying "inside" or "outside" their race. When applying that paradigm to class, I realize it would be hard for me to avoid a cross-class relationship even if I wanted to (there are relatively few people, women, and lesbians, in particular, from my "class"). Negotiating relationships across class has been a profound experience, something requiring intense amounts of trust, faith, love, and belief in myself as an individual who really is doing her best, doing her thing, never thinking she's more than one individual person here on earth, not trying to take up more than my own space, being humble in the lap of power.

S: Class shaped the signifiers of gay sexuality for us. The language was different, though the passion was much the same. To understand gay life in the islands, just check out a hotel performance of "Hawaiian" music. The "ladies" so like drag queens, with branches—I do mean branches, as in limbs, boughs, pieces of trees—in their hair. False eyelashes, heavy makeup, fabulous gowns, crowns, broad gestures, and the hair! One feels like calling out "surf's up!" at the sight of those incredible 'dos! Talk about gender fucking! We invented the term.

Perhaps the "lady" performers in the hotels are so like drag queens because they, too, are imitations of "women," middle- and upper-class white women of whom we knew none to temper our imaginations. This is what Donna Reed looks like in the colonies. And in spite of all the show, and the early ages at which so many of us "lost it," we were in many ways sexually conservative. We were shy about our bodies, shy about showing off, and definitely not into public displays of sexual debauchery. Perhaps the stereotyping of so many people of color as sexually out of control shaped our expression.

We certainly had little to lose. Finding one's way into Waikiki's sex industry and gay community often meant finding one's way out of home and family.

C: My mother modeled for me what I was to do with the money I got from her and her father. Although my mother didn't grow up around out and proud gay and lesbian people, our extended family of artists, curators, educators, patrons, and collectors involves many gay men and a sampling of lesbians. This community represents an incredible cross-section of different classes because you have artists, patrons, and viewers, the politics of the work, and a position on the fringe of the business world (except maybe in New York, where it can seem more like the center). Class and race politics are played out here as anywhere, but art-world people come together in a way that doesn't happen in other wealthy circles where no one sees people of other races and/or classes unless there's an employee-employer relationship.

Many women with inherited money have archaic relationships with the men who control it. The men are their fathers, brothers, grandfathers, trustees, lawyers, or financial advisers they inherited along with the money. Even now (what, with all that women's lib and stuff?!), women don't know what their assets amount to, whether they have stocks or bonds, or if they've invested in "socially responsible companies" or nuclear weapons and tobacco. They don't know where the money is kept, who benefits from it in addition to them, or who ultimately controls it. They just know they get a certain amount in a check every month.

A lot of younger women today have feminist moms and single moms, and the next generation is going to have us as moms and dads—queer moms and dads—in interracial relationships, with various levels of access to money but a commitment to sharing that wealth, to redistributing that power, and to living real, emotional, honest lives. As I think about being a parent, as I continue to live in this raucous world, I'm involved in a rigorous self-interrogation. How can I be a better ally? How am I sustained in that process? What kind of cross-class strategies can we use to achieve justice, to secure a society and a world in which everyone can participate fully?

S: In Hawaii, being gay meant that if you could negotiate your way through the complex web of power inequities, exploitation, and violence that so often shaped the cross-class and cross-racial relationships between working-class gay men of color and middle- and upper-class white men in Hawaii, one could move, just a little, up the class ladder. Much like women who marry for money, we were never secure in our positions, we were often beaten or otherwise intimidated, and our status was contingent on the continuing approval of our lovers, but by climbing in this way, we did get to taste something different. We got to experience what it meant to be "classy."

I went from being a down-home boy in faded jeans and corduroys, T-shirts, and sweat jackets to being a fashion plate in a short minute. I wore feathered hair, shoulder-length, faded orange by the sun, with silky shirts or velours, and wide flaring polyester Angel Flight pants. I didn't just walk, I swaggered.

In the bar district, I would park myself across the street from Hula's, the most trendy and popular of gay watering holes, and wait for the men to come by. "Hey, Mister, can you buy me some beer?" Success might mean dinner, maybe a show, a party in a hotel room, or entrance into the bar (without I.D.) and an education in living the high life. I learned how to navigate my way through French restaurant menus and cocktail parties. No matter how foreign the flavors of the food or drink were to my working-class tongue, I savored the experience and forced myself to adjust. After all, that was what it meant to have class.

I can still remember the faces of some of those men who occupied the darker corners of what I jokingly refer to as my "seedy side life." Some of them were so kind, whatever their motivations. Some I remember best for the bruises they left on me. But in the end, I always went back for more. This for me was another route to class mobility, illusory as it was. This was how the deep yearning for validation through power and ownership that capitalism instills in so many of us was played out in my gay life. And I did play.

C: I feel comfortable about ways I've shared resources, lived communally, and made good use of time and space in this crowded city. I've lived with several people at a time for a variety of reasons. Besides having excellent companionship, we only needed one TV, we got a much larger space for a much lower price than our friends, and for the most part we all liked each other a lot. Some people might feel threatened to find that most of the resources being shared belong to them alone, but I felt much more taken advantage of because I'm really neat. I pick up after everybody. And it pisses me off because—although I know that if I just left the clothes on the floor or the dishes in the sink, they'd get attended to sooner or later—I just can't live in a huge mess. As you well know, in the home I share with Melanie, neatness isn't the issue. We're both totally anal.

Taking a lead from my mother's example, I originally formalized my own class-activist response when I joined the board of directors of the Astraea National Lesbian Action Foundation. Astraea was and remains unique: it's a multiracial, progressive funding organization that fosters lesbian visibility and activism across the country. The office, staff, and board of directors is New York-based and includes women of different class backgrounds. During my tenure I drafted the policies and procedures for the Community Funding Panel (CFP), designed like the Funding Exchange (FEX) Network of Community Funding Boards.

FEX was always working with two distinct constituencies: the funders/founders and the community-based activists who gathered to make financial allocations. At Astraea, our board evolved from a single group under incredible pressure to raise money, oversee financial reports, make all general grantmaking decisions, and troubleshoot for the executive director (who suffered from burnout!) to a more equitable and resourceful system of the two boards. Finally, the CFP allowed for more women to share the workload. Furthermore, CFP women now come from all over the country instead of only the tri-state area to participate in a proactive program of empowering, mobilizing, and funding lesbians.

While still on that board (and afterward continuing on the CFP), I was asked by Helen Hunt to join the board of directors of her newly reorganized foundation, The Sister Fund (formerly Hunt Alternatives Fund). Since we didn't have to raise funds, this new board work gave me an opportunity to focus on systematically supporting organizations that could network with and benefit from the programs of other grantees. At The Sister Fund, we're strategizing to leverage our grants and technical assistance with a broad vision for a multicultural feminist movement. That movement is closely tied to the lefty queer movement you and I are struggling to participate in, the one we are struggling to mobilize.

In the multicultural, multiclass, and multigenerational community of The Sister Fund staff and board, I have learned about spirituality and faith. I have learned to value my values and myself and to value others regardless of whether they spend their days as activists or organizers, as teachers or writers, as nonprofit directors or spiritual ministers, as students or artists. We have quite a dialogue, which is never only about money and always infused with the scars of different class experiences, the emotional demands of capitalism.

Now I'm also working with twenty-four other young women and men (suddenly at thirty *I'm* the oldest) to create a fund for young women nationwide. (Years ago I fantasized about a similar cross-class group of only girls-that-dig-girls pooling various amounts of money and funding a lesbian revolution. I wanted to call it Dykes Who Give It Up.) In this current manifestation, The Third Wave Fund, we are black, Latino/a, Asian, Native American, and white. We are lesbian, gay, bisexual, and straight. We have different financial backgrounds and different kinds of life work, although much of it falls within the creative, activist, and nonprofit realms. We've chosen several areas for the fund to focus on: fighting for reproductive rights and providing money for abortions when necessary, providing scholarships for full-time or part-time education, and supporting micro-enterprise by granting loans to small businesses owned and managed by young women. We're organizing to respond to the issues of the day, whether that's voter mobilization, education, and registration; fighting the religious right; or organizing campus activists. All of our work takes into account the young women most blocked by our current social system; our grantmaking will focus on women of color, lesbian and bisexual women, and poor and working-class women.

All of this "redistribution of wealth" work adds up to one component of my class view and my forms of activism. Basically, I make certain priorities about how I want to spend my time. I don't want money to be the thing that rules my life. I hear about other people who spend all their time dealing with where it's going and where it's coming from, and that's fine. But that's not what I want to do with my life. I want my money to effect a more just society. I want to make videos, make love, and make revolution.

Postscript

After reading through our stories written above...

C: A problem for me is that I feel like I wrote a lot of direct biographical information in an effort to clarify my history and individuality outside of assumptions about very rich people. I don't want to spend all my time here shaking this chip off my shoulder.

S: A problem for me is that I wrote a lot of biographical information about myself and my experiences growing up very poor, and while I think there are valuable lessons in that experience, I also think that people have a way of deifying poor people rather than taking the experience as it's described and using it to challenge themselves. That is not very useful because the working class is so much bigger than poor people.

C: I imagine that people reading this want me just to put forth my stories and that they're not necessarily looking to me to interpret or theorize about capitalism because owning-class people are seen as the problem. The problem is capitalism, not the individuals who are rich and poor and working-class and middle-class. But the solution could be about what individuals in those classes do with their experiences, and I think that's why you and I have decided to have this conversation together. There is merit here if we can get to it.

S: The merit in this, I think, is that dealing with the issues of class and the painful injuries of capitalism requires more than theory and analysis. There's a personal dimension to this that I think stops people from successfully getting to the meat of the issue. Whether it's understanding how we're limited by our class experiences, whatever those experiences may be, rich or poor, or just getting hung up on guilt, many of the barriers are personal. As political people, I think that we so fear psychologizing problems and ignoring the social dimensions of them that we end up forgetting about people, whom we cannot forget in this society that is so based on individualism.

C: Feminist writers and writers of color talk about not being silent for a reason. There's a reason to tell our stories, whether they're about hearing our mothers talk in the other room with their friends and trying to recall what they were saying, what their friends looked like, how they acted, how they responded to the world around them, and how all that made us feel. That's how we learned to be the way we are today. We need to tell these stories because these are the ones never talked about. The silence can be deafening if all we hear is the sound of Wall Street men and politicians daily barking rhetorical responses to the media's representation of how people think—and what they want—in this country.

S: Even this would-be Third World working-class revolutionary loves fashion, enjoys TV, and aspires to living comfortably. People don't want to hear these things. I think that poor people and working-class people often avoid really looking honestly at the personal dimensions of the problem because it means acknowledging that we carry around a lot of bullshit about class.

C: . . . and a lot of pain. But I don't see rich people running out there to tell their honest stories, either, which brings us back to why we both wrote our class autobiographies in this particular form of exchange. We know that neither of these stories has ever been told in this way or, more importantly, to this end.

The authors would like to thank Ivy Young, Stephanie Clohesy, David Becker, and Mab Segrest for their feedback on this article and their support for this work.

Contributors

DONNA ALLEGRA has been anthologized in *SportsDykes, Lesbian Erotics, All the Ways Home: Short Stories about Children and the Lesbian and Gay Community, Queer View Mirror, Dyke Life: From Growing Up to Growing Old—A Celebration of the Lesbian Experience, My Lover Is a Woman: Contemporary Lesbian Love Poems,* and *Lesbian Short Fiction.* Her pieces will also be published in *The Wild Good: Lesbian Photographs & Writings on Love* and *Close Calls: New Lesbian Fiction.*

DAVID P. BECKER has been funding within the lesbian and gay and other social change movements for twenty years. He is also a writer and college teacher living in Portland, Maine.

ALLAN BÉRUBÉ, an independent scholar and a founder of the San Francisco Lesbian and Gay History Project, has, since 1978, written, lectured, and presented slide shows on U.S. lesbian, gay, and transgender history. He is the author of the award-winning book *Coming Out Under Fire: The History of Gay Men and Women in World War II* (Free Press). He co-wrote the 1994 Peabody Award-winning documentary film based on his book. In 1994-95, he was awarded a Rockefeller fellowship at the Center for Lesbian and Gay Studies at CUNY, and in 1996 he was awarded a MacArthur "genius" grant. He is currently writing a history of queer work and gay activism in the Marine Cooks and Stewards Union from the Depression to the Cold War titled *Shipping Out* (Houghton Mifflin, forthcoming).

VICTORIA A. BROWNWORTH is a working-class lesbian and award-winning journalist who writes for many national and international publications, including *The Nation, The Village Voice, Ms., OUT, Curve,* and *Poz.* She is the editor of five books and author of seven, most recently, *Too Queer: Essays from a Radical Life* (Firebrand). She lives in Philadelphia with filmmaker Judith M. Redding and their seven cats.

JUSTIN CHIN is a writer and performance artist. His solo work has been presented nationally. He is the author of *Bite Hard* (Manic D Press), and his writing has appeared in *Men on Men 5: New Gay Writing* (Plume), *Eros in Boystown* (Crown), *Best Gay Erotica 1997* (Cleis), and *Flesh and the Word 4* (Plume), among other publications. He was also on the 1995 and 1996 San Francisco National Poetry Slam teams.

ELIZABETH CLARE is a poet, essayist, and activist living in Michigan, transplanted from Oregon. She has an M.F.A. in Creative Writing from Goddard College. Her poems and essays have been published in a variety of anthologies and periodicals, including *Sojourner: The Women's Forum, Sinister Wisdom, The Disability Rag, Hanging Loose,* and *The Arc of Love: An Anthology of Lesbian Love Poems.*

KENNETTE CROCKETT is a transplanted journalist now working and living in Los Angeles. Her work has appeared in *Girlfriends, The Chicago Tribune, Genre,* and other publications. She and her partner, Monica Warden, have collaborated in love, life, and the pursuit of good writing. Kennette has an M.A. in English literature from DePaul University and a B.A. in English literature from Mundelein College, both in Chicago. She has used her writing talents in the fields of teaching and development. Born and raised in East St. Louis, Illinois, Kennette has put down roots in two other cities (Chicago and Los Angeles). She thanks her parents, Kenneth (her namesake) and Shirley Crockett, for their love and support.

AKLILU DUNLAP makes his home in Minneapolis, where he practices law and champions civil and human rights causes. When not traipsing through the halls of justice, Dunlap can be found in the kitchen, defying yet another culinary tenet. His fiction, poetry, and essays have appeared in *Amethyst, Colors, The Ebbing Tide, Evergreen Chronicles, Modern Words, North Coast Review, Owen Wister Review, Whiskey Island Magazine,* and *Wolfhead Quarterly.* His new work will appear in forthcoming issues of *Artword Quarterly, Next Phase, New York Native, The Northern Reader,* and *The Poetry Page.*

MICHIYO FUKAYA (born Margaret Cornell), a Japanese American lesbian poet and activist, was also a single mother of a mixed-race daughter living on welfare, a survivor of childhood sexual abuse and sexual assault, and a woman of color in an all-white environment. Her life and work are documented in the collection *A Fire Is Burning, It Is in Me*, edited by Gwendolyn L. Shervington (New Victoria Publishers).

B.MICHAEL HUNTER, a.k.a. Bert Hunter, is a graduate of Adelphi University and Northeastern University School of Law, and a member of Alpha Phi Alpha Fraternity, Inc. His work has appeared in *One Teacher in Ten: Gay & Lesbian Educators Tell Their Stories, The Road Before Us: 100 Gay Black Poets, Queer City/Portable Lower East Side,* and the award-winning *Sojourner: Black Gay Voices in the Age of AIDS,* published by Other Countries Press, for which he also served as managing editor.

JOANNA KADI is a writer, poet, musician, and critic living in Minneapolis. She is the editor of *Food for Our Grandmothers: Writings by Arab-American and Arab-Canadian Feminists* (South End Press, 1994) and a book of essays dealing with race, class, sexuality, and imperialism, *Thinking Class: Sketches from a Cultural Worker* (South End Press, 1996). She has had numerous essays and short stories published in local and national publications. She teaches classes in critical thinking at the Centre for Arts Criticism.

WILLIAM J. MANN is the author of the novel *The Men from the Boys* (Dutton) and the forthcoming *Wisecracker: The Life & Times of Billy Haines,* a biography of the openly gay actor and designer (Viking). A widely syndicated journalist for the queer and alternative press, he is the winner of a 1996 fiction-writing grant from the Massachusetts Cultural Council. His fiction has appeared in *Men on Men 6, HIS: Brilliant New Gay Fiction, Happily Ever After,* and *Shadows of Love.* His essays have been included in the anthologies *Sister & Brother* and *Looking for Mr. Preston,* as well as in *The Advocate, Harvard Gay & Lesbian Review, Frontiers,* and numerous other publications.

JOHN ALBERT MANZON-SANTOS has been published in *Chrysalis/HRS Literary Magazine, ColorLife! Lesbian, Gay, Bisexual, Two-Spirit People of Color Newsmagazine,* and *Witness Aloud/Asian Pacific American Journal.* He dedicates this piece to his niece and nephew, Aimy and Tommy Ko-Garcia, and to his cherished friend Haruko Kuroiwa Brown (December 12, 1921–June 6, 1996).

MIRANDA MELLIS is a poet, dancer, and painter born in 1968, raised and still living in San Francisco. She makes her living variously as a child care worker, home health care attendant, and bodyworker. Her solo work has been seen at 1800 Square Feet, New College of California, and the Bay Area Dance Series. She has performed at Luna Sea, Theatre Artaud, and many other venues. Since 1988 she has collaborated and performed with the Knee Jerk Dance Project, former members of CONTRABAND, and S.A.M., the writing performance trio she cofounded in 1992. She is currently dancing with Dominique Zeltzman and self-publishing *Terminatrix Progeny*, a book of poems and performance texts by S.A.M. (to order, call 415-550-1617). She was brought up by working people, artists, activists, and queers aiming to make revolution. She is a second-generation dyke.

SCOT NAKAGAWA is a longtime community organizer for grassroots economic development and political empowerment projects in low-income communities. From 1992 to 1996 he worked for the National Gay and Lesbian Task Force as a Fight the Right organizer and field director. He is currently executive director of the McKenzie River Gathering Foundation, an organization dedicated to supporting grassroots social change through fundraising, grantmaking, and philanthropic reform.

SUSAN RAFFO has worked as a park ranger, waitress, activist, managing editor of *The Evergreen Chronicles* (a journal of gay, lesbian, bisexual, and transgendered arts and cultures), taxi driver, technical writer, educator, and salesperson. Her poetry, fiction, and essays have appeared in numerous periodicals and anthologies.

WILLIAM REICHARD holds an M.A. in Creative Writing from the University of Minnesota, where he is currently completing a Ph.D. in English literature. He has work published or forthcoming in a number of literary journals, including *Spoon River Poetry Review, Outerbridge, Folio, Modern Words, Connecticut Review, The James White Review, Seattle Review,* and *Black Warrior Review.* He also has work published or forthcoming in the anthologies *The Perimeter of Light, Reclaiming the Heartland: Lesbian and Gay Male Voices from the Midwest,* and *Gents, Badboys, and Barbarians.* His novella, *Harmony,* won the 1994 *Evergreen Chronicles* National Novella Competition. He is a poetry editor for *The James White Review.*

HAROLD McNEIL ROBINSON attended Saint Olaf College in Northfield, Minnesota, where he received a B.A. in English. He returned to his place of birth, Brooklyn, New York, in 1983 after alternately teaching and training in Minnesota, California, Saudi Arabia, and Yemen. He is a cofounder of Gay Men of African Descent, and is currently an associate staff analyst with the New York City Department of Health. His work has appeared in Assotto Saint's *The Road Before Us: 100 Gay Black Poets* and *Here to Dare, The Portable Lower East Side's Queer City* (contributing guest editor), *Other Countries, Sojourner*, and *Lisp*. He has participated in numerous readings, including New York City Hall's Out in Government observance, Poet's House, Dixon Place, and the four-man show Lifeforce at Harvard and Rutgers Universities.

RUTHANN ROBSON is the author of *Lesbian (Out)law: Survival under the Rule of Law*, as well as two short story collections, *Cecile* and *Eye of a Hurricane*, and two novels, *Another Mother* and *A/K/A* (forthcoming).

CATHERINE SAALFIELD is a producer/director, writer, teacher, and activist. Her most recent production is the half-hour videotape *When Democracy Works*, about the rise of the religious right, their attacks on most Americans, and our collaborative strategies for resistance. In 1994, she was senior associate producer/segment producer of the four-hour public television series *Positive: Life with HIV*. Her other videotapes include *Sacred Lies Civil Truths, Cuz It's Boy*, and *Among Good Christian Peoples*, among others, as well as work with the collectives DIVA TV and Paper Tiger Television. Saalfield was the founding director of BENT TV, the video workshop at New York's Hetrick-Martin Institute, where gay, lesbian, bisexual, and transgender youth produce a monthly half-hour public-access TV show. She currently serves on the boards of several nonprofit organizations.

TOVA is a jewish working-class lesbian writer mom aquarius living in seattle with her partner, anne, their not-quite-two-year-old, mayim, and their cats. she'll be 40 by the time this is published. she's an editor of *Bridges: A Journal for Jewish Feminists and Our Friends*. she writes poetry, fiction, and nonfiction and has been published in numerous journals, magazines, anthologies, and newspapers. she's trying to make a go of it as a freelance writer and just got hired to write an on-line vegetarian food column. she's hoping to have a poetry manuscript published soon, as well as a cookbook she's co-authoring. she loves to garden and spends too much time on-line. reading her own bio makes her a bit tired.

JANE VANDERBOSCH was director of Wisconsin's largest GLBT center until 1995. Disabled since, she has begun writing again, both poetry and prose. Her most recent poetry collection, *The Long-Term Memory of Cells*, is currently looking (on its own, of course) for a publisher.

CARMEN VAZQUEZ is director of public policy at the Lesbian and Gay Community Services Center in New York City. A published author and public speaker, she has served as coordinator of Lesbian/Gay Health Services for the San Francisco Department of Public Health, founding director of the San Francisco Women's Building, and member of the board of directors for the National Gay and Lesbian Task Force. She is currently on the board of directors of the OUT Fund for Lesbian and Gay Liberation, a project of the Funding Exchange. Born in the hills of Puerto Rico and tempered in New York City's Black Harlem projects, a self-described "Butch-Puerto-Rican-Socialist," Carmen lives in Brooklyn.

MORGAN GRAYCE WILLOW holds an M.A. in Creative Writing from Colorado State University. Her awards include a Loft-McKnight in poetry, a Minnesota State Arts Board Fellowship in poetry, and a Metropolitan Regional Arts Council grant to produce a poetry/performance series at the Minnesota women's correctional facility. She has taught at The Loft in Minneapolis; for the COMPAS Artists-in-the-Schools and Literary Post programs; and for Arts, Etc., an education and therapy center. Her chapbook titled *Spinnerets* was published in 1987. Her poetry and prose have appeared in *Bloomsbury Review, Sing Heavenly Muse!, The Evergreen Chronicles, Hurricane Alice,* and *From Wedded Wife to Lesbian Life: Stories of Transformation,* among other publications. Morgan lives in Minneapolis, where she works as an American Sign Language interpreter.

JUDITH K. WITHEROW was born in 1944 in the Pennsylvania Appalachians. A mixed-blood Native American lesbian, she was raised in rural poverty. She resides in Morningside, Maryland, with her partner of 20 years, Sue. Judith has many illnesses, including multiple sclerosis and systemic lupus. She is a storyteller, writer, and poet, and the winner of the first annual Audre Lorde Memorial Prose Contest for Nonfiction, April 1994.

Index

265

About the Editor

S usan Raffo has worked as a park ranger, waitress, activist, managing editor of *The Evergreen Chronicles* (a journal of gay, lesbian, bisexual, and trangendered arts and cultures), taxi driver, technical writer, educator, and salesperson. Her poetry, fiction, and essays have appeared in numerous periodicals and anthologies.

About South End Press

S outh End Press is a nonprofit, collectively run book publisher with more than 180 titles in print. Since our founding in 1977, we have tried to meet the needs of readers who are exploring, or are already committed to, the politics of radical social change.

Our goal is to publish books that encourage critical thinking and constructive action on the key political, cultural, social, economic, and ecological issues shaping life in the United States and in the world. In this way, we hope to give expression to a wide range of democratic social movements and to provide an alternative to the products of corporate publishing.

Through the Institute for Social and Cultural Change, South End Press works with other political media projects—*Z Magazine*; Speak Out, a speakers' bureau; Alternative Radio; and the Publishers' Support Project—to expand access to information and critical analysis.

For a free catalog, please write to South End Press, 116 Saint Botolph Street, Boston, MA 02115; call 1-800-533-8478; or visit our website at http://www.lbbs.org.

Other Titles of Interest